M. V. MURATOV

L. N. TOLSTOY

AND

V. G. CHERTKOV

Translated by

Scott D. Moss

Hermitage Publishers

2002

Muratov Mikhail Vasil'evich (1892-1957)
L. N. Tolstoy And V. G. Chertkov
Translated from Russian by
Scott D. Moss

Copyright © 2002 by Scott D. Moss

All rights reserved

Library of Congress Cataloging-in-Publication Data:

Muratov, M. (Mikhail), 1892-1957.
    [L.N.Tolstoi i V.G. Chertkov po ikh perepiske. English]
    L.N. Tolstoy and V.G. Chertkov / M.V. Muratov ; translated from
Russian by Scott D. Moss.
       p. cm.
    Includes index.
    ISBN 1-55779-138-4 (pbk.; alk.paper)
    ISBN 1-55779-144-9 (cl.)
      1. Tolstoy, Leo, graf, 1828-1910—Friends and associates.
      2. Tolstoy, Leo, graf, 1828-1910. 3. Chertkov, V.G. (Vladimir
Grigor'evich), 1854-1936. 4. Novelists, Russian—19th century—Biography.
I. Title.

    PG3409.M813 2002
    891.73'3—dc21

                              2002032726

Published by Hermitage Publishers
P.O. Box 310
Tenafly, N.J. 07670, USA
      Tel. (201) 894-8247; Fax (201) 894-5591
      E-mail: yefimovim@aol.com

The entire Hermitage catalog could be seen on
www.hermitagepublishers.com

CONTENTS

From the Editor *6*
From the Translator *8*

I
Tolstoy in 1883 *15*

II
The Youth & Adolescence of V.G. Chertkov *28*

III
The Beginning of the Friendship *53*

IV
The Common Project *75*

V
Rzhevsk *100*

VI
At The Crossroads *136*

VII
L.N. Tolstoy and V.G. Chertkov 1897-1902 *169*

VIII
L.N. Tolstoy and V.G. Chertkov 1902-1906 *209*

IX
The Last Years *243*

Notes *297*

Index *314*

Illustrations *320*

FROM THE EDITOR

In 1879 Lev Tolstoy, being at the height of literary recognition and personal prosperity, experienced an emotional crisis, which turned his life inside out. He described this crisis in the book *Confession*. All his previous life appeared to him as erroneous, bringing any person and all mankind to an impasse. From that time on he tried to look for new paths and devoted the last 30 years of the life to this search.

His main companion in this search was Vladimir Grigorievich Chertkov, acquaintance with whom had begun in 1883. Chertkov, like Tolstoy, came from a rich aristocratic family, began a successful military career. But soon, like Tolstoy, developed a deep disgust for the socio-religious structure of the Russian State during the second half of 19th century. And like Tolstoy, he was distressed by the position of proprietor and landowner, rejected doctrines of Orthodox Church, considered it his obligation not to participate in any forms of state violence against his fellowman. Their emotional bond and mutual understanding developed into close long-term friendship. They not only wrote each other the most detailed letters, but also gave their diaries to one-another to read and enthusiastically commented on them. Chertkov became the main publisher of Tolstoy's new works in Russia and abroad, he organized archives, which carefully assembled and stored Tolstoy's manuscripts, copies of his letters to different people, and notebooks. Subsequently this archive has played an important role in the preparation of the 90-volume collected works of Tolstoy.

We know, that second half of Tolstoy's life ended, like the first, in deep emotional crisis. His attempts to live up to the precepts of Christ – as he understood them – resulted in the heavy conflict with his family, with "members of his household". At 82 the world famous writer damned by church as a heretic, the spiritual leader and the example for hundreds of thousands followers, secretly abandoned his home, having in terms of belongings only those clothes which were on his back. In a few days he died in a small railway station and did not have time to write the second "Confession", reflecting his spiritual search of last thirty years.

It seems the value and importance of Muratov's book, being offered now to the reader in English translation is that it, to a great extent, compensates for this gap. Since the relationship between Tolstoy and Chertkov as shown in their letters are presented with such total sincerity and confidence, this book acquires a confessional character. And if it is possible for us to learn something from the great seafarers of the Oceans of Spirit, such books will be always invaluable "maps", important support in the choice of our own individual path.

I.M. Yefimov

FROM THE TRANSLATOR

Much has been written about Lev Tolstoy, his works and his philosophy in the near century since his passing. Yet who was Vladimir Chertkov? Why is it that we know so much about Tolstoy and so surprisingly little about his number one disciple who devoted his life to the publication of Tolstoy's works and the dissemination of his teachings? I posed this question to myself in 1999 and set out to find the answer.

My journey began in 1983, when, in my final year at the Hackley School, I was intrigued at the possibility of studying Russian with Professor Nicolai S. Tchertkoff, whose sincerity and mastery of teaching coupled with his love of the language and culture became the impetus for much of the last twenty years of my life, and I am confident this will continue for many years to come. I only had a passing knowledge of Tolstoy then, as much as most people knew of him – author of *War and Peace* and *Anna Karenina*. I had no idea of whom Chertkov was or the fact that the Tchertkoff who was inspiring me at that time was any relation of his. I subsequently learned that he was. And although he has moved on to teach at the Horace Mann School to inspire a new generation of students, our friendship has grown and remains one of the most important in my life thus far.

I graduated successfully and went on to study Russian, first at Boston University and then at City College, City University of New York. During my sophomore year I learned about the Alexandra Tolstoy Russian Summer Institute at the Tolstoy Foundation in Valley Cottage, New York. Indeed I had grown up in this small suburb of New York, just minutes away from the Foundation, but had never ventured over to discover what it was all about. Now was the perfect opportunity. I contacted my high school mentor once again and posed the question of whether the ATSRI program was worth further investigation and Mr. Tchertkoff highly recommended it, even informing me that his aunt, Mrs. Rodzianko was on staff that summer teaching a course on history and civilization.

I attended the summer program in 1986 and not only came away with a richer knowledge of language and culture, but also a full understanding of the history and goals of the Tolstoy Foundation, something that was to serve me well in the following years. I found out that Alexandra Tolstoy, youngest daughter of Lev Tolstoy and her close friend Tatiana Schaufuss founded this organization with the goal of helping refugees fleeing the communist block in Eastern Europe and the Soviet Union and resettle in Western Europe, South America, Australia, Canada and the U.S. Since it's inception in 1939, TF has had a rich history in resettling not only Russian and Eastern-European emigrants but also varied ethnic groups from around the world. The values of assisting those in need lay in the teachings of Lev Tolstoy, imparted to his daughter during the late 19th century and were carried to fruition through her humanitarian works at the Foundation named after him.

This influence was so great that I returned the following summer to volunteer at the Tolstoy Foundation Nursing Home where I was privileged to meet many pre-Revolutionary Russians whose stories filled me with the romanticism of life in St. Petersburg and elsewhere before 1917, and of course, practice my language skills as many Residents did not speak English! I have spent the last fifteen years at this facility, working in different capacities, yet my bonds with these Residents have left indelible marks on my soul and have made an indescribable difference.

As fate would have it, life presented me with another twist of circumstance in 1997. My high school Russian teacher, Mr. Tchertkoff (whom I had begun to address as Nicolai Sergeyevich in traditional Russian style, now that we had been acquainted for fourteen years!), had admitted his mother, Anna Tchertkoff, (neé Rodzianko) to our facility. She was the granddaughter of the last Speaker of the Third and Fourth Imperial Duma under Tsar Nicholas II. We started talking about what had been happening in our lives since we last met. He informed me that he founded a humanitarian, non-profit organization in 1993 – the Tchertkoff Memorial and Cultural Foundation – the mission of which was to discover and restore those monuments of Russian culture made by his family in the 18th and 19th centuries. Among them is the restoration and reopening to the general public of the Tchertkoff Library *"Rossika"* founded in 1831 by Alexander Dmitrievich Tchertkoff (1789-1858). The library, which consists of 50,000 volumes of rare books written in many languages of Europe about the Russian history, became the First Public Library of Moscow in 1863 and Tolstoy used it in 1864 when he was writing *War and Peace*. In 1834, 400 miles South-West from Moscow in the Voronezh Province, Alexander also built on his estate a sugar factory, which still produce sugar today for the past 168 years. After discussing this project for a few hours, I joined TMCF and designed the website, which documents these projects in Russia.

1999 celebrated the 130th anniversary of the founding of Chertkovo, a town of 13,000 in the Rostov Province, which has been divided, since 1991, between two independent States: Russia and Ukraine. A railroad track, which crosses the town, serves as a border between these two countries. Chertkovo was named after General Mikhail Ivanovitch Tchertkoff (1829-1905) – nephew of Alexander – because he built a thousand-mile railroad track from Voronezh to Rostov-on-the-Don on the land that belonged to the Tchertkoff family since the time of Catherine the Great. Due to this event, Nicolai Sergeyevich organized a family reunion, to which I was invited, – a two week adventure through Moscow and the south of Russia – exploring the regions which were the cradle of the Tchertkoff clan, culminating in the three-day celebration of this anniversary. Among the places we traveled to were the towns of Vladimir Chertkov's (1854-1936) estate also located in the Voronezh Province – Lizinovka and the homestead of Rzhevsk, including the school that he established for the purpose of educating peasants working on his land. He strongly believed that peasants could, through education, emancipate themselves from the "exploiting class".

I realized then that from all the research we had done on the Tchertkoff family, we had very little information on the only man Tolstoy considered his friend and confidante. Further delving, with the aide of Vladimir Boikov, an historian specializing in the history of the Tchertkoff family, lead to the discovery of a book written by Mikhail Muratov in 1934, published by the Tolstoy State Museum, entitled "L.N. Tolstoy and V.G. Chertkov Through Their Correspondence". I was sure that this book could only be found in Russia and would certainly look for a copy during my next trip. Over dinner at Nicolai Sergeyevich's one night, I mentioned the existence of this book, which I was told, had biographical information on Chertkov. He looked at me with a puzzled look on his face, and mumbling the author's name over and over, walked over to his bookcase, stood up on a small stool and reaching up the highest shelf, pulled down a copy of this very tome! Needless to say I was quite surprised!

I took it home that night and immediately started reading it, however I soon discovered that even though I have a fairly good command of the language, it is based primarily in the realm of healthcare and noticed that I began looking up every third word in the dictionary. After several hours of this, I decided something had to change. The next day I decided to attempt translating this work, simply for my own edification as well as to retrieve any biographical information on Chertkov that I could find in it's pages. It never entered my mind that this translation would ever see the light of day, that it would be worthy of publication and that anyone outside the world of academia would be interested in such a topic.

The basic translation was completed seven months later, but I knew there was still a lot of work to be done, including finding someone to proofread the manuscript to make sure my translation was up to professional standards. Indeed translating quotations that used language in a style from over a century ago was somewhat of a challenge. I turned to my friend Alla Katkowski, who, with her husband and son made invaluable corrections to half of the manuscript and to whom I will be eternally grateful. Yet it wasn't until I approached Igor Yefimov, himself an author of books concerning Tolstoy and the driving force at Hermitage Publishers, that I found a kindred spirit and proposed he become involved in my project. A few days later I received a letter from him stating that just the fact that I spent seven months translating a work of over five hundred pages without any hope of it seeing the light of day was nothing less than "heroic" and that he would be delighted to become involved in publishing this work!

And so, the translation of Muratov's work was born, a mere sixty-eight years after the original Russian version saw the light of day. Since this work uses terms commonplace in life of the 19th century, I wanted an opportunity to explain a few points in Muratov's book that may not be clear to the modern reader:

The first is the concept of the patronymic or *otchestvo*. Russians do not have middle names, as we understand them in the West, instead they take their father's name and add masculine endings "*ovich*" or "*evich*", or feminine endings "*ovna*" or "*evna*" to it. So for instance, Lev Nikolaevich Tolstoy is Lev, *son of Nikolai*, Tolstoy and Sofia Andreyevna Tolstaya was Sofia, *daughter of Andrey*, Tolstaya. In addition, adding *a* or *ya* to the ending of a woman's family name differentiated her from her husband or father.

Second, units of measurement appear unchanged in the text, including *verst*, which is 1.1 miles or 1.6 kilometers, *pood*, which is 36 pounds or 16.38 kilograms, and a *desyatina* of land is 2.7 acres.

Thirdly, to point out that Chertkov had a habit of "renaming" members of his family, such that, although his wife was Anna Konstantinovna, he often referred to her as "Galya", his son, Vladimir as "Dima" and his daughter Olga as "Lusya".

After this translation was completed, I found out that my former teacher Nicolai Tchertkoff, while on a trip to Paris, found two books written by Vitali Shentalinsky. These books were translated into French and published by Robert Laffont. The first one is entitled *The Resurrected Word in the Literary Archives of the KGB* (1993), and the second one has for title *The Surprises of the Lubianka: New discoveries in the Literary Archives of the KGB* (1996). After the fall of communism and during the first years of the Yeltsin democratization process of the New Russia, the KGB archives were open to researchers. Shentalinsky, a novelist and poet who presided at that time in Moscow the Federal Commission for the Legacy of Writers Victims of the Repression, had access to the archives and was doing a research on the fate of writers after the revolution. There he discovered a letter Chertkov wrote to Felix Dzerzhinsky, then head of the Cheka (former KGB), appealing to him to release Tolstaya from the Lubyanka jail. He explained in his letter that her actions were above-board and there was no justification in holding her. This letter was published in the second book in a chapter dedicated to Tolstoy and the fate of Yasnaya Polyana after the revolution and entitled "The Fall of the Tolstoy House":

"Honorable Felix Edmundovitch!

Last night, the daughter of Leo Tolstoy, Alexandra Lvovna Tolstaya, was imprisoned in the Lubyanka. During the search her private correspondence was confiscated, and she was told that she was arrested because of a denunciation. Knowing that A.L. Tolstaya never participated in any political plot, and being totally absorbed by the preparation work for the first publication of her father's manuscripts, I suppose that she is a victim either of deletion or of a misunderstanding. In any case, A.L. Tolstaya is not a person who is hiding from the authorities, and it seems to me that all suspicions against her could have been verified without subjecting her to a preventive detention. Furthermore she has a poor health and her incarceration can have a very negative impact on her. In the hope that you will find these considerations fair, I dare to ask you if it would be possible to release A.L. Tolstaya until the Instruction will determine if this case comes from a mistake or a misunderstanding.

Sincerely,

V. Chertkov."

His letter didn't remain unanswered. Dzerzhinsky gave the order to release Alexandra Lvovna and all her private correspondence was returned to her. Chertkov's success in winning the release of Alexandra Tolstaya was in part due to Lenin's positive attitude toward the Great Russian writer. Didn't he say after all that Tolstoy was the mirror of the Russian Revolution? Tolstoy once said about Chertkov that if he had wanted to invent for himself a friend, he couldn't have imagined anybody better than him. If it was not for Chertkov's intervention on Alexandra Lvovna's behalf, she would have disappeared in the darkness of the Gulag and there would have been no Tolstoy Foundation. Millions of Russian refugees fleeing from Stalin's death camps wouldn't have been saved and emigrating to the U.S., my life's path wouldn't have taken me to the point it is today, and I wouldn't have had the opportunity to work on the Muratov book in the first place. So the story has come full circle and in a round-about way – I owe a dept of thanks to the man whom I wanted to learn about in the first place!

Lastly, I want to take a moment to thank those involved in this work, for without their support and guidance, it would not have been possible:

To my parents, Leland Moss and Gail Baymiller, whose strong belief and commitment to providing the best education possible and their never-ending belief in me, gave me continual encouragement to pursue my interests, I am eternally grateful.

To my sister Robyn: thanks for sharing my enthusiasm for this work as well as all the motivational talks to keep me going during this long process!

The Katkowski Family – for their proofreading and correction of this manuscript, and for sharing their love of Russian literature with me over the last fifteen years!

To my friends at TFNH, in particular Theresa Pietrantonio, Anna Chemerov, Harriet Wise, Nancy Esposito, Deborah Kline, and especially Nancy Gronwoldt for their continual interest and support during the course of this work at a time when I needed them most!

To Igor Yefimov, my editor at Hermitage Publishers – for his interest in this work, in Russian culture and literature overall that he has shared with me and his enthusiasm in turning the rough manuscript that I presented him into the work that it is today – I am in his debt!

And a very special thanks to Nicolai Tchertkoff... – what can I say? A mere expression of thanks cannot do justice for what I owe him! He has changed the entire course of my life, by getting me hooked on loving Mother Russia, her language and culture as much as he does, by teaching me in school, by becoming my mentor, and my friend. He has shared his hospitality, his insights into life, around the table, in typical Russian fashion, and his country during the most amazing trip I have or will ever experience! I hope this translation will serve as a testament to his ability to impact the lives of his students!

SDM, Nanuet, New York, June 2002

I
Tolstoy in 1883

In 1883 Lev Nikolaevich Tolstoy turned 55 years old. Despite approaching old age, he was strong and healthy and many could be jealous of his ability to work efficiently. Those who looked at his life from the outside would think that his life was happy and fulfilling.

War and Peace and *Anna Karenina* were long since published and were declared the most well known artistic works of Russian literature of that time. He not only was undoubtedly first among Russian writers, but more often he was more and more informed that his name had been gaining worldwide recognition.

The main part of the year was spent at his estate, Yasnaya Polyana. It was a noble estate of average size – without palaces, columns or English parks, like those created for themselves by the grandees living in the country. It was constructed in such a way that it was comfortable to live in, freely and simply. From the two white turrets at the entrance was a wide road that led to the estate, lined with leafy birch trees. The road continued toward the two-story white house with a balcony on the sunny side and a shaded, glazed terrace. Near the terrace grew an old elm tree with wide spreading branches, familiar to Tolstoy in his early childhood years. Nearer to the house itself was the park, with its four paths, all lined with lime trees, a gazebo and ponds. Beyond the park was an old apple orchard of 35 desyatins in which Tolstoy himself planted many of the trees. Behind the estate was a grove of young oak, and not far away began a dense reserve forest Zaseka spreading out for many versts.

In Moscow, where Tolstoy spent the winter months, he had a spacious house, far away from the city noise. On the quiet, narrow Dolgo-Hamovnicheski Pereulok was a factory and small houses that were densely populated by the poor. Despite this location, the place was calm, behind high and thick wooden fences, reminiscent of a small country estate, with a garden. A two-story house of 17 rooms, painted light-brown, stood on a wide courtyard, with communal buildings, cottages for servants, a hut for the caretaker, stables and shed. The house was constructed such that a large family could live comfortably, and adults and children could live their own independent lives, gathering at the tea or dinner table or sitting around in small groups at the lit lamp in the living room, and besides that, receiving every guest, working, studying or entertaining exactly as they wanted.

Tolstoy's wife, Countess Sofia Andreyevna, energetic, strong and still young at 38, presided over the household and remembered everything which was necessary such that life in the house continued without any interruptions: about what kind of products to order to run the kitchen, that it was necessary to order the coachman a new caftan, thickly lined with cotton for appearance, the fact that one of the children's grades had slipped and he needed a tutor, that is was necessary to buy tickets for the opening night of the new play, that there would be something to talk about with guests, decided that it was time to begin a new edition of her husband's works, to talk to the typesetters about more advantageous terms for her husband. She knew very well that she had to organize their life such that it would be exactly like the lives of those in the class in which the Tolstoys were, which meant that it was necessary to make sure that there was an impeccably clean tablecloth on the table, that the maid had a starched apron, and albums were put out in the hall for guests to look at. She put all her strength into these things and although everyone in the house knew that when she succumbed to irritations that would suddenly seize her, she could yell at one of her family members, create a bad scene with the tutor, did not jibe with that outward veneer which she always strove to strengthen in the way of life for her family, or to show strange pettiness in some kind of financial matter - that everyone felt that she was the one who remembered everything essential, such that life at home rolled on non-stop of it's own inertia. It was very important to her that everything went this way and, probably many guests, being in the home during these years, would readily agree with Turgenev, who kindly told Tolstoy during one of his visits: "You did right that you married your wife."[1]

Tolstoy had many children and around him many noises and tones were created. The eldest of his sons, Sergei Lvovich, turned 20 years old and studied at the university. The youngest, Alyosha, was only 2 and just learned to walk. The eldest daughter, Tatiana Lvovna, a nineteen-year-old girl, studied at the school of fine arts, lively and sociable, equally capable of organizing a fun game for kids gathered in the Tolstoy home, as well as holding a conversation in the living room, gladly volunteering a free minute to show her father something or another, copying for him a small letter, writing a response to a letter addressed to him or to run another of his errands. The youngest daughter, Masha, a skinny, plain, kind, and sincere girl – studied at home, occupied with resident teachers and governesses living at the Tolstoy's, who taught the children foreign languages.

The Tolstoy family kept growing and therefore expenses grew as well, but the expenses which would have suggested trouble in other conditions must not have caused the Tolstoys alarm, for at the same time revenues grew from his artistic works, continually republished, because the demand for them continued steadily to grow. Each year the value of his spacious land in the Samaran Steppe increased, which he bought very cheaply at some point, and now, at the insistence of Sofia Andreyevna, leased to the peasants.

But, despite this outward prosperity, Tolstoy, remaining alone in his small, simple and comfortable study, where noises of the full life of the house almost did not penetrate, often was displeased with himself and felt sad and depressed, which was reflected by many entries in his diaries.

Indeed few knew at that time, that discord, which was becoming deeper and deeper, existed in Tolstoy's house. And almost no one knew that Tolstoy, who was world renown, steadily and sharply felt his loneliness.

At forty-seven, he was getting on in years, at a time when many others had already ended their search, using their views and convictions which were developed earlier, Tolstoy as is well known, came to the conclusion, that there is something in his life, not thought through, and values, which he tried to create, needed verification and justification. He himself wrote about this subsequently:

"Something strange began to happen to me, there began to come moments of bewilderment, pauses in life, as if I didn't know how I shall live, what I should do, and I got lost and became depressed. But this passed and I continued to live as before. Then these episodes of bewilderment began to repeat themselves more frequently, always in the same way. These pauses in life always voiced the same single question: Why? And then what?"[2]

A review of former values began: his wealth proved to come from exploitation of a someone's hard work, church decreed, regulated belief, giving prepared answers to all questions, became unacceptable.

As a result of this work, he wrote to his relative A.A. Tolstaya, whom he treated with respect and friendship, although her devotion toward orthodoxy caused arguments between them, reaching confrontation.

"Check the ice you are walking on: is it firm? Try to pierce it. If it breaks, it's better to walk on dry land. And if it will hold you, then wonderful, we're all going to the same place... I broke my ice on the hard ground and already I am not scared of anything because I don't have the strength to break that upon which I stand, and that means it became genuine."[3]

This review of his worldview lasted a number of years for Tolstoy. Only at the end of 1882 was it basically finished - more accurately - it was a totally defined point of departure and Tolstoy was able to write to Nikolai Nikolaevich Strahov, critic and author of the articles about philosophical questions, with whom he had an ongoing correspondence:

"To speak about changes I have not changed at all; but the difference between my past condition and my present are the same, like between a person being built and one who has already been built. I hope to cut down the scaffolding, clean the litter around the house and live unnoticed and peacefully."[4]

His new convictions came in obvious contradiction with the way of life of people in his circle and also in the life of his family, using all the income from his land that belonged to them.

Tolstoy's wife, Countess Sofia Andreyevna, in her better moments could, with sentimental tenderness, read the thought of Marcus Aurelius in French translation, but vehemently refused to change the accustomed lifestyle, wanted to live "like everyone." And during that time, when Tolstoy intensely worked out his new views, she looked at him with bewilderment, with vague fear, and hope that this incomprehensible passion would finally pass, not leaving a trace.

"Lyovochka always works, as he calls it, – wrote Countess Sofia Andreyevna in 1879 to her sister T.A. Kuzminskaya, – but it seems, he writes some kind of religious dissertation, to show that the church is incompatible with the teachings of the Gospel. You couldn't find ten people in Russia who would be interested in that. But there is nothing to do, I only wish that he would finish this soon and everything would go away like a disease."[5]

And many years later, looking back at this almost finished long-lived life, she wrote in her autobiography:

"My life and I remained the same. He left and not in everyday life, but in his writings, in sermons to the people, how it was necessary to live."[6]

There were always many guests in the Tolstoy home, and Tolstoy, it seemed, never could complain about the lack of company. The most distinguished representatives of Moscow intelligentsia sought circumstances to meet with him, were in his house, and he in his turn was in theirs. But this relation usually only strengthened a sense of loneliness in Tolstoy. Returning to himself after lively discussions with guests, Tolstoy wrote with relentless clarity in his diary:

"Idle, empty, indirect, dishonest conversation: gossip, showing off their knowledge and wittiness. I took part in everything and left with a feeling of embarassment."[7]

In dealings with these people, Tolstoy suffered, just as Levin in *Anna Karenina,* meeting with his neighbor Sviyazhsky – a smart, cultured, honest and liberal person, whose life went smoothly and pleasantly and still seemed to Levin strange, unknown and incomprehensible. Every time, when Levin tried "to reach the very foundation of his view on life... tried to penetrate beyond the reception rooms opened for everyone in Sviyazhsky's mind", he noticed that Sviyazhsky easily got confused and gave the conversation a different direction. Tolstoy kept up his acquaintance with professors and writers, who were at his house, and at the time felt that he could not discuss with them questions that seemed the most essential and important to him because there was nothing beyond the reception rooms in their minds. And Tolstoy sometimes repaid them for this with sarcastic ridicule. Managing to get away from Moscow in spring to the countryside, Tolstoy wrote to his wife:

"Starlings right in front of my fortochka in the birdhouse show all their skill and sing as orioles and as quails and as corncrakes – and even as frogs, but can't sing as themselves. In my opinion I say: that birds are like professors, but are much more pleasant." [8]

Tolstoy often strove in conversation with acquaintances to state his views, but usually if the collocutor did not manage to change the topic of a discussion, the conversation would leave only an unpleasant taste and a disappointing feeling of mutual incomprehension.

V.V. Stasov, who was a well-known musical and art critic, good-humored, effusive person, perhaps to some extent, styled his effusiveness in his behavior, tireless and heated debater, being at Tolstoy's was always ready to start a debate, but, returning home, with characteristic straightforwardness wrote to Tolstoy:

"I don't even want to think about that dark and incomprehensible "corner" which scared and troubled me both in the first and the second day, as if running into clouds, coming from God knows where, but then to make up for it, what a magnificent hot July day all the rest was."

"Thank you for your good opinion of me," Tolstoy answered him, "but I can't hold out, and not say that everything good which you like in me comes out *only* from that dark corner, of which you are so hateful."[9]

Looking at the wide circle of people, found to be in constant relations with Tolstoy during those years, when his life-understanding was worked out and studying his correspondence and unpublished diaries, it is possible to notice a few people with whom he had inner closeness.

One of them was Nikolai Nikolaevich Strahov, a refined connoisseur of literature, possessing almost encyclopedic erudition in various spheres of knowledge, because the rest of his pleasure was leisurely, solitary intellectual work of acquiring the riches of philosophical works. He worked in the public library, wrote critical articles and small philosophical works, and was not able to participate in life, as much as scrutinize it, glancing at it from the side.

Tolstoy wrote to him at the beginning of their acquaintance:

"Do you know what struck me more than anything else in you? The expression on your face, when you, not knowing that I was in the study, walked from the garden through the balcony door. This expression, alien, concentrated and strict, explained you to me. I am sure that you are destined to purely philosophical activities."[10]

And Strahov himself wrote about himself to Tolstoy:

"All this time I did not live, I only accepted life, as it came, tried with the least expenditure of strength to satisfy its demands, and as much as possible, walk away from its misfortune and discomforts. For this, as you know, I am totally punished. I don't have a family, no property, no position, no circle; I have nothing - no ties which could bind me to life. And besides that, probably as a consequence, I don't know what to think."[11]... "And all the best feelings, which I discover in myself, guard them all, foster in myself, hold on to them, but not in my power to give them impulse and fire. Such is my fate, life has shaped up in conformity with these characteristics."[12]

In Strahov's literary activities his very large erudition was clearly demonstrated, he diligently studied and expounded on foreign views and gave them his appreciation, but his own personal creation was not significant and did not even satisfy himself that much.

Tolstoy valued in him a smart and attentive co-conversationalist and talked a lot with him about life and about faith. Strahov was always able to point out literature on questions which interested Tolstoy, to find and send books necessary for him, attentively and with sympathy read his writings and give it critical evaluation, but he was not able to become for him his companion on life's journey - and in one of his letters, Strahov wrote about this to Tolstoy:

"Why do I understand your feelings, but don't share them? I will say, as if in confession. Because I don't have such strong feelings as you do, don't want to coerce myself or pretend, and where can I obtain this selflessness, this zeal with which you feel, which endows your heart? Be tolerant of me; don't repel me for this difference. Your aversion to the world, I know it, because I also experience it, but experience it in such a mild degree, which doesn't smother or torment, but I don't have the attachment toward the world at all."[13]

Tolstoy understood this, and related to Strahov with respect and good will, but knew that he could not lean on him, and told about this one day with some bitterness:

"Strahov, like a rotten tree – poke it with a stick, thinking it will be unyielding, but no, the stick passes throughout wherever you poke, there is absolutely no middle in it, everything in him has been corroded with science and philosophy."[14]

Another person with whom Tolstoy could share thoughts, which occupied him during these years of sudden change was Vasili Ivanovich Alexeyev, resident tutor of the Tolstoys', teaching their children for nearly four years from 1877 to 1881. This was a person not totally ordinary, and his life did not go exactly as planned. Finishing the university and becoming a teacher in the technical faculty, he became closer to a revolutionary-minded group of youth, though his views did not totally coincide with their ideas, which defined the world-outlook of the majority of his comrades. Together with A.K. Malikov, he considered that the key to freedom is to be found first of all inside a person, and to build public life on new foundations was possible not necessarily by means of propaganda, but by the many paths of self-education. After search and arrest, he, as soon as he was freed, left with N.V. Tchaikovsky and a few like-minded people for North America in order to try out settling in conditions free from administrative interference and organize a commune with their labor and work the land. The commune was created but collapsed, Alexeyev returned to Russia and soon after that assumed the responsibility of home tutor for the Tolstoy family.

The position of teacher, living at the Tolstoy's, always had a certain duality, – he was the educator of the children, it was necessary to treat him such that the children felt his authority and considered his words, and at the same time Countess Sofia Andreyevna was able to let him know that he was just an employee in the house and should know his place. But Tolstoy's attention, always with sharp interest scrutinizing new people, was attracted by Alexeyev's unusual views and his endeavors to implement them. Tolstoy's first step toward rapprochement, and conversations between them brought the beginning of mutual friendliness.

Alexeyev believed that the government sooner or later should be replaced by a world federation of communes and denied the admissibility of war earlier, than these views grew in Tolstoy with enough clarity. Tolstoy talked to him many times about these themes. Beside that, he respected Alexeyev for that benevolence and gentleness in relations with people, which was characteristic of him.

"The only conclusion that I see", wrote Tolstoy to Alexeyev, "is to live well, always to turn the nice side to all. But I still cannot do this like you. I remember about you - when I stop short on this. Rarely can I be like this, I am hot-tempered, easily angered and unhappy with myself."[15]

These friendly relations between Tolstoy and the teacher of his children were unpleasant for the mistress of the house. Sofia Andreyevna knew that Alexeyev sympathized with Tolstoy - in those aspirations that went contrary to the gentry ways of life for which she spent much of her strength.

And when, one day, immediately after the murder of Alexander II, Sofia Andreyevna, listening to the conversation which went on in the other room, heard that Alexeyev supported the idea of Tolstoy appealing to the new Tsar with a letter about pardoning the assassins, she ran into the room and spoke in a voice which escalated to screaming:

"Vasili Ivanovich, what are you saying? If you were not talking to Lev Nikolaevich who does not need your advice but to my son or daughter, I would have ordered you immediately to get out of here!"[16]

And swiftly stretching her hand foreword she pointed to the door. And that was the very day at lunch, apparently after the conversation with Tolstoy, Sofia Andreyevna, in front of everyone apologized to Alexeyev and said that she appreciates him as a sincere person, but he decided it was time to leave the Tolstoys and soon fulfilled his intention.

With his departure from Yasnaya Polyana, Tolstoy lost the only person in the house who subscribed to his views with real sympathy. Tolstoy continued to maintain ties with him through correspondence, but Alexeyev did not belong to those people who lived such an intensive inner life that it was strikingly felt and would be necessary to others from a distance. An attentive and understanding collocutor, an attractive person for Tolstoy, he did not possess strong original ideas or outstanding will. He himself was inclined to search for support and Tolstoy had to write to him, trying to help in the moments of depression:

"I very highly appreciate, like and believe in you that your life won't be wasted in vain. It is only necessary to sharpen the knife when it becomes dull."[17]

There were a few other people with whom Tolstoy felt such bonds, but studying his relationships with these people, it is not difficult to see the limits of their friendship. Two of them were friendly not only with Tolstoy himself, but also with Sofia Andreyevna – in her perception they were people "of their circle" and their position allowed them to be accepted as welcomed guests in their home.

One of them - the artist N.N. Ge, who, having read Tolstoy's article in 1882 "*About the Census in Moscow*", without objection accepted his understanding of Christian reading and came to Moscow especially in order to meet with Tolstoy and declare to him that he agrees with him about everything. By this time Ge turned 50, he already had a widely well-known name, but he was characteristically greatly effusive, and he was always ready to energetically express his feelings. Appearing for the first time in front of Tolstoy, he immediately embraced him and announced that, as a sign of gratitude for his companionship, he was ready immediately to paint for him any portrait - his daughter or his wife. Tolstoy was friendly toward him, but there was something in Ge's character, which was alien to Tolstoy.

"I see, as you, my dear, I walk firmly, well, and I will drag myself after you. Although I will sometimes get my nose smashed, but I will start to climb,"[18] – Ge wrote to Tolstoy at the beginning of their acquaintance.

And Tolstoy, who himself accepted every thought new for him only after long thought and persistent analysis, could say, about Ge, that he later wrote about one of his like-thinkers:

"He's too agreeable"

At the same time for Tolstoy, restraint in communication of his feelings, there must have been something alien in that constant readiness for excessively endearing words, which was also characteristic of Ge, not always, perhaps, understandable, that in this sphere, there was nothing worse than exaggerated expression.

The second person, sharing Tolstoy's views and at the same time preserving friendly relations with Countess Sofia Andreyevna, was Prince L.D. Orusoff. Soft and delicate, understanding Tolstoy's opinions not only mentally as much as having a feeling for them, he was always ready himself to take part in spreading ideas close to Tolstoy. He translated the thoughts of Marcus Aurelius into Russian and Tolstoy's "*What I Believe*" into French. But despite the fact that, accepting Tolstoy's views, he remained the Vice-Governor of Tula for a long time and in questions of raising his daughters, he backed down in front of his wife, the daughter of the rich factory owner Maltzev, whom Sofia Andreyevna called vulgar.

Tolstoy felt friendship toward Prince Orusoff, understood a lot in his life, by his own experience, but knew that in the moment of fatigue or hesitation, Orusoff could not provide him vital help.

People with whom Tolstoy met during the time of his search, close to him in opinion, had much more integrity and consistency, but did not belong to his circle.

Such was V.K. Syutayev - a peasant in the Tver region, not able to read and write, independent of Tolstoy, and earlier than he, worked out a life-understanding, very close to Tolstoy's views. Throwing away church ritual, Syutayev believed that what was important first and foremost was the inner world of the person, which must completely define his external life, just as the cause stipulates the following consequences.

"Everything in you and everything now", - Syutayev said, and these words made favorite sayings of Tolstoy, which he often repeated in the last years of his life. Hearing about Syutayev, Tolstoy went to visit him in the fall of 1881 in his village and found with joy that they both, beginning their journey, were at absolutely different ends and totally different conditions but reached the exact same point.

In accordance with his views, Syutayev tried to reorganize his life, but for him it was much easier to do than for Tolstoy.

Visiting Tolstoy in Moscow during that time, when Tolstoy, after his work on the census of population in Moscow, was occupied with the thought of how to help the city poor and alcoholics who were at life's lowest depths, Syutayev immediately offered a way out, which would, in his opinion, save children, teenagers and youth from this environment:

"Lets take them under our supervision. I am not rich, but I'll take two... Another ten people will take more. You take and I'll take. We will work together, he will see how I work, will learn how to live, and we will sit at one table together and he will hear words from me and from you. This is alms."[19]

These words touched Tolstoy, but he could see that it was easier for Syutayev to accomplish his plan in his hut than Tolstoy in his house with lackeys in white gloves.

In the sphere of thought, a lot came to Syutayev much easier than Tolstoy. Syutayev was not able to extract from the data of knowledge open to him, accepting the Bible in its entirety but interpreting it allegorically, believed in the authority of the tsar, to whom he tried to reach, in order to ask him to order that the Gospel be interpreted in the way that Syutayev understood it, and as a result of this attempt he returned home under guard.

Many problems facing Tolstoy did not exist for Syutayev. Tolstoy could think of Syutayev with tenderness, often said that this barely literate peasant possesses much more education than learned professors, although he had to realize that his own external life and Syutayev's were like two parallel planes: Syutayev was for Tolstoy a person close in views but living on another planet.

And to some degree, it was possible to say the same thing about two other people about whom Tolstoy responded with great warmth in letters and diaries in the beginning of the 1880s – a teacher at the railroad school - V.F. Orlov and the librarian at the Rumyantsev Museum, N.F. Federov. One – Orlov, former revolutionary charged with participation in the Nechaev affair, – had worked long and hard on his worldview; the other N.F. Fedorov whose principles required being satisfied with an insignificant salary, a sizeable part of which he spent on others, author of the original teaching about the resurrection of all the people in flesh – both of them attracted Tolstoy with their exceptional strictness toward themselves and consistency in life. But with both Tolstoy was much decidedly separated, acquaintance with them did not leave a significant trace in his life and, finally, they were not recurring guests in his home, the whole style of which was alien to them.

Tolstoy knew that sometimes it was possible to meet people who perhaps understood and were interested in his views, but in his house in such an environment in which his life went he was alone. And the feeling of loneliness, especially agonizing because there were people around him, close outwardly, but alien inwardly, sometimes grabbed Tolstoy with such force that he could not cope with it. Receiving in December 1882 a letter from a young man unknown to him, M.A. Engelgardt, writing to him on his views of church rituals and government authority, Tolstoy accepted him as a person close to him and wrote him a letter which was the outburst of the long-held pain of loneliness:

"You probably don't think this, but you can't imagine to what degree I am alone, to what degree my real "I" is despised by everyone around me. I know, that enduring this until the end I will be saved, I know that only in the trivial things a person is capable to use the fruits of his labor or at least to see this fruit, but in this affair of God's truth, which is eternal, does not allow a person to see the fruit of his work, especially in the short period of his short life, I know all this, however often I am depressed. And therefore a meeting with you and hope, almost belief, to find in you a person sincerely walking with me along one road toward one and the same goal, for me is great joy."[20]

This hope of Tolstoy's was not justified. Further correspondence revealed that the views of M.A. Engelgardt were very alien from Tolstoy's and their paths could not cross.

But in a few months, Tolstoy met a person who immediately occupied an important place in his life.

At the end of October 1883, a young man came to the door of Tolstoy's Moscow home, in a coat sewn by an English tailor, very simple yet very expensive, tall and stately, with a peaceful assuredness in movement, which was characteristic of people, accustomed since childhood to feel their independence and to receive the signs of respect from those around them. This was Vladimir Grigorievich Chertkov.

II
The Youth & Adolescence of V.G. Chertkov

Three sources of power – wealth, aristocratic origin and eminent rank – were at the disposal of V.G. Chertkov's family.

In the southern region of the Voronezh province, on the way to the Territory of Don Cossacks, the Chertkovs had an extensive estate – all together around 30,000 desyatin of land, with fields of black earth, steppe and forest in which there were many wolves and foxes. In the center of their holding, in the settlement of Lizinovka, stood a large manor house, but Chertkov's parents always lived in Petersburg where their ties and interests were centered.

Chertkov's mother, with whom he felt especially close, Elizaveta Ivanovna was born Countess Chernysheva-Kruglikova, occupied an eminent place in Petersburg society, singled out among her circle for her beauty, intellect, from childhood educated authoritativeness and at the same time tact – that ability to hold oneself with people which in high circles was valued not less, than intellect, and generally entirely replaced it.

She had close family ties with the Decembrists: her uncle, Count Zahar Chernyshev was sent to Siberia for his participation in the Decembrist uprising, her aunt was the wife of another Decembrist – Nikita Muravyov – and followed him into exile, but monarchist traditions, although softened by Western European culture thanks to personal and long journeys abroad, remained strong in her family.

Chertkov's father, Grigorii Ivanovich, was aide-de-camp under Nikolai I, Adjutant-General under Alexander II and Alexander III. He was well-known in military circles as someone with special knowledge of front line service and military bearing, which officers acquired, beginning their career in the guard of Nikolai I and at the same time he had the rare reputation in court spheres of a person straight and trying to accomplish his task as he understood it.

An aunt on his father's side, Elena Ivanovna, was married to Count P.A. Shuvalov, one of the most influential and most reactionary courtiers of Alexander II, his father's brother – Michael Ivanovich Chertkov Adjutant General – was Ataman of the Don

Cossack Army and Governor General of Voronezh, Kiev and Warsaw. He was also a member of the State Council. The Chertkov family with all its ties belonged to the most select circle of Petersburg aristocracy, occupied a place on the highest rung of that social ladder, on the summit of which was the tsar's throne, and used the imperial favor so much so, that Alexander II and Alexander III visited their home.

Chertkov, in the mature years of life remembering his childhood, the brilliant position his parents occupied in high circles and his upbringing, which they gave him, he distinctly felt that many traits in his character depended on the fact that he was born and grew up in a lordly environment.

Describing his parents in one of his diary entries, he wrote that although "they belonged to a number of the most respectable of "respectable people", at the same time, the status which they occupied, must be negatively reflected on his development:

"How much the best traits of my parents reflected negatively on me, I now understand, when I reminisce, that everything I now say about their merit and honor, how they used it, was well-known and highly valuable to me, as if I shared some of their own superiority over others when I was still small. That's how I grew up, assured of my own innate advantage over other people, proud of the dignity of my parents, their relatives and friends, entourage of servants, rising from their seats in the ante-room when I passed from my rooms into my parents' part of the house, swimming in all kinds of luxury and almost not knowing rejection in satisfaction of my desires."[1]

He had two brothers: one, Grigorii, was older by three years, the other Michael – two years younger, but both died, one in early adolescence, the other in childhood, and all the forces of maternal and paternal love were concentrated on the only surviving son. And since childhood he was accustomed to people regarding his will and were ready to give him any pleasure appropriate to his age. Days passed easily and pleasantly, but these pleasures, which they brought, did not leave a significant trace in his memory.

Many years later, thinking about his childhood and trying to point out such joy which occupied a big place in his inner world, he wrote in the entry of his diary already quoted before:

"Searching for such joy that could move me during reminiscence of it, I can stop now only abruptly, now and then, and for a minute, with a renewed impression of some kind of totally far-away childlike relationship to the surrounding life – like it was something strange – like a different world, contemplating from within one's one small, comfortable and isolated little world. The mood now, from time to time, but not for long, restores me to a better soul-felt moment; external access to an instant renews when I by chance in a dark night glance out the window of the top floor of the city house and I will see there somewhere far away from me lit lamps of peopled streets with warping here and there carriage lights: probably, I am carried back to this time, when, after a tiresome journey by rail, our whole family settled in for lodging for the night at one of the best hotels of the foreign city."

The Chertkov children continually received wonderful presents from their parents and relatives, belonging to the same circle of rich aristocrats, around them were servants who carried out their wishes, but Chertkov, remembering his relations with people, around him in childhood, left in his diary one of these experiences, not totally noticeable to others, and perhaps not even to those close to him:

"I have yet another reminiscence which indeed touched me: my younger brother, Misha, who was about six and I was eight are sitting in some house away from everyone, on the stairs, holding, holding one another, hugging and confessing and telling each other that we love each other very, very much, and that we couldn't express in words and that no one knows this and no one could comprehend it."

There were always many people in the Chertkovs' home who served their family: porters, coachmen, lackeys, maids, and a cook with a whole slew of helpers in the kitchen, over which he was the head. And around the children were also people, who had to dress, feed and teach them. Therefore, the situation in society and this material independence, which was guaranteed by a wide landed estate, and the way of life of the Chertkov's more closely resembled English landlords and perhaps, they realized this themselves, gravitating toward English aristocracy and giving their children a similar upbringing.

Chertkov had English nannies during his first years and then his upbringing fell into the hands of English governors and the English language came to him as naturally as Russian and French, without which it was impossible to get around in fashionable salons. Chertkov was not sent to school, though his parents could have chosen any privileged educational establishment – the lyceum or the corps of pages; they decided that in this way it would be easier to protect him from illness and their large fortune enabled them the opportunity to invite any teacher to their home.

His childhood passed uneventfully. He quickly grew into a young man who could expect a lot from a life ahead. According to all accounts he was very handsome – slender, taller than most other people, with big gray eyes under beaked brows, and especially witty, having a unique ability to speak paradoxically. He had a gentle and at the same time canorous voice, and pleasant infectious laughter. Truthfulness, sometimes even too straightforward, and a steadfast readiness to lend money to friends who found themselves in difficult circumstances were among his characteristics. And only if somebody had to act in defiance of his desires, it was felt that it was not easy to deal with Chertkov, because it could be easily said of him that:

"Whatever he wanted, he wanted very much."

Chertkov's friends could only be his own age and come from those aristocratic households which had ties to his family – those known as the golden youth, keenly knowing everything concerning societal decorum, and almost always lacking some kind of intellectual interest, with their understanding about honor and at the same time not used to holding back their desires, greedy in the most primitive delight, hidden behind a brilliant veneer. And very early – barely in his teens, – Chertkov indulged himself in all those passions, which his friends flaunted in front of one another, like heroic deeds of mettle: women, wine and heated gambling totally consumed him.

Nineteen-year-old Chertkov voluntarily joined the Life Guards of the Cavalry – one of the most brilliant Guard regiments, and that revelry which captivated him earlier, became for him in its own way a demand for good form: such that, whoever tried to live differently, in this environment would be looked at with bewilderment and mockery, sincerely considered to be a bad friend and a strange person.

In Petersburg, as in various big capital cities, there was a special class of women who considered their profession as having affairs with rich and well-known people – mainly guards' officers – having liaisons with them for months, weeks, or even for a few hours. It was not difficult to start a friendship with these women in a few of the chic restaurants or in the Summer Garden, a favorite place for such meetings. Drinking bouts with trips in carriages or revelry until morning, heated games, when handfuls of gold money were thrown on a green cloth, everyone increased the stakes, and the desire for good luck consumed him with such force that he could not and indeed did not want to resist. Sometimes, when passion for the game went too far, and losses made too excessive, friends tried to restrain Chertkov, and sometimes he tried to restrain them.

"Under fear of being humiliated in front of all my friends, I promised them under no circumstance to play roulette until February 1, 1873", – wrote one of Chertkov's society friends at midnight on December 13, 1872 and delivered this written obligation to him, which was preserved in Chertkov's archives until the present day.

But Chertkov himself, not to a lesser degree needed to hold himself in check because soon that very friend had to write him a letter, in which, through friendship, brought his attention to the fact that his losses in roulette remained high and convinced him to abandon cards and wine.

Yet yielding to all the enjoyment that was offered by life in the circle of golden youth, unaware of either external or internal obstacles for the realization of his desires, Chertkov from time to time felt, that there was something in his life that should not be and strove to find some moral law that would subordinate his behavior.

Still an 18-year-old youth, he wrote a letter in which he tried to state his thoughts about the meaning of conscience to one of his friends – a young man belonging to one of the most aristocratic Russian families and yielding to the same delights as he himself. In the response, overflowing with indecent jokes, which were considered, it seems, an indication of good tone during friendly conversation, in the circle of golden youth to which they belonged, Chertkov's friend tried, in his turn, to state his ideas about conscience, making big mistakes in Russian, which probably, he would not have made if he wrote it in French. Calling Chertkov's letter "philosophical", he tried to prove that the demand of conscience is relative because, Europeans hear the voice of conscience saying: "Don't avenge your enemy, throw away your gun"; and the Asian hears: "Grab the sword, run and rip the pants off your enemy."[2]

These attempts to think seriously about his life for long periods remained weak, and outwardly Chertkov continued to live the same life as anyone who totally did not strive to change his behavior. In 1876, one of the Chertkov's friends, congratulating him on his promotion to officer, wrote him that now he will have new friends – "they are merry people, sometimes have feasts and you will appreciate that."[3]

And at the same time discord grew in Chertkov's life, which continued inconspicuously and, with each year it was felt more and more, but was not apparent to others.

"A 22 year old guards officer, – wrote Chertkov afterward, remembering this time, – I plunged into dissipation." All three classical vices – wine, cards and women – I handed myself over without restraint, living, like in childhood, with rare intervals of spiritual sobering up. In these periods of internal lucidity, I felt repugnance toward my dissolute behavior and agonizingly oppressed by my situation. Searching for a way out, I intensely asked myself questions about life and religion."[4]

Together with a few of his friend-officers, Chertkov began to imagine how to run his life on a more serious footing, at least in the form of work on self-education. There was an effort made to organize in the regiment club readings and discussion, and with this goal, the well-known Professor Bestuzhov-Rumin was invited to give lectures about Russian history. But the division commander, finding out about this unusual occurrence, ordered that these discussions be stopped, probably, scared lest they not cross those strict limited boundaries which had to form a circle of thought of an exemplary guards officer. Chertkov, in these periods when he sharply felt the necessity to comprehend his life, strove to understand the very fundamentals of his world-picture, had a feeling that the conversations which arose after the popular scientific dissertation in the regiment club, could not give him anything in this respect.

Chertkov's mother, Elizaveta Ivanovna, was very religious. Her faith was not limited to her trips to church during ceremonial days and the fulfillment of rites that were part of daily life, with observance demand for decorum and tradition established by her environment. Together with a few families belonging to Peterburg's high society, she became a follower of the English preacher Lord Radstock, who in the 1870s, began sermons about Evangelist ideas among English aristocrats, and then spread his activities outside the boundaries of this circle.

Belief in the divinity of Christ and the redemption of mankind in his blood and the saving necessity of prayer, independent of various church rites, and persuasion that in the Bible and Gospels, as in writings inspired by God, it is necessary to search for answers to all questions about life – lay in the sermons of Lord Radstock. Chertkova, together with the family of her cousin, V.A. Pashkov, later sent into exile abroad for sermons of his creed, in the name of which followers of this movement in Russia were at one time called Pashkovites, totally accepted the Gospel readings preached by Lord Radstock and tried to convince her son of his truth.

Promising each believer salvation of the soul, this teaching did not require of them a change in social attitudes nor simplification of the way of life established in the high society circle and at one time enjoyed considerable success in this environment. And sometimes it could happen that a young society lady from an aristocratic family could send a young man a greeting card, on one side of which was drawn the image of a basket with roses and forget-me-nots and in gold printed "think about me" – and on the other side she concluded with Evangelical text: "Come to me all ye that labor and I will give thee rest."

Even in early childhood, his mother trained Chertkov to read the Gospels and to turn to this book in times of uncertainty, but it was characteristic of him, aspiring to strive independently to explain to himself questions facing him and not accept on faith words of others, directing his thought to one or another ready channel. The dogmatic side of this Christian reading, which Chertkov's mother shared, left him alien. Gospel stories about miracles produced skeptical reaction, but ethical precepts attracted him and from time to time began persistently to think about how to accomplish them.

Among the duties of guards officers came the periodic duty in military hospitals. And finding himself in the ward for sick soldiers, Chertkov felt how much suffering was hidden by the external brightness of the exemplary military hospitals. In December 1877, returning from duty in the hospital, Chertkov wrote his mother:

"In the wards where sick and wounded were brought from a battlefield, everything is arranged in the best possible way. High princes, ladies and nurses visit them, and all the staff it seems, are in their place. In other wards, there is a different picture; it's not worth writing about, because it's very distressing. But here every book left for reading is read with gratitude, every kind word calls for tears."[5]

The guards' officer on duty is given the right of supervision of the hospital's condition, but in fact this right was almost never implemented and Chertkov himself subsequently remembered this institution with bewilderment:

"Young guard officers, changing daily, who did not even know how to manage their own money were entrusted with the task which was beyond the capability of even the most capable administrator and not without preparation, how we visited our hospitals, but after continuous and solid introduction about all there is to know about the very difficult task. It is understandable that under such conditions, activity of an officer arriving in the hospital for one 24-hour period could be limited only to external formalities...

During inspection of the numerous wards and barracks for verification of satisfaction of their maintenance and care of the sick, an officer embarrassed by his inexperience, suddenly fallen into this situation from totally another world, everywhere meeting medical assistants and staff stretched out in front of him, whom it would cost nothing to bluff if he would get it into his head to check the hospital order and to disclose abuse. It is difficult to comprehend who would need this comedy of fictional control, which we, young officers, were forced to play in military hospitals. But I myself am forever grateful for the chance of having these duties forced on me – the chance to look, although with one eye, at the reverse side of life – at the more tragic serious side surrounding conditions, which are usually hidden from young eyes in my situation."[6]

Here, carrying out the obligation of duty officer, he ran across the disgraceful treatment of a political prisoner in the prison section of the hospital, Chertkov abruptly interfered with the order of the hospital administration and only thanks to the position which his parents occupied in society, this interference did not have any unpleasant consequences for him.

And although at the end of his duty, Chertkov again threw himself into that rotation of temptation and delight, which quickly fascinated him, everything more urgently and agonizingly became a need to break those forms that took over his life and to find a new life's path.

"Five years ago", – wrote Chertkov in the beginning of 1884 in his diary, – "after repeated, but futile efforts to overcome the evil in me, I finally began to notice that even the very desire to correct myself becomes weaker. I doubted in God's existence, the Gospels lost their authority for me. In time I clearly realized my situation, and then felt that I might quickly get closer to despair and lunacy. Only God knows, how close I was to one or the other and what horrible suffering I lived through in the continuance of these horrible times."[7]

In Chertkov's language were two words, which he always pronounced with great contempt – "be evasive" and "to try to get out of." He considered it an unworthy thing to hide from deciding those questions that faced him, but, it was unclear even to him, how he should live further.

In order to understand these arising doubts, to look closer at other ways of life and remain alone with himself, he decided, for a time to abandon his accustomed life, take a vacation for several months and go to England.

He shared his thoughts in a letter to one of his society friends, Rafail Alexeyevich Pisarev, who was ten years older and more serious than his other friends. Pisarev, at this time left his regiment, went to his estate in the Tula region and devoted himself to work in local administration earnestly propagating schools in his region and finding teachers for them. Pisarev knew Chertkov as a good friend and brilliant guardsman, and at first skeptically regarded the question of his internal life, doubting its seriousness:

"You start the wrong way and nothing will come of your observations of English life" – instructively wrote Pisarev to Chertkov. – "In order to observe it is necessary to be acquainted with the observed occurrences, and this is done through study of their basic principles. Tell yourself honestly that you are going to England because you like living there and to fritter away your time and don't deceive yourself or others embellishing your trip with the best intentions and complex goals."[8]

And in conclusion Pisarev appealed to Chertkov with a request of a friendly favor, sounding a little bit odd after the instructive tone of the letter, – he asked to find out: "how much would it cost in England to buy male and female Borzoi."

To take a multi-month vacation and not leaving the regiment was not difficult for the Chertkov family due to the place it occupied in society and responding to a request of Chertkov's father to extend the vacation beyond the established limits, the Commander of the Life Guard Regiment, Baron Fredericks – the future Minister of the Imperial Palace under Nikolai II – answered with refined civility:

"My General! I am hurrying to tell you, that I am under your orders for the leave extension of your son since you desire it, and I am pleased to know, that you are satisfied with how he is spending his time. He is a charming boy who has the esteem and the affection of his comrades, which I share as well, and I hope that, once his leave will be over, I will see him again in the regiment."[9]

In London Chertkov, thanks to close family ties with the house of the Russian Ambassador in England, Count Shuvalov, arrived in that narrow circle of aristocratic families, in which he moved in St. Petersburg: invitations to a party or lunch at Prince Shuvalov's or Countess Panin were interchangeable with invites from Lord Northampton and Duke Bedford and instead of Petersburg's aristocratic yacht club, he visited London's Piccadilly Club and Cricket and Skating Ring Club. Nevertheless Chertkov, on the advise of his friend, G.S.W. Burnsby, who was his Governor, rented an apartment in a rural area, two hours from London. He lived in the house of the local minister, in circumstances much more modest than those which surrounded him in Petersburg, but from time to time traveled to London where he carried on the former society life. Aside from that, he read a lot, choosing mainly compositions on social science and questions of religion and ethics, and it seems that during this time, he began to form those experiences and skills of intellectual work that he could not have created in years past.

At the end of December 1879 Chertkov wrote his mother a letter from England:

"I can tell you a few fragments of my last thoughts: 1). In order to be useful, a person must define his position in the world around him; 2). He must therefore look at himself not subjectively but objectively; 3). He can only reach such a view when the strength of all his aspirations are concentrated not upon himself, but on some kind of high goal, located outside himself." And he wrote further that concentrating all his thought on Christian study "can indeed be useful to fulfill the problems of his life"[10].

It became more and more clear to him that he needed to give up his old way of life, quit the regiment and find some project that would justify his life in his own eyes.

In order to live like everyone, it was not necessary to search and think, it was necessary only to stay in the frame of the accustomed way of life. Many comrades and friends were on this beaten path, and to go on it was easy and simple. The new life's path was unclear; he himself had to search and meanwhile, questions arose, which had to be considered from various angles. Chertkov, having a premonition about his coming loneliness, began to think about what he should strive for next to find in his close circle of people, whom together could discuss questions put to him and in that task tried to implement their life-understanding. At the same time, analyzing his life, he began to feel that it was built on the basis of overt injustice: those means which he could spend with such sweep, were provided by his parents' lands – in the final count by peasants working on it for paltry compensation, and it was impossible to hide from oneself that namely their work created refined luxury surrounding him. The thought occurred to Chertkov that, deciding to reorganize his life, it was necessary first of all to strive to use the means received from his parents for the benefit of the peasants who created it, and for that it was necessary to move into the village in his parents' estate, to meet with needy peasants and find out what perhaps would be useful to them. In such a way projects took shape, as if at some point at which life's journey must turn to the other side: resignation, circle of new friends, activity in the village.

In the beginning of 1880, Chertkov returned to Petersburg and told his mother and father about his decision to leave the service. They both saw the future of their son in totally different tones: it was absolutely clear that he, without any effort could go on the path which his father and uncle went, and finishing his days, occupying the proper place: "Adjutant General, member of the Government Council Vladimir Grigorievich Chertkov."

Resigning from the service, disregarding such a career, was an action that would cause society salons to begin to speak with perplexity and disapproval, like about something incomprehensible, unusual, and, like everything unusual, almost unpleasant. Chertkov's mother tried to investigate the motives of his decision, it was more difficult for his father to do this, but he had to come to terms with his son's decision, knowing his obstinacy and swiftness in carrying out his wishes.

Chertkov's friends were glad to see him again after his return from England and he could again devote himself to the usual entertainments and noisy drinking bouts.

"Dear friend, Chertkov, – wrote his comrade Prince Vasilchikov, soon after his return to Petersburg, – this evening we are repeating our trip to the gypsies and are strongly counting on you. In order to go there, all the company is gathering at our place at 9 o'clock. I hope that you don't refuse us."[11]

And during that very time, his friend, the sensible R.A. Pisarev, receiving a letter in which Chertkov wrote him about his desire to interpret and again organize his life gave him instruction:

"Don't long for ideals, which we did not attain and open a road to those good instincts which are in you but which can disappear."[12]

Before his resignation from service was finalized, Chertkov wrote to his parent's estate manager, Vladimir Sergeyevich Shramm that he planned to settle in at the estate and asked that he make the necessary arrangements.

Shram served the Chertkovs for more than twenty years. He enjoyed the absolute confidence of his landlords more so, that his father and grandfather ran the estate before him. All management of the Chertkovs were concentrated in his hands: he himself thought about when and what kind of crops to produce, how it was more expedient to buy and sell horses, sheep and milk cows, how to rent out unnecessary land to peasants at such a rate so as to receive a bigger return, and what kind of fines to assess for pasturage of cattle on the landlord's land, wedging between wooded fields and meadows belonging to the villagers. Chertkov's parents felt that thanks to Shram they were delivered from the necessity to know specifically how their wealth was produced, – this was a boring task and completely unpleasant. And Shramm understood that he could act, as he liked, if there would be a regular transfer of money in Petersburg, from time to time send out accounts, strictly send congratulatory letters during Christmas, Easter and New Year's. He absolutely never spoke about managerial tasks with the young master and knew this man only superficially– as a lover of horses and dogs, passionate hunter, ready to gallop like crazy at full speed with his dogs after a full-grown wolf or quick-legged fox. And during the span of several years, Shram considered it necessary from time to time to write Chertkov respectable letters, in which he announced only about perspectives for the hunt, and how its going in the landlord's kennel:

"I very much regret, that sad circumstances did not permit you to visit the estate this summer, however, now that it was not successful, God willing, will be successful next year, I will try to save the foxes and rabbits for you."[13]

"I found thoroughbred English pups, excellent and beautiful dogs, I was looking for them for a long time, and finally got them. They themselves are good for our place, and cross-breed them with the borzoi are still better, you saw this in Bibishka and Ubee."[14]

Finding out that Chertkov decided to stay at the estate, Shram decided beforehand that he must organize his life such that it is befitting to live like a big esquire settled in his holdings. He took appropriate measures and wrote Chertkov that he already hired a coachman and his wife who will fill the responsibility of laundress, found a gardener, is looking for a cook and advises bringing a valet with him from Petersburg.

In the spring of 1880, Chertkov left Petersburg and settled in his family's estate in Lizinovka. A year later, in the spring of 1881 he returned for several months to the regiment and then resigned from the service and settled in the village. Here he had the total possibility to organize his life, although with less brilliance than in Petersburg, but everything was comfortable and carefree.

Using total independence as a rich and highborn landowner, he was able to carry out social works in the branches of local government, which were left to representatives of the privileged estate, and in the same way to justify his life in his own eyes, believing in himself, that he is doing a worthwhile deed. His wealth and position immediately opened for him access to this work, and very quickly he became a member of the local council, administrator of schools, honorable world judge and member of the office of peasant affairs, which investigated complaints of peasants against the actions of the local authority. And again facing him was the ready, well-trodden rut in which went the lives of many noblemen, leaving an official career, – free and easy life in the country estate, winter – trips for several months to the capital, in order to hold on to former ties, visit society salons and – from time to time – noisily boozing; in the future – wedding to a girl "of our circle" and a position of the marshal of the nobility.

Chertkov indeed went to the village as a young rich esquire, planning to do a great favor for those peasants, at the expense on which he lived, having an unclear understanding of their needs.

But that love of independence that spoke in all of Chertkov's life, interfered with his keeping in step with others in this situation as well.

R.A. Pisarev, with whom Chertkov often shared his plans concerning his activities in the village, gave him prudent advice:

"I am rather afraid that you, not knowing the task will begin to break and destroy everything in your own way or undertake various improvements and not finish anything; I am afraid in general, that you will make the same mistake as [the main character in] "Morning of the Young Landowner" of Turgenev or Goncharov - I don't remember."[15]

Pisarev's apprehensions were a bit exaggerated. Chertkov was not able to "break and destroy" to the end because the land did not belong to him, but to his parents. He could spend at his discretion very large amounts of money that his parents gave him every year at his full disposal, but he was not granted the right to change the order established on their land.

Chertkov's projects went in a different direction, scrutinizing the work of the zemstvo, he notices it's weak sides and conceives the idea of implementing on his parent's estate those measures to which the zemstvo does not pay attention. In that way the project came about to organize a trade school, in which children of the local peasantry could learn, free of charge, shoe-making, joinery, cooperage; also the thought arose to oppose the village store owners, selling wares at triple the price, and organize a store in which the wares were at a fixed price, in order to cover the expense but not to make a profit, and set up a community savings bank.

All these things were new. They gave Chertkov the goals to apply his talent and energy which before he generously wasted in drinking bouts and revelry and which now demanded use. But honestly analyzing himself, Chertkov felt that all these things, useful and necessary, in and of themselves, couldn't give him total satisfaction. He felt the necessity to think through his life-understanding, to find those basic prerequisites from which all his ideas and all his activities would grow as a logical result.

Spending a few months every winter in Petersburg, where his mother, melancholy from living apart from him persistently called, he tried to create a circle of friends who also strove to think through their life-understanding. In such an environment, where Chertkov used to abide, it was easier to find friends for noisy revelry, than for taking part in a circle of thinkers, but he found a few people not alien to this aspiration. And one of them, Prince Vasily Pavlovich Golitzyne, a student of Petersburg University, having lived through a period of intense search and with such peaceful elation, which can be found in the early years of life, sharing these thoughts and feelings with Chertkov made him one of his closest friends and was ready to carry on endless conversations with him.

"Its funny, – wrote Golitzyne to Chertkov in the winter of 1881, that even though I spent 15 hours in your apartment, there are still things to talk about, although in writing."[16]

Gallitzin actively began to search amidst the society youth, in which he himself belonged, for people wishing to join the yet to be planned circle and announced his success to Chertkov with joy:

"Concerning our religious association, talked much with Count Geyden and he is ready to join us with joy and faith in success of our activity. The plan of activity and the methods are already designed. When we see each other, we will talk about it."[17]

And another friend, Captain of the Life Guard Cavalry, D.F. Trepov wrote him about the organization of the circle:

"I passionately wish to organize the circle of conversation on various themes, prepared beforehand, in one word, that which you and I wanted to organize in the regiment, but unsuccessfully. I already spoke with a few people who relate very sympathetically, especially Count Kutuzov. It would be preferable to organize this circle soon, as in the proverb "strike while the iron is hot", therefore I ask that you give me information that you have, about such circles and if possible, as soon as possible."[18]

So appeared a small circle in which Gospels were read, and questions discussed arising from these readings. And in close ties with it arose another circle – in considerable degree from the same people – which should have to carry out Gospel ideas in the form of charity: "The Association of Christian Aide."

Both of these circles arose before Chertkov moved to the country and gathered for a short time after his departure from Petersburg.

Golitzyne was pleased with both circles. He wrote with pleasure to Chertkov about which passages from the Gospels they read during the meetings, and about that for charity they succeed in finding new means. Chertkov took part in both circles, but the self-analysis, which forced him to abandon the accustomed way of life and move to the country, shows itself here as well as exposing those contradictions that others preferred not to see.

Those brilliant society youth, who from time to time came together at meetings of the circle, felt a necessity to infuse the spirit of new interests in their lives different from the ones they were used to, giving up their time in the evening in high society salons, balls and drinking bouts, but did not intend to change their lives in their basics and refuse prosperity and privilege which they used.

Like other members of the circle Chertkov could sometimes order the harnessing of a trotter and call upon people whose fortunes were at the bottom of the barrel in order to donate 10 or 20 rubles from the sum the circle had, but he felt something false in such good deeds. And it is possible that still at this time sarcastic thoughts came to his mind, which he told of many years later, saying that to devote oneself to philanthropy is more repulsive than riding on a trotter, because in philanthropy is it possible to imagine that you are serving the people and as riding on trotters there is no such hypocracy.[19]

As it was to be expected, these circles proved to be short-lived – they existed only 2 or 3 winters, and slowly died down completely. Chertkov took part in these meetings – sometimes they were organized in his apartment, but he felt he must go on his path about which he subsequently wrote in his diary in January 1884, summarizing the meaning of events that were experienced in the last years:

"The time came to break consistently and relentlessly not only my former way of life, but also an understanding and ideas given by education and background. Breaking continues until this day, breaking, relentlessly collapsing of customs and views, inculcated since childhood, and replacing them with totally new understanding about life and relationships toward people."[20]

Spending most of the year in Lizinovka, Chertkov unyieldingly strove to implement those intended measures, many of which he brought to fruition. A good building was built for the trade school, experienced teachers were found, and 60 peasant boys studied there - their studies being paid by Chertkov. A village store and savings bank were organized. A first-aid station for peasants began to operate regularly - organized by Chertkov's mother who instructed him to invite the zemstvo doctor twice a week to take care of the sick there.

Chertkov's friend, Pisarev, somewhat skeptically relating to his beginnings, went there in the fall of 1881, wrote him, returning from the estate:

"Returning from Lizinovka and summing up my stay at your place, I was very happy to come to a pleasant conclusion based on those impressions which you and all of Lizinovka made on me."[21]

And in another letter, written the year after, Pisarev gave credit to Chertkov's energy:

"Reading your letters, I am certain more and more, that our roles have changed: before I had to inspire you into activity, now it is the opposite, your letters have on me the same effect as mine had on you."[22]

These activities gave Chertkov some satisfaction, and probably this prevented him for the first time to feel with all sharpness the contradictions between his aspirations and his lifestyle, which contained all the habits of a rich nobleman inoculated from childhood.

In the respectful letters that Chertkov, living in Petersburg, received from the manager of the estate of his mother, it is not difficult to notice these social boundaries:

"All of your orders have been fulfilled, – wrote Shramm in the winter of 1881, – the school children are sewing so diligently that soon they will bankrupt me of the supply of hide, the sick, situated in the casualty ward, are being cured, your horses and retinue are in good health."[23]

But continuing to think about his life, Chertkov made a few attempts to simplify his way of life: he moved from landlord's home luxuriously furnished to the empty workshop of the trade school and tried to introduce the elements of equality in his relations with the staff. With the young village lad who carries out the duties of clerk and copier, he talks about questions of life-understanding, gives him to read a few pages of his diary and persuades him to also start writing a diary.

Elizaveta Ivanovna Chertkov, noticing that her son's life is again leaving the prepared course, and he again thought up something unusual for the people in his circle, wrote him in the winter of 1882 with alarm and easy reproach:

"It seems to me that you are too disposed to confuse democracy with Christianity, which advises each of us to remain in our social position; harm from this for all situated around you is obvious. Remember my word (I would be glad to be mistaken), your servants will not be suited for any job after working with you... To know that you eat worse, dress worse and drink unlike anyone in your circle does not please me; but note that I don't add much importance to this, I am only stating my impressions."[24]

And as though wishing to remind her son of the brilliance of the "high society" life, from which he strove to leave, she in one of her letters gives the unique scene of their social life, writing about the tsar's visit to their home, who wished to spend the evening with them together with two high princes and a few selected guests. The whole etiquette of the gala reception in the high society home was held with great care, with the exception of one detail: Chertkov's father, due to the illness of his legs, couldn't meet his guests at the bottom of the stairs and gave this mission to his cousin Grigorii Alexandrovich Chertkov:

"Our evening took place and seemed very successful. Our guests gathered about ten o'clock. Grisha Chertkov met them at the bottom of the stairs and I on the stairs. There were: Mikhail Nikolaevich with Olga Feodorovna and their son, the Tsar with the Empress, and already when we sat down to tea, an embarrassed Maria Pavlovna arrived with Vladimir Alexandrovich. Papa opened the door between the first room and the red living room which gave new beauty to the whole apartment, in the living room was covered the large round table for tea, around which the ladies sat and I poured them tea... There were Betsy Shuvalova, Nellie Bariatinskaya, Countess Vorontsova with her husband, aunt and uncle Chertkov, Gagarin, Cherevin and Levashov. After tea, everyone went into papa's study and walked around the room for a long time, looking at everything, finally sat down to play cards. The Tsar with his party sat at your round ancient table of Louis XV, which was dragged from your room and which everyone loved. The Empress sat with the ladies and cavaliers at the committee table and played their games. Papa was near them... At one all went to dinner: the red living room was filled with three round tables decorated with white English plates and flowers, everything looked very formal. The Empress invited papa and uncle Gagarin to sit near her. The Tsar at another table sat between Countess Vorontseva and me... Dinner was wonderful, everyone was happy and nice."

And in conclusion Elizaveta Ivanovna, as if remembering about those new interests that her son lived for, added:

"I don't know if you are interested enough in this kind of thing to enjoy reading my detailed description."[25]

The negative attitude toward the external brilliance of high society life, appearing in Chertkov, distressed his mother and father, but what still alarmed them more was the rejection of established traditions in the sphere of faith which with every year became clearer and clearer in his letters to his mother. Analyzing his life-understanding, Chertkov, as he often wrote to his mother, strove to find a "clear meaning" in Gospel sermons and to reject everything that contradicts him in social life and in church teachings. In the process of this critical work an abrupt reevaluation of worth happened; church sacraments and rituals completely lost fascination in his eyes, it began to appear senseless reading that all people not belonging to the predominant church are condemned to eternal suffering, actions tied to force and especially war became unacceptable to him.

He had to think in solitude and these views were not brought into a system, but he talked about them more and more often, surprising others with his opinions, so differing from customary views, that a few were ready to consider his words witty paradoxes, got into arguments and energetically defended his point of view. His mother, feeling that her son was going farther and farther from her path, experienced this with great pain, often getting into intense arguments with him, but at the same time – sometimes with tenderness and pride – thought that in breaking up of previously formed beliefs, he would only strive to carry out his obligation just like he understands it. And in correspondence, writing in pencil during one of these moments, probably after a long conversation she wrote:

"My boy, I don't want you to think that I don't sympathize with your internal life; a few things aren't my taste, but my goal, like yours is that there should be nothing done against your conscience. As long as you act in accordance with it I will sympathize with you and ask God always to support you in fulfilling every goal, and that He does not allow, that even I would be able to disturb or distract you, when His will has been declared. Good night, my boy."[26]

In 1883 Chertkov turned twenty-nine and feeling the pressure of accumulated energy he was ready to devote it fully for such matters in which to implement a new life-understanding, already formed for the last year, although he still did not think it totally through to the end. Activities in the village that occupied him during this time, seemed useful, but he could not look at it as the goal of his whole life. Thinking about his traveled path, Chertkov himself realized precisely how far he went internally from those interests, which people in his circle lived.

At the end of 1883, answering a letter from his mother who was trying to convince him that government service and company of people, equal to his position, may be useful for him in educational relations, teaching him to face higher demands, Chertkov wrote:

"Now take my situation. I am almost 30, at my disposal more than ten thousand a year, and at the same time I deeply believe in certain basic principals and consider spreading this belief to be the main mission of my life. Where can I better reach these goals and have a big influence? There where my actions will be less limited, where initiative and direction stay in my hands and where I can support my projects with my material wealth? Or there where I will soon be only an executive, where I will continually reconcile with more or less important circumstances directly contradicting my convictions, where I will for that social service let go of many of the things that depend on me? I will lose my money on one thing, my attention on another – and I will do this only for the hope that my work will have some educational influence on me?."[27]

He tried to organize his new life on the basis of those views, which he strove to work out, not accepting on faith prepared opinions and he knew well there was no return to the past: his decision to throw away his brilliant career he called his "recovery" and wrote in his diary that only from this day he indeed began to live life. Nonetheless, studying Chertkov's diaries and letters, it is possible to notice that his life, although it went tensely, gave him little simple and clear joy.

In Chertkov's life there were many contradictions, which, as is shown in his diary, he experienced with great pain, fought with it, but was not able totally overcome it. He refused luxury surrounding him in Petersburg, and creating the trade school for peasant children, strove to return to the peasants' part of the means, which they paid his parents in the form of rent. But some habits inculcated in him since childhood continued to live in him, and considering wealth evil, he in many ways remained an esquire who does not know the worth of money.

He was able from to time to hold himself to the rule of cleaning his own room, but at the same time kept the whole staff of servants in the house; traveling to Voronezh for a meeting of the gubernia zemstvo conference, he did not sit alone in the first-class car, but in the crowded car of third class causing perplexed smiles from the local residents; but staying at the hotel, gave the lackeys the tips in the sum, which probably well exceeded this economy.

He did not pay much attention to those external barriers that separated him from people, located on another step of the social ladder, and would himself directly and simply speak about what interested him with teachers teaching children in school, where he was a trustee, and with neighbors on the estate and with the coachman who served him. But at the same time everyone felt that he was not accustomed to meet opposition to his will, and this alienated him even from those people who had good relations with him.

Those friendly ties that Chertkov created with those of his age from his youth became completely weaker right after he changed his views. Comparing those letters saved in the archive with those correspondence before he quit the service, sometimes it is possible to think that they are related to another person, so much have they changed the social structure of people with whom he corresponds. He himself wrote his mother that his correspondence with former friends almost came to nothing and he considered it quite comprehensible.

"As long as some new beliefs relating to questions of life have been developing in me, as long as these beliefs have been moving away from the beliefs of people with whom I was close earlier, my relations with my former friends, not that then lose interest, but were becoming less communicative. When our main ideas separate, then the conversation about trifles either accepts the most superficial character or goes soon toward basic question in which there is no agreement."[28]

He wrote his mother, that on the other hand he had started friendships with those people with whom he came into contact during his work in the zemstvo; but the word "friendship" in this case could be used only with some strained interpretation: concrete matters which involved Chertkov with these new people were for him mostly "trifles"; and the "main thing", meaning his life understanding, was alien to those around him. In this sphere of his life, which Chertkov himself considered most vital, he was alone.

In June 1883 Chertkov received a letter from Pisarev in which he wrote about his upcoming marriage and persistently asked to come for the wedding that would take place at the beginning of July. Pisarev belonged to the group of those few friends from Chertkov's youth with whom he did not lose touch in the new conditions of his life. Beside their personal friendship, they became close in general interest, because both of them worked in the zemstvo, although the building of a new world-outlook which was carried on by Chertkov was to a certain degree alien for Pisarev and interested him little.

Pisarev's estate was located in the Tula gubernia and Chertkov had to travel a long time by rail and by horse, but he gladly accepted the invitation and got ready to go. There were many guests at Pisarev's wedding and among those arriving from Tula was the public prosecutor of the county court, N.V. Davydov. The man was lively and sociable, well-read and a pleasant co-conversationalist. Davydov easily started an acquaintanceship with the most varied people, was a desired guest of families that, sometimes it seemed, had little in common. He did not think about basic questions of life, lived easily and not too complicated, could, wearing a uniform and appearing in court in his official role, send the condemned to jail or hard labor, but in ordinary time relate benevolently toward people, willing to render various services to his multitude of acquaintances and strive in their interests. He was well-acquainted with the Tolstoys, whose estate Yasnaya Polyana was located 12 versts from the city of Tula, was often in their home and Tolstoy related to him amicably.

Having met Davydov and talking with him, Chertkov slowly switched to topics not usual among the circle of guests gathering to celebrate a wedding. With characteristic humor, Chertkov loved to discuss his opinions, so much unexpected by his collocutors, that they did not immediately find words for retort and with some confusion stopped before conclusions, seeming to them paradoxes that they could not accept and were not always able to disprove. Davydov was not only a smart and polite collocutor, but also a public prosecutor, who must stand guard in favor of the government power and the Orthodox Church, and Chertkov with peculiar pleasure could tell him of his views on the incompatibility of any coercion and military service in particular, with Christian dogma that he realized in the last years.

But Davydov knew one of the main rules of that science, which the French call "*savoir vivre*" – the science to live: not to think about problems of life very seriously. Chertkov's words surprised him not by the revealed contradiction between the demand of Christian ethics and service to the government about which Chertkov spoke. Being at Tolstoy's, Davydov heard more than once such opinions, and now he was totally amused by these coincidences in opinions of these two unacquainted people. And listening to Chertkov he repeated the same thing several times:

"Yes but Tolstoy says the same thing. You repeat Tolstoy's words – you need to absolutely meet with Tolstoy."[29]

And Davydov, being always ready to do the favor pleasant to his collocutor, offered to introduce Chertkov to Tolstoy.

Chertkov knew Tolstoy through his literary works, but had no idea of his religious-ethical beliefs: up to this time Tolstoy wrote little about these themes and almost every article in which he talked about them could not appear in print as a consequence of the censor hindrance. And Chertkov listened to Davydov's words about Tolstoy's new views with great joy because he felt totally alone in his search.

After spending some time as Pisarev's guest, Chertkov returned home but he made the decision to meet with Tolstoy in the near future.

Davydov, on his behalf, told Tolstoy about Chertkov, the former having already heard about him from one of his visitors, G.A. Rusanov, living in the Voronezh gubernia, a story about Chertkov's activities that were unusual for a landowner.[30]

In September Davydov wrote Chertkov that Tolstoy was in Yasnaya Polyana and was leaving for Moscow not earlier than October. Chertkov then prepared to go to Yasnaya Polyana, but some business concerning work in the zemstvo held him back. At the end of October Chertkov left the village and, staying at one of the best Moscow hotels – the Slavyansky Bazaar, – found a telegram sent to him by Davydov:

"TOLSTOY IS IN MOSCOW!"

III
The Beginning of the Friendship

Very few pieces of information about Tolstoy's and Chertkov's first conversation were preserved, but it is possible to precisely imagine for yourself it's basic tone. In youth Tolstoy was shy, but with years that awkwardness, which he felt somehow, meeting with unfamiliar people, went away and he learned how to speak with them freely and simply. But Tolstoy was unable and did not like to hold a conversation that he considered unnecessary, usually immediately trying to direct the conversation such that it would give him interesting material. Attempting to separate the basic core of the conversation from useless peel as soon as possible, he persistently strove to discover for himself his collocutor's moral position, often asking one question after another, as much as it was possible to do this, while not violating the demand for tact.

Chertkov had two characteristics interesting for Tolstoy: first, he was a new person for him, organizing his life differently than other people in his circle, and second, because, abandoning his brilliant career and settling in the village, he was guided by the desire to find such a path on which he would be able, although to a certain degree, get closer to implementing his new life-understanding.

Both characteristics were close to Tolstoy himself and learning of Chertkov from mutual acquaintances, Tolstoy was glad during the first meeting to pose these questions that seemed to him most important, but the answers for which he had to seek alone so far.

Chertkov still in his youth adopted the ability necessary for a high-society person: to enter confidently to the living room – a science, which, judging from his letters to his mother, he did nor master immediately, – and, if he wished, to support any conversation. But he, like Tolstoy, always became bored by the conversations that were carried on only for the sake of decorum and loved to joke, that people supposing, like Middle Age scholars, that "nature can't stand emptiness" are most of all afraid of silence during a meeting and are scared to rush to fill it with unnecessary words.

Chertkov, after following Tolstoy into his study – a secluded, peaceful and bright room with windows looking out over the garden and courtyard, with long cloth green curtains, with simple soft black armchairs and a big writing desk on which set two candles in ancient copper candle holders, stood a copper inkwell in a green malachite stand and paper lay in a pile, in the very beginning of the conversation felt that he could directly and simply speak with Tolstoy about those questions, which he constantly thought about by himself in the last few years. Many years later, Chertkov wrote about this in his memoirs about the meeting with Tolstoy:

"I met with him, like old friends, since it seemed, that he from his side already heard about me from a third person. He at that time was finishing his book *What Do I Believe*. I remember that the question about the relation between teaching of Christ and military service was already then in my conscience decided unfavorably, and that I had no one sharing my opinion (at this time I had not heard about Quakers and other pacifists). Starting a conversation with each new acquaintance on religious grounds, I hurried to produce this probing question. In Lev Nikolaevich, I met the first person who, completely and with conviction, shared the same view on military service. When I posed my usual question and he, in response, started to read his handwritten manuscript of *What Do I Believe* lying on his desk, which was categorically opposed to military service from a Christian point of view, I felt such joy from the acknowledgement that the period of my spiritual solitude had finally ceased, that immersed in my own deep thought, I could not follow the long passages which he read to me and regained consciousness only when, reading the last lines of his book, he distinctly pronounced the words of his signature: *Lev Tolstoy*.[1]

Conversing with Chertkov about these questions which were close to both of them, Tolstoy, also it seems, immediately felt that they were speaking the same language, although his collocutor did not totally rush to agree with his words completely – Chertkov was not inclined to deny his opinion in those few situations when he came to different conclusions. Wishing to firm up their budding acquaintanceship, Tolstoy introduced Chertkov to his family, invited him to lunch and asked him definitely to come to his house on the return trip from Petersburg, where Chertkov decided to go to visit his parents. In several days, returning from Petersburg, Chertkov stopped on purpose in Moscow, went to Tolstoy's, was at his house two times and each time felt that strengthening sense of mutual internal bonds which were experienced during the first meeting.

This was apparent in Chertkov's correspondence with his mother: nothing has changed in his external life in the first months after meeting Tolstoy. Those projects that occupied him when he was living in the countryside went smoothly, as if in the path of a big wheel and carried him with it even when they stopped to occupy his thought with former intensity.

Returning to Lizinovka, Chertkov immediately found himself in the familiar situation of the way of life that he created, in the center of varied beginnings, each of which needed his work and attention. It was necessary to find out what was happening in the trade school and to give further orders concerning the expenses and it's needs, to go to the first aid post, listen to accounts about work in the Lizinovka Savings Bank, to order a photo projector for reading with pictures, at which on winter evenings not only children gathered but adult peasants as well, to spend a few days making trips, visiting schools in the neighboring villages, which were under his supervision in his zemstvo work. Finally is was necessary to discuss with the manager Shramm about plots of land which Chertkov's parents assigned for his disposal, in order to organize a small model farm there, with the help of an agronomist.

These new projects strongly interested Chertkov, he wanted the fields of this village to become model plots where peasants could be introduced to an attainable agronomical science and he himself intended, under the leadership of a specialist, to study farming closer.

Returning from Moscow after his meeting with Tolstoy, he purposely went to the Tula district to his friend Pisarev, with the idea of introducing and discussing this plan with Professor Stebut, supervisor of higher farming courses, owner of Pisarev's neighboring estate. And, although all of these projects, some started earlier, some just conceived, seemed urgent and necessary, he could not devote his former enthusiasm to them, since he was constantly reminded of those thoughts which made him go to Tolstoy and lay the basis for their conversation. These thoughts seemed to him more important than all his projects, since thoughts had ultimately to define each part of his activity, although in reality everything often turned out completely different: each new project began to live a life of its own, pushing aside motives which gave it birth and advancing his next work, dull and small, but totally unavoidable.

Feeling himself exactly as if in captivity, in creating those very projects, Chertkov wrote his mother:

"Despite the fact that I harnessed myself still tighter to the zemstvo yoke, I cannot not feel every day and every minute that I have too many projects, that I cannot manage all of them well and that its better to do little and well than take on a lot and not follow and not watch for the general idea and order."[2]

Returning in his thoughts to the conversation with Tolstoy, Chertkov took a few English books on the question of religion out of his library and sent them to him. The letter that he sent to Tolstoy with this package was the first after their acquaintance but written like they had been friends for a long time and parted only the day before.

Not trying for any kind of artificial appeal, Chertkov began the letter with simple and direct words:

"I am sending you a few books. Perhaps some of them will prove useful to you."

After giving a list of the books and concisely having said that they might be interesting to Tolstoy, Chertkov mentioned his life in Lizinovka and only at the very end of his letter was it possible to notice the feeling remaining in him after the new acquaintance:

"It is wonderful here now. The first snow just fell and became very enjoyable. Tomorrow the boys begin work in the trade school; it will be lively and still more enjoyable. Goodbye, Lev Nikolaevich, thank you one more time for your kindness toward me."[3]

Part of the texts which Chertkov sent Tolstoy were concerned not only about the study of Christ but about his divinity; the views expressed in which Chertkov still did not totally renounce at this time, despite some steps he made in this direction. He did not totally agree with Tolstoy on this point, but dealt with this disagreement with the serenity of a man confident in himself and independent in his judgment.

"Your comment regarding your pleasure to find out that I don't agree about everything with Tolstoy surprised me and forced me to smile," – wrote Chertkov to his mother. "Indeed mama, you suppose that I have so few of my own convictions relating to these questions that I would agree to everything with the first new acquaintance."[4]

But Chertkov felt during this time that this "new acquaintance" occupied such a considerable place in his life, like none of his former friends. Making entries in his diary and analyzing his actions with nagging thoroughness, Chertkov prepared to show this diary to Tolstoy.

"I want him to read it because I want him to see me better and could help better"[5], wrote Chertkov in his diary.

Tolstoy received the books Chertkov sent him, but, with the exception of one, they were of little interest to him, – he saw in them theological discussion, which he knew of already and of which a lot was alien to him.

Tolstoy answered Chertkov with a letter written very warmly and at the same time with great straightforwardness:

"Dear nice and near to me Vladimir Grigorievich, I received your books and I thank you for them. I read them, and don't disapprove me as too proud, but I found nothing in them... But I like you so much that I cannot not tell the whole truth."[6]

Tolstoy gave the concise characteristics of every book, and wrote that whoever accepts Christian teaching must focus on it with all his strength in order to transform his life, and distraction and disputable and cloudy dogmatic discussion can't interest him.

Chertkov, still during these years when he experienced the torturous need to comprehend his life, came to the conclusion that the measure of value of every teaching must be it's realization in life. He often wrote about this in his diary. Tolstoy's letter called in him the sense of closeness that he poured out in a short reply:

"In almost everything I agree with you and recognize you as the spokesman of my best aspirations."[7]

Chertkov had a big supply of untapped strength and a great need to act.

He felt the desire to open his inner world to Tolstoy, introduce him to the very essence of his ideas, in order to fully explain the general points of departure, then – certainly to find some kind of life project, which could flow from his beliefs. Both of these aspirations were revealed in the very beginning of Tolstoy's and Chertkov's acquaintance.

Chertkov sent Tolstoy his notebook with excerpts from books read and entries of his thoughts. Then, coming toward the end of December 1883 to Petersburg, so as to spend the Christmas holidays with his parents, he made a stop in Moscow, so as to be at Tolstoy's, and on the way back again, staying in Moscow, shows Tolstoy what was done in the few days before writing in his diary, in which he remembered his entire life story and which led up to his strivings. And then Chertkov meets with Marakuyev, a book publisher for the masses, and a few prominent writers, as though preparing for a new project concerning the dissemination of his most important ideas.

Tolstoy in the beginning of his acquaintance with Chertkov was intensely busy with a series of works: proofreading his book "*What Do I Believe*", which they decided to publish without prior censorship in fifty copies, in the hope that, in such an insignificant circulation, it could avoid confiscation, scrutinizing the life of the city poor and putting in order those ideas that were then discussed in "*What Then Must We Do?.*"

He lived like a foreigner in his own house, trying to stick to his customs and rituals in a foreign state, but was powerless to change its way of life: he wore a sheepskin coat and felt boots in which peasants walk, learned to sew boots and invited simple people into his study, the appearance of whom brought perplexed smiles to society guests visiting the Tolstoy family.

In his house went another life with its worries, joys and work: Countess Sofia Andreyevna solicitously held connections with the most prominent noble families in Moscow and "introduced to society" her eldest daughter, enjoying her success. After evenings in the aristocratic home of the Samarin's, she wrote to her sister Tatiana Kuzminskaya:

"The ball and dinner were wonderful, the luxury was such that that there could be no better ball. Tanya wore a pink gauze dress, plush roses; I wore purple velvet and yellow shades of pansies. Then there was the ball at the governor-general's, evening and performance at the Teplov's and even a Christmas tree for the little ones, and today again a ball at Count Orlov-Davydov's and Tanya and I are going. She has a wonderful dress, very thin tulle, greenish-blue and lilies-of-the-valley with a pink tint all over. Tomorrow they are again dancing a huge ball at the Obolensky's. Tanya's and my legs are simply worn down."[8]

Tolstoy saw life at this time from another side, and remaining alone with himself wrote in his diary:

"After lunch I went to the cobbler's. How bright and morally refined it is in his dirty, dark corner. He works with a boy, his wife feeds"; "I was at the boot-tree maker's this morning. In the basement they intently cheerfully work and drink tea. Everyone works except me. I sleep. Sins: vanity, idleness."[9]

Tolstoy found for himself a few outlets, trying in his articles to discuss those thoughts that were useless to discuss at home. He worked persistently and painstakingly, many times reworking one phrase or another, striving hard for the possibility of fully expressing his thoughts, often complicating the sentences and making text cumbersome and unwieldy. But this work seldom found immediate response because it was difficult to reach a wide circle of readers. The book *"What Do I Believe"*, although only fifty copies were published with the hope that such an insignificant printing would avoid a ban, nevertheless was confiscated by the censure.

Tolstoy consoled himself in a letter to one of his acquaintances:

"It was published and was not permitted, but not burned, and brought to Petersburg, where, as far as I know, those who did not allow it, analyzed each and every chapter and read it. At least this is good."[10]

But Countess Sofia Andreyevna, with the preoccupation of a good housewife, counted up during this time expenses for the publication of this book and wrote her sister Tatiana Kuzminskaya:

"Instead of burning this composition prohibited by censors as it is required *by law*, they took them, all 50 copies, to Petersburg and read them in high circles *for free*. I said that I wished those people of substance would have paid 400 rubles for printing."[11]

Tolstoy, persistently developing his new views, as his letters and diaries show, was upset by his solitude and during this time seldom experienced the feeling of joyous uplifting. Chertkov, in his own way came to the conclusions, similar to Tolstoy, quickly understanding his complete thought, even before Tolstoy's words were spoken and at the same time always directly and precisely expresses his opinion, full of strength, which he was ready to give to the project, corresponding to his convictions, immediately occupied an exceptionally significant place in Tolstoy's life. Many events in Chertkov's life were close to Tolstoy by his own experience.

In Tolstoy's youth, just as in Chertkov's, he was attracted to passion and enjoyment, such as they were – the excitement of card games, carnal pleasures even if bought for money, the delirium of hunting, the sharp sensation of danger in war. And although remaining alone with himself, analyzing his feelings, he condemned his enthusiasm and wrote in his diary detailed developed rules of conduct, his life again and again slid down from those notches on which he strove to firm up.

Self-analyzing and aspiration to find the basics, which must determine the behavior of a person, characteristic of Chertkov were to a still greater degree characteristic of Tolstoy.

Still in youth, shy and awkward, he, unnoticeably for others, looked at the life of others opening up before him and in himself with such an attentive all-noticing glance, like a master looks at work, that he wants to understand.

Continuous introspection, which in a person with less reserve of life's strength would produce a burdensome condition of diffidence, became for him the source of creative work.

Like a watchmaker, who fastidiously dismantles the difficult mechanism until the tiniest screw, and then gathers it again letting it in motion, Tolstoy mentally dismantled his life until the last detail and restored it in an artistic work: that is how Tolstoy's first work *Childhood and Adolescence* appeared.

Most of all Tolstoy had to be impressed by that internal independence which Chertkov manifested by leaving a brilliant career opened to him and trying to live and think in his own way.

Tolstoy acquired literary fame early, could easily and pleasantly organize his life using a prepared template: consolidate his position in the literary world, joining a writing group of his choice, write books, the demand for which was guaranteed for him, and enjoy that material independence which his position could give him of a young, well-off, although not very rich landowner with a Count's title and ties to what was called "high society."

But his life's path went on the side away from the common road, with turns on which others looked with perplexity and often with condescending smiles. Despising literary and worldly ties, he retreated to his country estate with enthusiasm, given to farming, reading, hunting and studies with peasant children.

Married, he led the life of a landowner, earnestly working toward enriching his family and devoting himself to literary creativity.

He lived in such a manner for fifteen years; he made a total revision of his views, just as Chertkov did, not fearing to reach the conclusions that were incomprehensible and alien to his family.

Both of them were people not only much of the same culture but belonged to the same class, and those contradictions between views and lordly lifestyle, which they both experienced, were understandable and dear to both.

In his diary for 1884 Tolstoy often writes about Chertkov and always with the feeling of great closeness:

"I like him and believe in him." "He is burning with such enthusiasm." "I am tired, he is firm and unyielding."[12]

In the first year of their acquaintance, Tolstoy noted in his diary such words about Chertkov, which are not found about any other person:

"He is surprisingly in convergence with me."[13]

Closeness, born in the first meeting of Tolstoy and Chertkov, grew and strengthened during future encounters. Chertkov, returning to Lizinovka after the trip to his parents at the end of December 1883, when he, on the way to Petersburg and on the way back, stopped in Moscow for the meeting with Tolstoy, wrote him, that he wants to recount in his letters not about his external actions, but cover those internal springs which determined his behavior.

"You want to know what I do? I would like to tell you not about my actions, but my thoughts of them. Others consider these thoughts acting, originality or fantasy. And therefore they cannot help me in the examination of my conduct. With you, I feel myself on common ground, I know that you understand me."[14]

In long letters, often resembling intimate diaries, Chertkov told Tolstoy about his thoughts and feelings, especially staying on that which seemed to him the weakest place – on the feelings of sexual desire with which he fought and on the incongruity of his life and beliefs:

"In theory everything is well and beliefs in my mind are so clean and high, that they excite even sarcasm on the side of people comparatively gentle. But the real internal mood has nothing to do with the mental belief. In the mind there is Christ, unselfish service to God, direct understanding of teaching, absence of compromise, etc.; here, in the emotional sphere, is apathy, lethargy, pettiness, irritability, egoism..."[15]

Tolstoy, receiving such letters, was pleased, but along with it sensed the feeling of some alarm:

"Thank you that you write me, – answered Tolstoy. – I get excited about your every letter. I will tell you my feeling upon receiving them: I am terrified, fearful, – that you might lose your mind. And its not that I don't believe your strength, not highly appreciate you; but you, in my understanding, climbed horribly high (exactly where it is necessary), but it seems to me that you are not firm there. This comes from the fact that I like you a lot and that the project that you are working on, this bell tower, is very dear to me. I want to give you advice but fearful so as not to interfere."[16]

Chertkov was not inclined to accept on faith any kind of advice, but he felt that he needed support from another person, who already had come, to a significant degree, on the life's path that he decided to go. And in response, wrote Tolstoy:

"Why are you fearful to give me advice, Lev Nikolaevich? I feel sorry that you restrain yourself from this. I would understand your apprehension if you had reason to suppose that I would immediately, unquestionably implement your advice. In such a case it is indeed horrible to intrude on another person's life and be in charge of it.

But this is not the case, and your advice would serve me only as an indication of how another person, standing on common ground with me, would act in my place... If each person were so careful in giving his or her opinion, then continually each person would have to discover America and go through all the depressing and hindering phases of this process... Again, I respect your advice, as it would serve me as information. I need it a lot, I trust you, Lev Nikolaevich, even though I will not and cannot totally agree with it."[17]

Tolstoy did not have the idea to give Chertkov advice in the form of prepared rules, usually valid for everyone and unnecessary to anyone in particular.

Answering Chertkov's letter, he tried to give him those methods he himself used in times of depression:

"Your unhappiness with yourself, conscious of the incongruity of life with the demands of the heart, I know myself, but what I ask of you, don't talk about this, don't think about it to yourself. This could be compared with the traveler, going to Jerusalem, and continually thinking that he has gone so little and has a lot remaining. These thoughts can only weaken his energy. It is only necessary to think about the next verst, if it is necessary to think about the future."[18]

At the same time Tolstoy had in his turn the desire to tell Chertkov about those sides of his life that were a torment to himself. In March 1884 Tolstoy wrote Chertkov a letter in which he talked about his family discord, and then asked him to destroy this part of his letter. Chertkov fulfilled this request but it is possible to judge the mood in which Tolstoy wrote this letter by the preserved lines:

"I write about myself: I would like to say that I am healthy and fortunate, but I cannot. I am not unhappy – far from it... but it is so upsetting for me."[19]

Receiving a response from Chertkov, Tolstoy wrote:

"Your letter for me was joy and consolation. And as you see from my last letter, I need comfort, sometimes support of my spiritual energy."[20]

Living alone in the country and corresponding with Tolstoy, Chertkov sometimes felt himself closer to him then, than when he met with him every day in Moscow. Visiting Tolstoy in his Moscow home, Chertkov often met other guests, and then it came to carrying on a common conversation lacking necessary concentration. And even remaining alone with Tolstoy, not always immediately came to begin a worthwhile conversation: sometimes shown weariness – Tolstoy had from intensive work, – Chertkov had from Moscow commotion; often were cases, when conversation stumbled into the blocks hidden in both of their characters: persistence in disputing their views, which could escalate to heated arguments, even during full agreement on other questions.

Leaving Moscow, Chertkov in his letters continued mentally conversing with Tolstoy, but talked about what he considered important and with the same words used when talking to himself. For a long time giving up his diary, Chertkov sometimes for several days in a row wrote Tolstoy letters in such manner as though he was alone by himself writing his vital thoughts and experiences. Never giving himself the difficulty of thinking about his expressions, he himself sometimes warns Tolstoy about this:

"Lev Nikolaevich, this I wrote you on the spur of the moment... this is only a torn off part of me totally unexpectedly even for myself."[21]

Chertkov did not belong to the number of people, for whom reflection on abstract themes are the only interesting way of spending time, – intellectual gymnastics, not tied to common happenings. In the process of becoming acquainted with the thoughts of Tolstoy, he developed the desire to work on their dissemination.

Already in April 1884, living in the countryside, Chertkov began to translate Tolstoy's book *What I Believe*, not permitted in Russia, into English. He only partially devoted his time to this project and continued to work on the trade school and other of his beginnings; but they occupied his thoughts less and less.

A sudden event sharply disrupted Chertkov's country life, prompting him to leave Lizinovka for several months, and apparently hastened the process of slow internal exit from those projects that for a period of several years were the objects of his efforts.

In the beginning of April Chertkov was in Petersburg and celebrated Easter with his parents. Everything went exactly as it would usually in the Chertkov home on ceremonial days: the front rooms were decorated with flowers, a multitude of impeccably well-trained staff dressed with special care, all day guests visited – coworkers of Grigorii Ivanovich Chertkov in brilliant, general's uniforms, sewn with gold with ribbons from the shoulders and medals, arriving directly from the palace, and ladies, relatives of the Chertkov's, in dresses, specially made for the day, costing so much that each of them could feed several peasant families for an entire year.

Grigorii Ivanovich Chertkov suffered from gangrenous legs for a period of several years already, feeling not worse than usual in the past year, and Elizaveta Ivanovna, worrying about his health, did not have grounds to worry about him.

Chertkov related to his father with respect, but in their relationship they felt some alienation since they differed too much in their views of life; he was much closer to his mother, but in conversations with her he had to avoid topics which could call for sharp and futile arguments about questions of faith; acquaintances of their family arriving to congratulate with the holiday were alien to him, the festive atmosphere of his high-society home during the holidays was painful for him. And he wrote to Tolstoy:

"Arriving here, I immediately experienced the usual feelings of lying in a coffin and the lid put on."[22]

As soon as the chance came to leave Petersburg, Chertkov hurried to return to the countryside. But just as he arrived in Lizinovka, he received a telegram prompting him to quickly return: on April 23rd his father suddenly passed away from a hemorrhage in his brain.

The death of his father postponed those projects to which he devoted his strength since he moved to the country by many months.

Chertkov's external situation changed little: his father fearing that he, after receiving his own land, would give it to the peasants and squander his legacy on his undertakings, bequeathed all his fortune to Elizaveta Ivanovna and she was not able only to sell the real estate without agreement of their son. In such a case, Chertkov, as usual, would receive from his mother means, not being a landowner and not taking on any business responsibility.

But in the first few months after his father's death, he could not carry on the former way of life since he could not leave his mother, who was in deep grief.

Chertkov wrote Tolstoy that he would try to stay with his mother at least until the end of summer, spent a few weeks in Petersburg and then went with her to England, hoping that a change of environment could help her, more so, that her close friends and co-religionists were there – followers of the preacher of Evangelical Christianity, Lord Radstock.

Leaving for England, Chertkov brought with him Tolstoy's *What I Believe*, which he started to translate into English during this period, and with characteristic persistence in achieving the goal put to himself, began to work on it and prepare it for publication. But sharing the basic thoughts of this book, Chertkov during this time disapproved of that harshness with which Tolstoy was writing against faith in the divinity of Christ and thought that some passages could be found unacceptable by many readers. And Chertkov made the decision to do one of two things: publish this book in it's entirety, but in a limited number of copies in order to give it to people who would not be troubled by these opinions, or publish it, with the exception of those passages which were alien to him. He expressed this to Tolstoy with great clarity:

"But I am sure that you understand that there are passages in this book with which I completely don't sympathize and that I am unwilling to be an instrument in its publication and distribution. The word, spoken or communicated often acts stronger than many deeds – you probably agree with this. And since I cannot consider myself in the right to do what is against my convictions, in the same way I cannot consider myself in the right to publish what is against them."[23]

Tolstoy, usually totally not inclined to agree with people, intending to bring some kind of change to his work, told Chertkov that he completely trusted him in the choices of passages he desired to shorten, adding:

"I will even be very glad to see what is unnecessary."[24]

Then, beginning to vacillate, Tolstoy wrote that it is better not to remove anything, but later reproached himself for vanity and offered Chertkov to act as he finds best, even not showing him these cuts until the English text came out.

Five years ago, arriving in England in order to tear away from routine conditions, better to think about his life's path, Chertkov moved in English aristocratic circles, visited London's high-society salons and clubs, was a guest at the estate of a lord, acquaintance of his mother, hunting together with him and his guests for fox and even went with acquainted English officers on the parade regiment of kings cuirassier. Now Chertkov's attention was concentrated on something else: he worked on the preparation for publication of Tolstoy's book in translation, with great relentlessness analyzed his internal life and persistently thought about how much contradicted the wealth that he used, his beliefs.

"You ask how do I work for what's right in life? – wrote Chertkov to Tolstoy from England. – This question makes me blush, because all this time I am in a weak and vile enough mood…toward my mother I notice in me little love and compassion, and it seems, often distresses her. Even thinking about you, I notice nasty traits in my relations toward you. In my sincere friendship toward you often stir in basic feelings of self-satisfaction that I have close relations with such "wonderful" person as you… So in answer to your question, I can only say that I am base and nasty and don't deserve my grub."[25]

The correspondence of Tolstoy with Chertkov shows that these confessions not only did not alienate Tolstoy from Chertkov, but also on the contrary strengthened the feelings of closeness.

"I am glad for your truthfulness and learn from it."[26] – wrote Tolstoy to Chertkov in response to one such letter.

In another letter, Chertkov wrote about his relations toward ownership. He explained to Tolstoy that he now received from his mother for life 20,000 rubles every year and that this money finds its own way into his pocket. Refusing to take it from his mother, he would not be able to give it another purpose and would lose the possibility to help to the peasants and fulfill those measures with which he was occupied the last years, living in the countryside. But this calming reasoning, apparently, did not totally satisfy Chertkov and he wrote Tolstoy that he wanted to know his opinion. Tolstoy, already thinking about his relation to property and continually reproaching himself for the contradiction which created in his life the situation of his manor house, his rich surroundings, receiving this letter, made an entry in his diary:

"It is scary for him to refuse property. He doesn't know how they amassed 20,000 rubles. He should of. I know: by working people under the burden of tormenting work. I have to write him."[27]

Tolstoy told Chertkov his opinion. But by his own experience Tolstoy knew just how difficult it was to break years of a created life style, causing such inescapable pain to close people who have another point of view. And in the duration of many years Tolstoy and Chertkov continually had to return to one and the same thoughts about the incompatibility of their beliefs with material welfare, and this motif passes through all their correspondence.

Working on the translation and preparation for printing the book *What I Believe*, Chertkov often thought about the last works of Tolstoy. Chertkov had the desire during this time to express his belief that theoretical articles of Tolstoy produce much less of an impression than his artistic works, are understandable for only a narrow circle of intelligent readers and that he should direct his creative power along another channel. At the same time Chertkov – as he himself wrote about this to Tolstoy – somewhat afraid, that sharing these thoughts, he really strove to give Tolstoy advice, such as about what was necessary to write, encroaching on that sphere in which Tolstoy was much more competent than he. But the already developed habit of expressing himself with full sincerity in letters to Tolstoy prevailed and Chertkov began to share these thoughts with Tolstoy:

"Indeed now, that you clearly understand the goal and meaning of life, you don't use your gift to hand down what you acquired in your artistic works? Such works would have much more influence than your last unpublished writings, although it would present the same thoughts. Please excuse me if you don't like my audacity concerning these questions."[28]

In another letter Chertkov with great insistence wrote:

"You wrote a book for educated people in which you stated your faith. But of the simple people no one understands even a single full page from this book. I tried to read to simple people from this book, choosing the most comprehensible pages and I saw that many passages incomprehensible in words and methods of presentation, confuses them and sets them against thoughts."

Chertkov wrote further on how not once, living in the countryside, he noticed that the peasants had to read empty and bad books for lack of others and the most understandable for them were not ones of theoretical reasoning, but stories. He argued that Tolstoy, putting into his stories his life-understanding, could present it with new force:

"Here, Lev Nikolaevich, is what we need from you, I beg you for this, *almost* demand, but not demand because I cannot demand, but beg in the glory of God. Excuse me, if I said anything extra. Be angry with me if you want, but pay attention to my request."[29]

The summer of 1884, as the haymaking only just got started, Tolstoy totally left his writing. He felt great mental fatigue from intellectual work, from commotion and unnecessary relations with unintended acquaintances in Moscow and especially continuous discord with his family, which, as his diary shows, he felt during this time especially sharply.

Day after day he got up at 6am, went to the meadow, still covered with dew, stood in a row with the peasants and cut until lunch, glad, when it was up to him not to fall behind the cutters, and persistently finishing his portion if they left him behind. As his body became tired, he felt, he came to inner peace. With the peasants it was not necessary to hold intentionally artificial conversations, no one stood on stilts, everyone did simple and indisputably necessary work.

"How difficult it is for me, my position of well-known author, – wrote Tolstoy in his diary. – Only with the peasants am I totally simple, that is to say, a real person."[30]

And the very same day, when Chertkov wrote in London a letter to Tolstoy, asking him not to write theoretical articles, comprehensible to a few, but stories, accessible to every peasant,

Tolstoy early in the morning worked at mowing and wrote in his diary:

"Went to mow. We cut, cut and cut again. Am very tired. "Timofei, dear, round up my cows, I have a child." He – simple-unkind boy, tired out, but nevertheless, runs. Here – moral conditions. "Anyuta, run dear, and drive the sheep." And the seven-year-old girl flies barefoot through the cut grass. Here are conditions. "Boy, bring a cup to drink" The five-year-old flies and brings it in a minute. He understood and did it."[31]

Tolstoy still many years before worked with enthusiasm in the school for peasant children, put together the "ABCs" and books for reading in the first community school, and the letter of Chertkov with the request to write works comprehensible and accessible to every peasant, could only be met with approval. Tolstoy himself in the previous winter thought that it was necessary to create books, intended for folk reading and wrote about this to Chertkov already in February 1884. Receiving Chertkov's letter, Tolstoy answered:

"You tell me that I must do this. But, my friend, I only desire one thing from this, live only then that I hope to do this... I am afraid to say even that I hope to do what you request of me. But what you request from me makes me glad and encourages me... And thank God, I didn't do anything else this summer than prepare myself for this."[32]

Although the time of acquaintance between Tolstoy and Chertkov was less than a year, their relationship already to a significant degree took shape. Tolstoy had already, although infrequently, met people who sympathized with his views and understood his search. But Chertkov not only spoke with him in one language but also excelled at great internal activity. He not only agreed with Tolstoy's words, but also strove to build the path for his teachings, spreading works that were not allowed to be published under censorship and started ties with foreign publishers. At the same time Chertkov precisely and persistently expressed his opinion and was not inclined to passively accept Tolstoy's judgment; his independence together with the compatibility of their basic thoughts was giving special tone to their relationship, and made relations with Chertkov interesting for Tolstoy. At the same time, correspondence and conversations with Chertkov could not be gradually locked into a cycle of identical discussions on one and the same subjects, gradually killing off any kind of friendship. Their relations continued to develop and had to flow out into one common project for both of them. The undertakings, to which Chertkov devoted his strength, after settling in the countryside, now were turning into an already completed phase for him; other interests were gradually pushing them aside.

At the end of the summer, Chertkov returned together with his mother to the countryside and immediately fell into a routine chain of chores: the co-op of carpenters was building a long-planned addition to the trade school; in the farming school in which he was the superintendent, it was necessary to replace a teacher, poorly treating the students; it was necessary to give instruction for the organization of model farming of the village, the thought of which occupied Chertkov very much already several months ago. But now these projects lost a significant part of their attractiveness, and the doubts that were associated to them came out with new clarity:

"What tortures me is that it is up to me to decide that a teacher is incompetent and remove him from his position using my prestige and the fact that the school depends on me financially; at the same time I never participated in the most essential and the difficult side of carrying out school business, i.e. never fulfilled the duties of a teacher. I serve as a leader of such an undertaking in which I never was a worker,"[33] – wrote Chertkov in his diary.

"My farm doesn't provide me with a real occupation, because I myself don't work, don't participate actively and hang out near the workers like an ignorant spectator... I sleep a lot and not peacefully and in general I am not happy with myself and don't know what to hold on for."[34] wrote Chertkov to Tolstoy a month after his return from abroad.

He copied Tolstoy's book *What I Believe* in hectographic ink in order to increase the number of copies to fifty, separately hectographing the unacceptable passages, which he planned to give to a few people, began to translate into English Tolstoy's preface, unpublished in Russia due to censorship, to *A Brief Account of the Gospel*. But this was not enough for him and the need to concentrate his strength on the publication and distribution of books, revealing to people that life-understanding which was close to him grew stronger every day. He wrote about this to Tolstoy:

"But concerning publishing activities, I will tell you that it weighs on me until exhaustion this continual comparing of various important abstract questions *without* gradual obligatory work on any kind of practical project. When both activities go together that is OK; but one without the other is burdensome. And it seems to me that the interest which I feel toward this kind of occupation, namely a publishing activity, would satisfy the need for constant obligatory work, the use of which I would not doubt."[35]

"The best of all would be, if you in your free time would write tales and stories for people and allowed me to take publication on myself, the proofreading and other aspects of the project. I would publish them as a series, and, probably, would be inspired by the project and in St. Petersburg would become acquainted with writers whom I would also talk into taking part. It would be possible to secure the assistance of some artists who would supply drawings. Since I wouldn't strive for profit, such publications could be sold very cheaply."[36]

The more Chertkov thought about the new project, the more it captivated him and ultimately took control of him and literally did not give him peace. He did not belong to the type of people who, day by day, evenly and unhurriedly like a clock; go along their life's path. Not letting the ultimate goal go from view, Chertkov, however, periodically tested the ebb and flow of life's energy. And when he thirsted for activity, it produced such a need to move, work, state his thoughts in writing and aloud, that it was difficult for him not to give in; he did not sleep at night, kept thinking, and this went on until such time as weariness and mental as well as spiritual fatigue set in.

Tolstoy, reading the letter in which Chertkov with great insistence developed plans about his new activities and with total sincerity shared with him all his thoughts, expressing to him the most intimate side of his life – the constant struggle with sensuality, – wrote to him in response:

"I received your letter from the countryside with the diary and was very glad to get to know you the way I got to know you. I always want to know about you. I often think about you, how one thinks about people who are dear."[37]

"First of all remember that it is important to me, very important to know your mood, your mental sickness, important because I like you, very close to you and very scared for you, and still more because I suffered from the same thing and still suffer from the almost hopeless struggle against the same thing... Still – in your letters there is little simple love toward me, like toward a person who loves you. If it's like that in your soul, nothing can be done, but if there is some partition, break it dear. We both will feel better."[38]

"You worry too much my friend. You torture yourself very much... I would like terribly to live with you for some time. I want to see if you are always in such a tense condition, as such that I see you... Did you know, at one time I wrote about Peter the First and one thing came out all right: that was the explanation of Peter's character and all his evil deeds by the fact that he was constantly passionately busy – ships, lathe turning, travel, writing laws, etc. Idleness is the mother of vice – this is a truism; but these feverous hurried activities is the usual companion of unhappiness with yourself, and the main thing is you don't always know this."[39]

Chertkov's idea about publishing activities was very close to Tolstoy, but he did not share this enthusiasm with which Chertkov thought about it.

"It goes without saying that I sympathize with this and am glad to help you and I want to write for the people, but I know ahead of time, that this project will be much less, much, much less than what you imagine"[40], wrote Tolstoy to Chertkov.

In another letter Tolstoy wrote that he was glad to work together on a good project, but let him know that he cannot completely devote himself:

"I have mine, in my own work, I know that no one can help me."[41]

But Chertkov, once devoting his thought to the creation of a publishing house, could not just stop; not doing everything his means and energy would allow doing in order to carry the project to fruition. In November 1884, Chertkov left the countryside and, after making a brief stop in Moscow, settled in Petersburg where he immediately started the organizational work of the fulfillment of his projects. A new page opened in his life and at the same time a new phase began in his relations with Tolstoy: a common undertaking was started, which would bring them still closer together in common work.

IV
The Common Project

Thinking about plans for the publishing work, for the countryside, Chertkov did not immediately find that form which would conform to his aspirations. First he thought to start work at the publishing house with a popular magazine and during the second half of October, came to Moscow one day and visited the writer-populists Zlatovratzky and Prugavin and publisher Marakuyev beginning discussions with them concerning his plans.

But Chertkov immediately felt that they had another point of view:

"They all considered my desire to publish a periodic publication for the people a very good idea," – wrote Chertkov to Tolstoy, – "but they were very glad that I mentioned the newspaper format of the publication and persistently emphasized namely that such a format with a release one or even two times a week with the announcement of political, general, and remaining (as it is called) news of the day. I am more inclined to periodic release, not having a newspaper character, so that every issue would be one complete volume suitable for retail sale."[1]

And gradually he had begun to form another plan: organize a printing house, releasing books earmarked for the countryside, which could be used, although partly, to force out so-called popular literature.

The publishing activity for the countryside began operating in Russia already a long time and presented a very specific branch of the book enterprise: books earmarked for the semi-literate readers, released by semi-literate publishers and distributed by semi-literate sellers.

First it was a form of domestic industry, supplementary to the peasant household, where an artisan would cut out a picture in wooden block, made rough but with vivid cheap popular prints and sold them in the countryside for decoration of peasant houses; then captions appeared under these pictures, and finally entrepreneurs emerged who took it a step further: they began to publish small books using the same technique which were called block picture publications.

In such a way booklets appeared booklets with titles striven for effect and filled with the most unbelievable adventures: "The Story About the Adventures of the English Lord George and about Brandenburg's margrave Fredericka-Luiz With the Addition of the History of the Former Vizier Martsimiris and the Sardinian Queen Teresa", "The Story about the Famous and Strong Bogatyr Bova-Korolevich and His Wonderful Wife Druzhevna", "The Witch Beyond the Dnieper"; every possible fortune-telling book: books of dream-interpretation, "New and Complete Oracle Very Successfully Predicting the Future For Posed Questions, Composed of the Writings of famous astrologers", and similar publications.

These books were very cheap, first of all because there were no authors demanding the royalties, if one does not count those cases when the publisher bought some kind of drunken "author" for a few rubles, for total ownership of his writing, and secondly, because of the fact that they printed in such great quantity that the publisher paid attention to the price and not on the quality of the work. In the countryside they came in boxes called "peddler's boxes" in which the peddlers carried every type of petty wares, from needles, hairpins and thread to paper icons.

Attempts of intelligent publishers to release literature that could compete with the popular publications were unsuccessful: "educational" publications were more expensive than popular literature, their external format did not satisfy the taste of village readers, and peddlers refused to take them.

The absence of practical experience, dilettante and sometimes lordly attitude toward publishing work were the reasons why these publications were not successful in competing with the publishers of popular books. As a result, those books in competition with popular publications did not even reach the village reader and collected dust on the shelves of city stores.

Chertkov, thinking about the publication of books for the villages, came to an innovative decision: entrust the practical side of the project to one of the publishers of popular literature, who knew the path to advancement of popular books perfectly well, would undertake to publish and distribute good literature along with his own publications while completely not interfering, however, in editorial work.

In the beginning of the 1880s, among Moscow publishers of popular books, the young, energetic, well-mannered and quick-minded Ivan Dmitrievich Sytin began to move forward. Just as other publishers of this type, he released "English Lord George" and pictures of generals galloping on white horses with enemy soldiers running in front of them, but made a mark by his enterprise. It was possible to try to get him interested in new projects, if they promised him some profit, or – in any case – ask his advice.

In November 1884, passing through Moscow to Petersburg, Chertkov called on Sytin in his shop and started a conversation with him about popular publications. Many years later, Sytin reminisced about their meeting:

"On one lucky day in the shop a young man in an elegant fur coat called and offered, would I like to publish more interesting books for the people. He takes mediation between author and publisher upon himself. These books will be the works of the best authors: Tolstoy, Leskov, Korolenko, Garshin and others. They will pass to the publisher very cheaply. Part of the literary material will be free. But the pricing must be the same as for cheap popular books. If these popular leaflets sell at 80 kopeks per 100, then this must be the price for better quality books. They must have poor consumers and go as an alternative for existing vulgar publications. The gentleman offering this printing was V.G. Chertkov."[2]

Sytin possessed the flair of a businessman; able to immediately find the advantage it could bring in every offer, and never let go of the chance to move his business forward.

Chertkov's offer was unusual, but at the same time very tempting: it presented the possibility to receive the works of the most visible Russian writers for free, and this could not only give him monetary profit but also give prestige to the printing house, advancing him considerably among the popular book businesses and open up for him new perspectives.

The form of a new undertaking immediately took shape: Chertkov took the entire editorial work completely on himself, all negotiations with authors and artists, relationships with censors, and even proofreading, and Sytin could not interfere in this sphere of his work.

Receiving the prepared manuscripts from Chertkov for free, Sytin printed them on his account and distributed them together with his popular literature publications, holding on to the sums earned for his use.

Reprinting was permitted for all who wanted to, but this circumstance could not stop Sytin, in as much as these were agreed terms, printing had to be maximally cheap – other publishers, reprinting these books could not print them cheaper than Sytin and could not compete with his printing house.

Chertkov in the first conversation listed to Sytin books, which must be printed first: Tolstoy's *What Do People Live For* and *God Sees the Truth But Will Not Soon Tell*, and Leskov's *Christ Visiting the Peasant*.

Chertkov finally decided to devote his strength to printing work that was not tied to the necessity to publish releases of a fixed volume at a fixed time and, therefore, gave more freedom to the editor and author.

In two or three days after the conversation with Sytin, Chertkov, arriving in Petersburg, wrote Tolstoy a long letter persuading him to write for the future of the printing house, in the form which seems to him more comfortable, not limiting himself by the established framework:

"I allow myself, Lev Nikolaevich, to express my opinion to you that for the benefit of the readers, you should not calculate the size and in general think about the length of your stories. Send them the same length as they come out, just as in oral presentation when the storyteller is not inhibited by the worry of how many minutes and seconds it takes to tell about that situation which he wants to convey. And our printing business will consist of in order to glean through the length of each story the appropriate form: either pictures with text or booklets with pictures, and, if the story is not very long, with the largest popular typeface. Finally, books with ordinary script and large volume. If you will have this in mind, then probably you will be freer in narration and the choices of stories and will write totally, as you say, without alterations and abridgements that are necessary in such printings which must compete with many stories, written, for example, by the retired deacon, who for 2-3 rubles, cast off in one evening three separate stories about holy saints. That is what I wanted to relate to you, Lev Nikolaevich. I hope you don't think that I conceived the desire to give you advice about the writer's craft. I felt only an irresistible need to share with you these thoughts."[3]

The business thought up by Chertkov was new and represented such difficulties, that even those who wished him success, seemed that it was doomed to failure.

The artist I.N. Kramskoy who was acquainted with Chertkov and sympathized with his endeavors, wrote him:

"The business of printing anything "for the people", is a business to such a serious and large degree that I don't think there are many people suitable for it. But nevertheless, we will now discuss you. If a similar idea had come from a person who supposes that everything is possible and allowable to do anything in the world and still could knock down profit, then it would not be worth talking about. For you the need is different. You have the sincere desire to do something good for the people. In your opinion (yes, in mine too), your internal peaceful system needs a calming conscience (located at present in the alarming condition everyone who has a soul which is not asleep forever). You are not a lord giving generous tips and thinking that God established the social order until the end of time and if that needs correction in social relations that it's only the most trifle. In a word, for you is the question if it did not become completely crucial, then perhaps not today – tomorrow will be, and in such a situation, I suppose, the need and point of view of the business must be totally different from the commonplace. The best of all for you is to leave the venture alone and only join with the rank and file that already exists. They say that such a situation already exists, but I have only heard of it and do not know of it myself. *"The Rural Journal"*, published by the government. It would be much better than to planning something to start, to produce results first and then to leave it, because in this case the hopes already are in motion and that which will not be fulfilled will be soulfully felt."[4]

A difficult work expected Chertkov in Petersburg. It would go in two directions: it was necessary to prepare manuscripts for printing and start ties with the best writers and artists who would identify with the idea of the printing house so much so as to give their work for free or for insignificant compensation. At the same time it was necessary to familiarize himself with those popular publications already existing, choosing from them those few books, which could be recommended for village readers, and organize a small bookstore which would become the base of the new printing house in Petersburg, and at the same time where, not only its publications but also other popular books, receiving positive evaluation would be located. The printing house must serve as a binding link between the countryside and those who strive for it to work, and it was given an appropriate name *Mediator*.

In the first days after his arrival in St. Petersburg, Chertkov persistently occupied himself with this business that was new for him. First of all he invited one of his friends, Pavel Ivanovich Biryukov, to take part in it. He knew Biryukov from the circle of high-society people meeting for conversations on religious themes, which were organized by Chertkov together with Prince V.P. Galitzine and Count A.F. Geyden in 1881.

Biryukov went farther than Chertkov's other friends. Meeting Tolstoy through Chertkov, he expressed full agreement with his views. Leaving a career as a naval officer, he entered into service in the observatory that, however, took him comparatively little time. He had few original creative ideas, he was not good at extreme spiritual concentration or abrupt change in his path under the influence of a passion that suddenly gushed over him, but he was far from an ordinary man, he would calmly carry out his work well and be a very worthy coworker.

Biryukov agreed to devote half of his time to the printing house *Mediator* and took upon himself a significant part of the petty organizational work without which it was impossible to implement any kind of business.

At the same time, the day after his arrival in St. Petersburg, Chertkov was at Kramskoy's discussing with him the illustration of publications of *Mediator*, and Kramskoy, despite the doubts that he expressed earlier, gladly agreed to help the new business.

"He is glad that you took up the stories again, – wrote Chertkov to Tolstoy about Kramskoy; – ...offers to gather a few artist friends and convince them to contribute to the business of improving the content of woodcut publications. It seems there will be no shortage of assistance, since your participation in this work is winning approval and urge many on."[5]

Tolstoy began to write for the new printing house, but at the same time tried to hold back some enthusiasm for the work, which drew Chertkov in, to introduce a steadier pace to his activities.

"Worked for you yesterday – it didn't turn out, – wrote Tolstoy. – I don't despair; I will take it up again... You really excited me, so I began to fuss. And this is most harmful. It is important to live, and not write. Please, please, you should strive less – search for rest and quiet."[6]

That direction, in which Chertkov lived in the fall months of 1884, compelled Tolstoy to worry that when it disappeared, it might cause the condition of mental fatigue.

Even at the time of enthusiasm for new plans Chertkov did not stop his usual self -analysis.

"Since I started to think about my project of publishing a popular magazine, – he wrote to Tolstoy, – I continually catch myself on that I present myself for praise and approval of other media publications and the public in general for the fact that I undertook such a praiseworthy venture and run it so brilliantly, intelligently and nobly. I catch myself still on one display of the most trifling, childlike vanity: when I look from afar at my writing desk, illuminated by a lamp with a green lampshade, I imagine myself at this desk surrounded by papers and immersed in the most difficult and feverish editorial work – and this scene gives me some kind of self enjoyment... When I catch myself in these moods, and it is understood, I become very ashamed. One trick now destroys these moods, namely: reminiscence about death, about that my personality, no matter how much praise and how I would sit at the green desk, however, it would certainly die and this thought acts wonderfully sobering."[7]

Successful beginning work on organizing the printing house did not give Chertkov satisfaction strong enough that he could be completely content.

Following the receipt of a letter in which Tolstoy warned against excessive stress, Chertkov wrote:

"Emotionally I am in a bad shape, Lev Nikolaevich. I fell into such a mood that everything that I do, nothing is OK... It is so empty here, although I know, that people, the same people are around. But I don't have a humane feeling toward my fellow human beings in general. For me, the close are only those who give pleasure to *my personality*. And my personality only receives pleasure from those, in the past relations with whom I myself played a role, more or less worthy in my own eyes."[8]

Tolstoy wrote Chertkov in response to this letter:

"To write everything that I think and feel about you is not allowed because it is too much. I will say one thing: cold, reasonable, Christian life is Christian and holy life... Love is like that spring in the year, it comes and goes, but there would be no spring, if there were no fall and winter... A person always feels himself responsible. He can't control love, but in reasonable life he is in control. Here he directs all his strength toward love, cries when there is no love. He says such phrases about "percussion cymbal" and wants to feel himself not guilty. Horrible evil was made by Saint Paul's words about love... You probably think that I love you much less than I actually do."[9]

In the next letters Chertkov writes about the list of projects, asks Tolstoy, how, in his opinion, better to translate one part in the book *What Do I Believe* into English, the translation, which Chertkov worked on together with the Englishman K. Heath; tells about the writer–worker in the mint – V.I. Savihin and sends Tolstoy his manuscripts, wishing to know Tolstoy's opinion about if they could be used by the printing house *Mediator;* orders artistic drawings for Tolstoy's booklet *What People Live For*, *God Sees the Truth* and *Caucus Prisoner;* tells about the acquaintanceship with V.M. Garshin, who with joy agreed to write for *Mediator;* transmits the conversation with the publisher of *Russian Riches*, L.E. Obolensky, who through Chertkov asks Tolstoy for an article for his magazine. Preparing for publication in *Mediator* Tolstoy's story *Caucus Prisoner*, Chertkov writes Tolstoy on January 31, 1885:

"I was pleased with the story to a high degree. But I will tell you one thing candidly... in two parts sympathy and happy approval of the reader excites such actions of Zhilin, which at first glance seem a demonstration of intelligence, but in reality, more or less, are the deception for the achievement of his goals... I know for sure, that these two episodes must call forth approving laughter in such readers and, it follows, gives them still another push to that already too predominant direction, which acknowledges that it is incomparably more practical in achieving his goals not to be too scrupulous in the choice of means. Therefore, I would like it very much if you allowed me to leave out these few lines in popular print."

Tolstoy responded to this in full agreement:

"On the exclusion of those episodes which you wrote about, I gladly agree and am thankful. Only do it yourself. If I begin to do it, then I would redo everything and I need time for other things."[10]

In the winter months of 1884-85 Tolstoy was intensely busy with his work, and, as always in these periods, when creativity seized him, it was difficult for him to think about anything else. He, with great sympathy followed Chertkov's work, preparing for printing booklets for the new printing house, looking at manuscripts sent to him by Chertkov for his opinion, but letters were short and opinions superficial.

Tolstoy himself explained the reason, for why he was not in a condition to devote to these printings as much time as he wanted:

"I cannot occupy myself with the projects most dear to me. I am very gladly busy with my writing. Things became clear to me that before were not clear. If only other people realized half as much."[11]

Tolstoy finished preparation for print of the article *What Should We Do?* at this time. As always, many times redoing whole pages, crossing out, again rewriting and again crossing out whole phrases and words. Chertkov, receiving this article in the beginning of January 1885, reads it with joyful emotion and writes Tolstoy:

"It was very gratifying to realize how very analogous and parallel were our lives, our impressions, our thoughts and our conclusions of the past years. I totally, unconditionally agree with everything that you say; you said something that I myself discovered in a course of my life, but said it with such clarity, incontrovertible logic, persuasiveness and sincerity that literally during the reading, tears welled up in my eyes."[12]

Tolstoy gave this article to the magazine "Russian Thought" and it was typeset but never saw the light of day.

The portrayal of destitution of the city proletariat, the description of doss-houses, given together with a picture of the high-society life was completely unacceptable to the censors.

Chertkov strove to do all that depended on him so that the article would become published, and when Tolstoy agreed to put some excerpts into the journal "Russian Riches", Chertkov planned inevitable cuts.

Tolstoy's letter from March 26, 1885 offered Chertkov to make these cuts on his own discretion:

"I don't like castration, but if it is necessary, then I am very glad to give it up, namely in this deformity. My carte blanche to you continues."

Despite his full agreement with his thoughts expressed in the article "What Should We Do?", Chertkov considered that they would be much more persuasive if they were presented in artistic form. With the persistence with which he already more than once wrote Tolstoy about this, Chertkov again writes how strongly the artistic form affects the reader and how weak in comparison with it the impression from the theoretical discussion:

"You know, concerning this article, I remained of the same opinion, as in the beginning, that is, good in the real sense of the word... But since then I often had to watch the impression which it leaves on the most varied readers, and I understood that if you communicated the same thoughts, the same feeling in artistic images, in parables, then it would carry a stronger impression... It is impossible to object to so-called artistic presentation when it is indeed artistic, when content is justified and when it is written under the influence of high, sincere feelings. As much as I had to talk about your books, *not one* person took to disprove the thoughts in the booklet "*What People Live For*", it's simply impossible because there is nothing argued or concluded logically, but thoughts penetrate directly through the whole being of the reader. Beside that, "*What Should We Do?*" calls up other impressions. There is a part, corresponding with "*What People Live For*" and it's the strongest. But there are conclusions, logical conclusions, and definitions, somewhat understandable, for example about private property, about money... But for those who did not penetrate the basics, from which these conclusions flow, that are, for the majority of readers, conclusions which are not convincing. The smallest insignificance, omission, all this catches their eye and makes them biased against the general thoughts of the article."[13]

And after a year and a half, on 8 August, 1886, in the car of the express train returning from England to Petersburg, Chertkov again returned to this article and wrote to Tolstoy:

"I am writing in the car, on both sides by me fields, woods, houses and people are flying – hundreds of thousands, millions of people and all this is alien, some kind of panorama, and it occurs to me that they all live, each one has a whole world, each interlaced and bound with other people, living around him, – and I, as if not a person, but some kind of point which rushes from one end of Europe to the other... And as you know what kind of thoughts still come to mind... that all these millions of people, past which flies our train, to each, decidedly each of them would be pleasant and gratifyingly and reassuringly to read your latest stories and during time these stories would reach them. But your big articles, like *What Should We Do?*", these working millions don't need them, readers of such works live in the cities, where we make stops, which are designated in the guidebook with the word "buffet."

Tolstoy agreed with Chertkov, but explained why nevertheless continues to write theoretical works, not accessible for all:

"That which you write me about my writing is not only not unpleasant to me but useful and persuasive. I feel that I am convinced by your arguments, but... there is always a "but" – I am pulled toward theorizing nevertheless – and not from vanity – I truthfully know, – as for which, in order to be through with these lies in which I lived and with my friends lies. Imagine, you are taken away for the execution of truth from the hotel in which you stood. You do better, if despite the importance of what is in store for you, you don't forget to cancel lunch for which you invited guests, and pay the hostess and laundress and settle with everyone so as not to offend anyone. That is how I feel, that it is necessary to settle with my world – artistic, educated – to explain what and why I don't do what they are expecting of me. You think this is an excuse. Maybe; but the last one."[14]

Not limiting himself to one argument in order to convince Tolstoy to take up artistic works, Chertkov decided to resort to the original method.

In the small magazine *"Russian Worker"* which published moral articles and carried Gospel ideas, Chertkov suddenly found a small story "Grandfather Martyn", published without indication of the author, translated from French and reworked by a translator. Assuming that the subject of the story would interest Tolstoy, Chertkov sent it to him and attached blank pages to it. He hoped that, if Tolstoy, while reading begins to make notes and drafts, which the process of creativity would captivate him and the story would be written.

The assumption proved correct: on the basis of the material sent by Chertkov, Tolstoy created the story *"Where Love Is, There Is God"*

Subsequently, Chertkov often applied this method but in slightly altered forms: he took drafts of new works started and then left by Tolstoy, sometimes even a few pages, rewrites them, so that between the lines and in the margins remained a lot of empty space for new insertions, and sent them to Tolstoy, so as to seduce him into again taking up the work. And often Tolstoy, rereading the manuscripts sent by Chertkov, begins to correct it and gradually this work is transformed in artistic creativity.

A short time passed since the first meeting between Tolstoy and Chertkov but their relationship was already full-blown and already those basic lines on which further ties grew took shape.

In letters they continue to share their thoughts and experiences. This continual striving toward relations with each other expressed itself in the very quantity of letters: in 1884 Tolstoy wrote Chertkov 38 letters, – on average wrote more than one every ten days, in 1885 – 50 letters – almost one a week. Chertkov wrote Tolstoy even more often, and his letters often grew to many pages.

When activities in the printing house Mediator began to develop, correspondence between Tolstoy and Chertkov became especially animated since Chertkov continually sent Tolstoy manuscripts planned for publication asking his opinion.

In March 1885 Tolstoy's first three-fold stories were released, in blue and red folders with black drawings, composed in very large print, and priced unusually cheaply – a kopek or a kopek and a half per booklet. A small book warehouse opens in April in Petersburg in which were located publications of the new book publisher and popular books of other publishers assembled by Chertkov and Biryukov.

Biryukov ran the warehouse, two young men of the Lizinovka peasantry, assisting Chertkov when he lived in the countryside and taking advantage of his friendship, did the technical work. Chertkov himself took on the close participation in the decisions of all the projects concerning the warehouse but not taking on any work that required him to sit there in the early morning hours until closing time. More or less he spent the whole day in the warehouse. In his letters, he expressed to Tolstoy about how and who buys his stories and shares his observations:

"I sit at the table by the window, hidden from passersby by the book exhibit. Various people remain by the window reading book titles; themselves making various remarks, not knowing everything is heard in the room. It is possible to put together the most original book from all these overheard conversations."[15]

"The principle buyers of books on this block are those who are obtaining usually bad books and are mainly soldiers, artisans, factory workers and their children. And therefore every time that anyone of them comes to the store, we are glad as fishermen who have caught a fish. We follow, even as he "bites the bate" at the window – a title or picture is pleasing, a cheap price entices. They debate among themselves whether or not to go and buy. We hear all this and wait with excitement."[16]

Chertkov's letters gave Tolstoy the possibility to a certain degree to see those readers for whom he intended his books and to hear their response to his works.

Tolstoy, somewhat keeping Chertkov's enthusiasm in check during this period of the organization of the printing house, now devoted himself to the new project with enthusiasm.

Already in December 1884 Tolstoy writes Chertkov: "I am afraid that you are waiting for a lot… wait that nothing will come of this. I desire success very much, but continually reign myself in, i.e., doubt success."[17]

In the spring of 1885, Tolstoy is already closely involved in the work of the new printing house and to a certain degree it occupies his thoughts.

In the beginning of March 1885, Tolstoy goes to the Crimea, accompanying his hopelessly sick friend Prince L.D. Ourusoff there, and despite his new impressions, during the trip continues to think about stories for Mediator – about the "English milords", how he jokingly named them by title of famous popular booklets. On the trip from Sevastopol to Simeiz, Tolstoy wrote to Sofia Andreyevna:

"Ourusoff took the landau, which had no opening top and worse than a coach, and I climbed on the coachbox. I was riding, not really meditating, but new thoughts began forming in my mind of a good structure, one of which was: "Look! I Am Still Alive and Can Live." While in the coachbox, I was composing an English milord. It wasn't bad."[18]

"*English milord*" about which Tolstoy wrote, – text for popular pictures, was transformed into a small story "*Ilyas*", was finished in the coming days, but just returning from the Crimea, Tolstoy began another story for Mediator – "*Let a Flame Go – And You Can't Put It Out*" and wrote about it to Ourusoff from Moscow:

"Chertkov is arriving today, and I got scared of him as of a teacher, and this morning wrote the story in rough draft. Maybe it will be OK."[19]

Tolstoy's letters to Chertkov during this time are filled with opinions about the new manuscripts and pictures, earmarked for publication. At the same time, Tolstoy worked on folk stories.

Concerning the sketches of I.E. Repin, Tolstoy wrote Chertkov:

"Repin brought me great joy. I could not tear myself away from his picture and was moved. And how many people will be moved. I will try so that it can be done as well as possible. I am sending you the rough draft of my story. Excuse me, that it is dirty. I will give it to be typeset tomorrow. Also "*The Shoemaker*"; only there is no picture for the "*Arsonist.*" Could it be ordered from someone in Moscow? Today thoughts came to me about pictures of heroes with captions. I have two. One, a doctor sucking poison from a diphtheritic and dying. Another, teacher in Tula dragging children from his building and dying in a fire. I am gathering information about these, and if God allows, I will write the texts, order pictures and portraits."[20]

And after references in this letter works Tolstoy in 1885 writes one story after another: *"Does Man Need Much Land"*, *"Candle"*, *"Two Old Men"*, and finally *"Fairy Tale About Ivan the Fool."*

Organizational work in the creation of the new printing house finished, and business was pushed into production. It was possible to tear oneself from the work, give prepared manuscripts and pictures to lithographers and leave the warehouse to Biryukov. Chertkov did this and in May 1885 left for England where his mother spent the summer almost every year.

In London, Chertkov entered into negotiations with publishers about the publication in English of Tolstoy's works banned in Russia – *"Confession"*, *"A Short Account of The Gospels"* and *"What Should I Believe"* – and continued together with his English friend Battersby to prepare the translation of these works on which he worker even earlier for publication.

He managed to organize the printing of these books and soon after his arrival in England, announced to Tolstoy that he made arrangements with Battersby concerning proofreading which was put off until the time when Chertkov figured he would be in Russia already.

Tolstoy did not respond to this announcement, but when finally, after half a year that the book saw the light of day, he wrote to Chertkov:

"I could not tear myself away – read it yesterday and today... I was very pleased to see this book, hold it in my hand and think that it will find, perhaps, Englishmen, Americans, who will become closer to us through this book. The main thing, it was simply nice, I thank you for this."[21]

Chertkov shared his impressions of English life with Tolstoy – in one of the letters gives, not without sarcasm, an account of a visit to one English philanthropist and preacher, lecturing his visitors, that "a social inequality exists in human nature and is blessed by God"; in another letter talks about the acquaintance with Quakers, writes about books read and sends Tolstoy the composition of Ruskin. At the same time, Chertkov in his letters from England continues to write about individual books planned for publication at

Mediator, and concerning one of them – *The Life of Socrates,* composed by A.M. Kalmykova, and edited by Tolstoy, expressed his conviction that it is always necessary in every case to tell the truth:

"I would avoid a too extreme idealism of teachers which are introduced to the readers in our publications. As various deviations from the truth, such relations to the subject must certainly bear rotten fruit."[22]

Tolstoy responded that it was not necessary to add to Socrates that which he was not, not deliberately underlining those weaknesses that were perhaps characteristic of him and added:

"Your opinion is useful to me. If I finish this project – I will use them – your observations."[23]

Thinking about those conditions in which Tolstoy had to work, Chertkov worried about saving his manuscripts.

In such a manner Chertkov at this time began a project to which subsequently devoted a lot of strength.

"Why don't you ask your eldest son to help you in bringing your papers to order and maintaining them in order?" – wrote Chertkov to Tolstoy on June 9, 1885. – "This is so important, so that someone in your home keep the papers in order. Everything that you write is so dear to us, so close to everything good, that we recognize in ourselves, that we simply shudder from the thought that any of your writings could be lost from insufficient care."

In other letters from England, Chertkov tells Tolstoy about his relationship with his mother, analyzes motives in which he is guided by in his conduct and shares various thoughts that interest him.

Tolstoy, in turn, shares with Chertkov his thoughts about the printing house Mediator, in particular announces to him the thought of creating a *Cycle of Reading*, which was implemented many years later.

Understanding from one of Chertkov's letters that he lives very tensely and not peacefully, Tolstoy writes Chertkov:

"How I would like to see and know you more happy and less tense. But, perhaps, this is impossible. Maybe then you would not be what you are, mainly dear to me and everyone who loves you."[24]

From his side Tolstoy writes Chertkov about that sphere in his life that was for him a continual source of painful experiences –

about the contradiction between his teachings and the reality in which he had to live, about hiding the family discord from strangers.

"Written work doesn't go, physical work is almost worthless, i.e. not forced by necessity, relations with those people surrounding me – almost isn't – (the beggars come, I give them half a kopek and they leave), and in my eyes the systematic corruption of children goes all around me in my family, tying millstones around their neck. It is clear that I am to be blamed; but I don't want to pretend in front of you, bring forward peace, which is not there... I get confused, I want to die, plans come to run away or even use my situation and turn my whole life around. All this only shows that I am weak and nasty and want to blame others and see in my situation something exceptionally painful. It is very hard for me, now already six days, but there is one consolation – I feel this is a temporary situation..."[25]

Chertkov answered that this letter called in him the feeling of even greater closeness to Tolstoy because he himself could relate to such a condition.

At the same time, he expressed his opinion with great precision:

"I write, loving you more than I am able to say, and all the time realizing that I can totally make a mistake. But get ready to hear unpleasant things; I want to speak without reservation and softening, because, as before, love dictates this to me. You say that you live in a condition absolutely against your faith. This is absolutely correct and therefore totally natural that you have in time arisen plans to run away or turn around the whole family situation. But I cannot agree with that which shows you are weak and nasty. On the contrary, clear recognition of the possibility to become in cases of need independent of the surrounding situation, direct your practical life on new lines, shows only the presence of strength. And to run away or turn over your life – in my eyes is not such an action which is reprehensible under any circumstances."

Further Chertkov reminded Tolstoy of the Chinese saying which he heard from Tolstoy himself: "Renew yourself every day from the beginning and again from the beginning and always from the beginning", and wrote that this principle is able to force to change his life such that is it difficult to foresee.

"I don't say this in order certainly to carry out the fulfillment of the temporary desire to run away or something similar, – wrote

Chertkov. – To fulfill this intention is not allowed. It is possible only to submit to such need when you feel that it is almost insurmountable, when you know all it's strength…But first it is understood that one has to do everything possible in order not to change the front, carry into action all instruments of persuasion and attraction toward which you consider true."[26]

Tolstoy answered this letter that he wanted to do everything that depended on him to have an affect on his family:

"I am sad today, sick for the children, for my wife, for their senseless and pitiful life, but I am not angry, don't desire anything, but only think and search, how to lovingly help them. And if I will live, I will find it."[27]

In the same letter Tolstoy called Chertkov to come to Yasnaya Polyana as soon as he returned to Russia. In the beginning of August Chertkov returned to Russia and on August 16th arrived at Yasnaya Polyana with Biryukov. They did not find Countess Sofia Andreyevna at home and Chertkov wrote his mother that he was not distressed by this circumstance.

Sofia Andreyevna related very suspiciously to people who sympathized with her husband's theories, – even motives leading them to Tolstoy, for her was often totally incomprehensible.

When A.M. Kalmykova, working a lot on the creation and spread of popular literature, visited Tolstoy, Sofia Andreyevna was very surprised that a young woman, belonging to the "good society" was able to be interested in national education, and wrote her sister:

"A strange woman was at our house, Al. Mik. Kalmykova… She was on a journey from Petersburg and arrived to meet with Lyovochka to ask his advice on some kind of secret. She is lively, happy and her whole life was devoted to school activity."[28]

Chertkov was for Sofia Andreyevna a closest ally of her husband in that sphere of his life to which she was hostile. Chertkov's activities in publishing Tolstoy's works called in her apprehensions from the point of view of material interests of the family.

When Mediator, with Tolstoy's permission, gratuitously published two of his stories, releasing them at a price much less expensive than that at which they were published earlier by Sofia Andreyevna, and the demand for these stories from her printing house grew less, she offered Sytin to pay her compensation covering her losses of 1000 rubles.

Chertkov, finding out about this, wrote Sofia Andreyevna a letter with great straightforwardness stating that such actions are unacceptable and at the same time expressing readiness to pay her such a sum from his own means. The incident was settled, but the unpleasant aftertaste had to remain, and Chertkov did not have the grounds to consider Tolstaya among the number of his friends.

Chertkov and Biryukov spent three days at Yasnaya Polyana and felt themselves relaxed and content there. Chertkov spent all day talking to Tolstoy, as expressed in a letter to his mother. Together with Tolstoy the guests gathered mushrooms, read books aloud, destined for publication at Mediator. One evening, when in Tolstoy's study gathered his children and his guests, Tolstoy offered them to tell them a story and everyone did, beginning with the smallest and ending with the host himself.

The contradiction between conviction and the situation in the lordly house usually so distressing for Tolstoy in such good moments would retreat to background. But it was dug in so deeply that it had to reappear sooner or later. A few tens of feet from the estate was the village and even someone not sharing the views of Tolstoy could see the sharp contrast between the lifestyle of the peasantry and the situation in the Tolstoy home.

The artist Repin, visiting Yasnaya Polyana, wrote Chertkov:

"By the look of the Yasnaya Polyana inhabitants in their black dirty huts with cockroaches, without much light, chilled in the evening by kerosene wicks, which gave off a stench and soot, which made me sick, and I don't believe in the possibility of bright joyous mood in this Dante's hell."[29]

Chertkov in his own life also continued to feel these contradictions, which were in Tolstoy's life and writes about them to Tolstoy. In one such letter from Lizinovka, where Chertkov lived with his mother for a few weeks in the fall of 1885 and 1886, he wrote that when his mother left for two days to inspect the new country school, he immediately felt like he had rest from the conditions of a high-society home, which was preserved in the country life of E.I. Chertkova:

"In this case I feel a kind of strange freedom, it's not necessary to be home by curfew, not necessary to sit in chairs, keep quiet and be bored, watching how two lackeys in coats and white gloves bring us small cups of coffee..."[30]

Being in peasant huts, Chertkov repeats the expression of Tolstoy, calling the peasant world "great society", counterbalancing the exclusive high-society circle and writes in his diary:

"I spent the entire day in the "great society" and felt myself freer, healthier and in general better than I've felt in a long time. It pulls me, and how it pulls. And despite all the estrangement from them by upbringing, which, must be, as difficult to overcome as covering them with high-society luster, necessary for entering into the environment of aristocrats, despite that this exterior estrangement, I feel, that they are more gracious and more cordially ready to accept in their environment, in their lives, such a crippled person like me than aristocrats in their environment and lives not "pureblooded" and without luster."[31]

Returning to Petersburg, Chertkov energetically submerges himself into the work in the printing house from which he inwardly would not leave in England, or Lizinovka, planning and preparing books and pictures with text for publication.

In one of his letters to Tolstoy, he announces that he hardly sees any new people except in business, tied to publishing, because he devotes all his time to this work.

Despite censorship difficulties, the printing house strengthens and works successfully. Tolstoy sends one new manuscript after another.

Each one of them made Chertkov happy, but he almost always tried to draw Tolstoy's attention to one or another paragraph, which in his opinion would benefit from changes, and Tolstoy attentively listened to his words. So, receiving the story *"The Candle"*, Chertkov writes that the end of the story – death of the evil salesman, falling, stomach-down upon a stake – can prove to be unlikely, and, at the same time, call in the readers a feeling of rejoicing at others' misfortunes. Tolstoy, in his response letter, sends him another variation of the ending this story.

From various sides Chertkov was receiving messages that demand for the books of the new printing house grew and Sytin confirmed this, telling that his salespeople cannot fulfill all the orders.

In order to prepare new publications for publishing, it was necessary to have staff members sensitive to the ideas of the printing house who could rewrite books written for another circle of readers in such manner that they become accessible to the wider audience, make translations from foreign languages, at the same time abbreviating and treating them such that it would be interesting and comprehensible for village readers.

Many expressed readiness to participate in this work, but some turned out incapable, others limited themselves to one or two books; often the process of work proved that they too strongly disagreed in their convictions to those of Tolstoy and Chertkov, and couldn't work successfully with them on a common project. Only a few people approached this work with a satisfactory degree of closeness.

The closest of all linking her life to this new business was the continual contributor of the printing house, a student of Bestuzhovsky's higher women's courses, Anna Konstantinovna Dietrichs, who began to work at Mediator during the first months of it's existence.

Among the paintings of the artist N.A. Yaroshenko is one, widely known from the many reproductions – "Kursistka." A lean, thin girl in a small black cap, with a plaid on her shoulders and with a bunch of books under her arm, concentrated and serious, confidently walks forward. In it's time this painting received great popularity, but only a few knew that in front of them was the portrait of A.K. Dietrichs.

Very prone to illness and fragile, sharply feeling every new impression, demanding of herself and serious, Dietrichs attracted people to her and soon became an essential worker in the new printing house.

Other new workers participated only in the compiling and preparation for printing of individual books and stood on the side from the continually current editorial-printing work.

Chertkov's letters to Tolstoy in the winter months of 1885-86, filled with work-related announcements, shows that he intensely worked at this time and he enjoyed this work, even though it could not totally fill his life.

Tolstoy in his letters also gives much space to ordinary projects – gives opinions about manuscripts, gives advice, but at the same time, sad notes sound especially often in his letters of this period.

At the end of October, leaving Yasnaya Polyana for Moscow, Tolstoy writes that it is difficult for him to go, and in the beginning of December, in a letter from Moscow, writes how painful are those conditions in which he has to live:

"I have become weaker from the time of your visit, I write almost nothing and am sad. Everything is so melancholy, dead around me and one wants so much to condemn and be annoyed."[32]

This feeling became especially sharp in the middle of December 1885 and poured out in a letter to Chertkov, written with exceptional force, but remained unsent:

"It is tortuously difficult for me and there is no one who I'd like to share this weight more than with you, my dear friend, because it seems no one loves what is good in me like you do. All this is an animal-life – is not only simply an animal-life, but also an animal-life with separation from all people, with pride, – goes stronger and stronger. And I see how God's souls of the children – one after another – go into this factory and one after another put on and strengthen the millstone around their neck and perish. I see that I, with my faith, with my expression of it, in words and in actions, withdraw, receive the meaning for them of unpleasantness, incorrect occurrence – as are worms in hives, which the bees don't have the strength to kill, and they isolate them so that they don't interfere with them, and wild victorious life goes down its worn out path. Children *study* in gymnasiums, less even study at home the laws of God that will be necessary in the gymnasium. Stuff themselves, amuse themselves, buying for money labors of people for their pleasure and all are more and more confident that this is the way it should be. That which I write about this – they don't read, what I say – they don't listen, or with mocking answer as they only understand, what the discussion is about, what I do – they don't see or try not to see."[33]

Further Tolstoy wrote, that, asking himself, how should he act, he comes to the conclusion that he must, nevertheless tolerate and, better, quietly accept all the consulting in his home than call forward irritation and malice. But to fulfill this decision was difficult, and the restrained unhappiness broke through during those days when this letter was written.

Between Tolstoy and his wife came about an explanation in a very harsh form, about which Tolstaya wrote her sister, T.A. Kuzminskaya, in a letter.

But the explanation could change nothing, not one word of Tolstoy's, it seemed, could be heard by his wife:

"I ask astonishingly, "what happened?" – wrote Tolstaya to her sister. "Nothing, but if on the wagon is put everything more and more, the horse stands and cannot go." What was put is unknown... all these nervous outbursts and gloom and insomnia I attribute to vegetarianism and excessive physical work."

To argue, apparently was useless.

What remained was either to leave or strive to cope. Tolstoy chose the latter path. But in his letters to Chertkov, the sad notes were still heard showing how he was oppressed by the conditions in which he had to live.

Chertkov in his letters to Tolstoy, for his turn, continues not only to tell him about his activities, but also introduced him to the sphere of his personal life.

He writes Tolstoy about the new plans in publishing books, about the translation into Ukrainian of *Two Old Men*, meeting obstacles from the side of the censors, about publishing in the magazines *Niva*, *Book of the Week* and *Russian Riches*, stories of Tolstoy's *Three Elders*, *Godson* and *Does Man Need A Lot of Land*. Leaving in June 1886 for two months for England, Chertkov announces his work on the translation into English of the article *What Should We Do* and a few other works and that he is sending Tolstoy English books about Indian and Chinese religious teachings and about other questions interesting to Tolstoy. At the same time Chertkov shares his personal experiences with Tolstoy.

"I am feeling something like emptiness, or more like uncertainty. I think that this comes from the fact that I never attached or grafted anywhere. And the main point is that I don't have a house – in the sense of a family. I am everywhere a guest, mostly in my mother's house. It is my fault or is it simply an inevitable consequence of my situation, I don't know, but I do know that I am constantly more and more feeling the need to share my life with a wife."

In a few months, Chertkov wrote Tolstoy in even a more precise form:

"I think if I got married, then my wife would bring a missing warm element to our family life. I think more and more about marriage. What comes of this – I don't know. I know only, that I can marry only the one who shares the same goals in life as I have. To help each other hold the same road. To hold each other when you stumble, to help lift up when you fall. You were right this time when you told me to get married."[36]

At the end of August 1886 Chertkov visited Tolstoy at Yasnaya Polyana and told about his decision to ask Anna Konstantinovna Dietrichs to be his wife.

Tolstoy knew Anna Konstantinovna not only through letters and stories of Chertkov and Biryukov reporting about her work at Mediator, but personally: she was at his house with Chertkov, Biryukov and A.M. Kalmykova in March 1886 in Moscow and together with Pavel Ivanovich Biryukov at Yasnaya Polyana in May of the same year.

He supported Chertkov's decision with great sympathy and after his departure from Yasnaya Polyana wrote him:

"I am waiting for news from you and I will be very glad to know that everything will be as we desire."[37]

In the beginning of September Anna Konstantinovna agreed and on 19 October they got married. For a short time they left for Lizinovka, then returned to Petersburg in order to continue work at the printing house together.

Tolstoy wrote them in the country trying with his advice to help them in their joint lives:

"Don't strengthen your affection toward one another, but with all your strength use caution in relations, sensitivity so there wont be collisions... Not with anyone as with husband and wife is there such close encompassing relations and we always forget to think about them, be conscious of them, like we stop being aware of our body. And this is a shame... I love you and am glad for you."[38]

Chertkov wrote Tolstoy that he felt totally as one with his wife, being with her is better and going forward more confidently than without her.

Tolstoy could himself be convinced that this declaration did not result from a temporary infatuation and since then he often began his letters to Chertkov with a common address – to him and his wife.

V
Rzhevsk

Despite the fact that a new phase began in Chertkov's personal life, the winter of 1886-87 was the time of special intensity in his work of releasing popular publications.

His correspondence with Tolstoy during these months is full of diverse considerations about various books prepared for printing.

In long letters Chertkov tells Tolstoy about projects of the printing house and especially notes a new occurrence: the arrival of the first manuscripts of authors from that same environment for which was created the publisher Mediator – stories by a worker in the mint V.I. Savihin, *Two Brothers* by the peasant S.T. Semyonov, and *Division* by a waiter from the "Tula Inn", I.G. Zhuravov.

Each of these stories called for Tolstoy's and Chertkov's opinions and great editorial work.

Tolstoy is interested in various new books and suggests wide plans of development of the publishing house activities of Mediator:

"What did Potehin said about his stories "*On the World*" and "*Sick*"? Will he give them to the people – to Mediator – or to Sytin? I elicited from my wife [my story] "Polikushka" for Mediator and now I will ask every author who will give what. It is necessary to ask Grigorovich for something that suits our needs. The main thing, I think, is to give all well-known compositions of the Germans, French and English that run many editions, and mainly in translations and I would do something for this but the harvest is great here and workers are few. Voltaire, Rousseau, Bernardin de St. Pierre, Lessing, "Nathan the Wise", Schiller's "The Thieves", "Viksfield Priest", "Gulliver", "Don Quixote", Silvio Pellico, writings of Franklin, Plutarch, etc."[1]

But the wider the activities of the printing house expanded, the more severe the censorship became. Chertkov strove to lean on his high-society ties, but they helped him little in this case.

In his diary Chertkov made a note of one of these attempts:

"I was introduced to the President of the Censorship Committee, Kozhuhov, through P.P. Golitzine. We proceeded together to his apartment. He was very polite, asked that during all difficulties we appeal directly to him, but warned that they related very strictly toward the publications for the people."

"I relate to the business from the practical side, – he said. – I was not a bureaucrat all my life, I was Vice-Governor for a few years and I know well what goes on in Russia. And therefore, know that with the books designated for people's reading, it pays to be especially careful. Sometimes the author even does not want to suggest anything pernicious, but due to his carelessness the contents of books, if they fell into the hands of some kind of lady teacher, receives a totally false and undesirable interpretation. And these lady-teachers are especially skillful in such tricks. And therefore we are very strict in relations toward publishing for the people." I asked him to reexamine the stories "Switchman" and "The Three Elders", banned during the time of his absence from Petersburg. Yesterday he sent for me and announced that becoming acquainted with the contents of these stories, he was not able to disagree with the decision of the Committee. He read me the motives of banning, which reveal the full inability of the censors to understand the actual meaning of what they read."[2]

In order to work under such conditions, it was necessary to rework the entire system of tactical devices, and Chertkov used them with great persistence. The path of compromise by changing the essential meaning of a story, changing ideas contained in the works, he rejects in a very resolute manner, agreeing in cases of necessity to remove single expressions, but categorically refusing to change the thought of one or another part, dangerous from the point of view of the censors.

In relation to various books he uses various methods for receipt of censor permission: in one case strove beforehand to publish works in magazines which censors checked less strictly than the publications for people; in other cases sends manuscripts not to the Petersburg Censorship Committee, but to a different city, where at any moment the book would have a better chance to receive permission to see the light – in Moscow, Warsaw, Kiev, Odessa; in the third case tries to interest one or another influential person in the manuscript.

Taking on himself all the dealings with the censors, Chertkov not only saves Tolstoy from very unpleasant and sometimes fruitless efforts, but also at the same time resolutely insists that Tolstoy does not attempt to make any moves without first consulting him in writing.

When Tolstoy, without informing Chertkov, proceeded himself to the Warsaw censors with his *Alphabet*, designated for reprinting at Mediator and then announced to Chertkov that he wanted to give him a "surprise", Chertkov resolutely insisted that in order to avoid confusion, all business of seeing through censorship of books must be concentrated in his hands:

"Lev Nikolaevich, please, don't prepare any surprises for me with the presentation of works to the censors without me... I am afraid of these surprises more than fire. Thinking about them I want to laugh and cry. Laugh because I am touched that you want to give me a pleasant surprise. You can give me a better surprise – write something, but leave the censors to me."[3]

Tolstoy came to terms with Chertkov's wishes and wrote him:

"Very – I didn't laugh, but smiled reading your ironic reproaches to my surprise. I will not do them anymore in this fashion, although it seemed this one was prepared wonderfully."[4]

In such a way in the process of publishing work Chertkov made himself plenipotentiary and permanent representative of Tolstoy in all censorship business.

Carrying out negotiations with the censors and not knowing it's demands, Chertkov repeatedly asked Tolstoy that he work on his compositions, did not think about limitations, imposed by the censors, and wrote "about everything", remembering that nothing written would be lost and in one way or another, in Russia or abroad, would be published at last without various cuts.

Tolstoy also wrote Chertkov about his decision to write as he thinks, independent of censorship:

"It is true, it is necessary to do everything that is possible, under the existing conditions *to do*, as pertains to publishing activities, but to think and express your thoughts is necessary independent of existing conditions. Often this troubles me, for me and for others. What if we don't give an outlet to our thought under the pressure of existing conditions? It would be the most sinful suicide."[5]

In October 1886 Tolstoy begins with great enthusiasm to work on the drama *Power of Darkness* and in December Chertkov received the manuscript.

Chertkov quickly starts to make moves in order to receive censor permission for this work, trying to use his high-society connections for this. He announces to Tolstoy that through his mother, got an invitation to Princess Paskevich, whom he wants to ask to organize a reading of this drama, inviting to this evening her brother, Minister of the Imperial Court, Count I.I. Vorontzov-Dashkov, writes about his negotiations concerning this business with Count P.A. Shuvalov and the head of the Censure Bureau Feoktistov:

"Feoktistov himself took to be a censor and made such corrections, of which the original version of the 4th act was completely castrated, but the variant and everything else is not ruined. All sharp swear words, in the fashion of "dog" – were obliterated. The part about the bank is all crossed out. I have in my hands now the second copy with Feoktistov's notes for the insertion of the final corrections."[6]

In the next letter – 15 January, 1887 – Chertkov announces to Tolstoy that *Power of Darkness* is finally permitted without cuts and wrote him about his further plans concerning this drama:

"Trying to organize, so that this drama is allowed to be performed in booths or in factories. This seems to me more important than in imperial theaters. Only I don't know if it will happen this year."

At the same time Chertkov, in his usual expression of opinion to Tolstoy about his new work, indicated the fact that in the last act the repenting murderer Nikita says that both scheme and murder – his act, although really the idea of crime did not belong to him. Tolstoy agreed with Chertkov, changed the words "my idea" to the words "my sin", but wrote to Chertkov that, adding his usual demand for absolute truthfulness to each word in artistic works, he sometimes can be too pedantic:

"Never think that your observations of disagreement could call in me some kind of shadow of displeasure. I always want to agree and now agree, like yesterday, reading your letter. Yesterday, rereading the end of the drama, I recalled how I felt about it. But this is unimportant. It seems to me that in this you are pedantic. Not in life. In life one cannot be strict enough and I profited by you concerning this, but in artistic works."[7]

Chertkov, not long before the receipt of this letter, read the legend of N.S. Leskov "The Tale of Feodor the Christian", found that at the end of the book it was necessary to make a few changes, adding more strict moral criteria to the actions of this legend and Leskov gave his agreement to do this.

Announcing this to Tolstoy, Chertkov wrote him commenting on the receipt of his letter:

"Well, after your observation, I again believed your feeling and your thoughts concerning the ending and I vow to you that, I cannot still see exaggeration in this. In general it is difficult for me to make distinctions between what goes on in artistic form and what we must try to conduct practically in our behavior. By the way, I repeat, I will remember your observations, I probably need them, if you saw the need to announce it to me."[8]

"Thank you that you accepted my observations with love, – answered Tolstoy, – perhaps, they will be useful to you, your strictness concerning truthfulness has already been useful and helped me for a long time."[9]

Finishing *Power of Darkness*, Tolstoy did not give himself rest; all winter of 1886-87 and the following spring Tolstoy continued uninterrupted intense work.

Already in September 1886, he began to write a long letter to Anna Konstantinovna Dietrichs who asked his advice on questions posed by thoughts of life and death and this letter grew into a big article "About Life."

Finishing *Power of Darkness*, Tolstoy with enthusiasm gives himself up to this work and in the beginning of April 1887 writes Chertkov that already doesn't think of anything else day or night for one and a half months.

At the same time Tolstoy works on "Suratov's Coffee House" and on a calendar of sayings and on a tale about the first centuries of Christianity "Walk into the light while there is still light", which he leaves unfinished.

Summing up this winter, Tolstoy writes Chertkov:

"Winter ended and I without repentance glance back, I hope and believe that you did also."[10]

Chertkov could say with complete truth the same thing about himself: he also worked a lot and intensely this year and with satisfaction, noting how developed were the activities in the printing house, often wrote about what great joy it gives him working together with his wife on common projects in which they gained full mutual understanding.

Nevertheless, Chertkov continues to write that his life is a lot unlike what he wanted it to be and that he still is often upset by those contradictions that he couldn't settle. He lives with his wife in the house of his mother, toward whom he always maintained great respect for her sternness about everything connected with her convictions. Chertkov himself considered that he inherited the ambition to fulfill in his life that which he considered his obligation from his mother and father, and in one of his letters to his mother, he wrote:

"Probably from you I received my need to try to be always consistent in my own convictions just as in big things as also in insignificant ones."[11]

But exactly this mutual inflexibility in questions related to their convictions was the source of many difficult experiences for them both at this time. E.I. Chertkova, in the words of her son, directly stated that the views of Tolstoy were imbued with the spirit of the anti-Christ.

"I am highly convinced and see from the Gospels that anyone who does not believe in our Savior resurrected from the dead, is saturated with this spirit and since sweet and sour water cannot run from one source, I cannot accept a teaching coming from that same source."[12]

Chertkov reminded his mother of that path which he took toward his convictions, showing that he made them totally independently and that it is useless to try to change his mind.

"The main change in my life – leaving regimental life and moving to the countryside, where I lived completely as I liked for a few years, went against the desire and advice of those who were around me, and even my closest friends. Then, my life in the countryside was totally unlike that of the landowners around me with whom I had good relations. All this happened during the time when I was still unacquainted with L.N. Tolstoy, who you now consider my tempter."[13]

But all this couldn't make Chertkov's views more acceptable for his mother and in his letters to Tolstoy in the winter of 1886-87, he often writes how many difficulties are brought in his life by this divergence in convictions with his mother colored at the same time by the feeling of great attachment to one another.

Another side of Chertkov's life, which continually disturbed him, was that money which he received from his mother and which he continued to use not only for the trade school, printing house and his other activities, but also for expenses for his life, coming often to significant sums. In one of his letters to Tolstoy, Chertkov tells that one day after an argument with his mother, in which he proved to her that revenue received from the estate, in the final analysis, is based on the enforcement and exploitation of the peasants, he together with Anna Konstantinovna came to the conclusion not to take more of these means and suspend activities in all of his establishments, including the book warehouse, but in a few days backed off from this decision, offering that it would change nothing in reality. The profit from the estate will, as before, go to the office of the estate and if he refused to accept this sum, he would lose the possibility, although only partially, to return it to those from whose it was borrowed. His mother will give them other purpose, or will save them in the hope that he in time will use them and the peasants' life wouldn't become easier.

But the thoughts did not hide those contradictions created in his life from Chertkov, and he writes Tolstoy that he continues to live "on lordly grub."

Finally, the work itself in the printing house filling the days with business negotiations and correspondence with various people, although it does give satisfaction, becomes so time consuming, that he does not feel belonging to himself as he would like to. Chertkov writes about this to Tolstoy on 12 July 1887:

"And it turns out, that the wheel turns and carries me with it. And I would like to end my obligatory mechanical participation in this business, not because I am tired of it, but because it ties me and I want to be more free."

As a result of these thoughts, Chertkov begins to raise the decision to reorganize his work, trying to combine it with his life in the country.

In the spring of 1887 the Chertkovs leave for Lizinovka and continue to carry on editorial publications of *Mediator*.

Manuscripts and booklets are to be sent to the country to Chertkov, and after editing and earmarking them for printing he directs them for censorship, giving necessary instructions to P.I. Biryukov, manager of the book warehouse in Petersburg, or to one of his other coworkers and then the manuscripts proceed to Moscow for the typography of I.D. Sytin. And although in relation to such a method of carrying out business, correspondence of Chertkov with various people must strongly increase, life in the country, more peaceful and measured, than in the city, gives him the possibility to try to fulfill some of his planned work.

In April 1887 Tolstoy, in answer to Chertkov's request to finish his manuscript "Walk To the Light While There Is Light", left unfinished, wrote that it wouldn't be completed and instructed Chertkov to look at it, exclude the excess, expand it and then to print it.

The summer of 1887 Chertkov intensely works on this project, inserting new speeches into the conversation between the heathen and the Christian in defense of Christianity.

Tolstoy receiving the manuscript with insertions made by Chertkov, answered that, taken without relation to the text, they make very good impression on him, but long discussions of the Christian weaken the impression and does not reach its goal:

"Pamfilii must with a sad face keep quiet during all speeches and this is stronger. And for every objection there is always another objection and for every proof – there is antiproof."[14]

At the same time, Chertkov plans some other work, but does not successfully begin it this summer. One event is approaching in his family about which he already wrote in the fall to Tolstoy: the birth of a child. When it got close to the due date, Tolstoy writes Vladimir Grigorievich and Anna Konstantinovna a thoughtful letter:

"Dear Friends Vladimir Grigorievich and Anna Konstantinovna: hold on tight – the upcoming time will be difficult for you – a test in the fullest sense of the word."

And reminding them of the fool gardener Grisha, described by him in *Childhood*, who, praying, appealed to God with the words:

"You are my host, my feeder, my physician, my pharmacist", Tolstoy gives at the same time a list of practical advice and makes a reservation:

"Please don't think that I want to philosophize; I simply want to give advice as an old man and father of a family."[15]

While expecting the baby, Vladimir Grigorievich and Anna Konstantinovna move from Lizinovka to the Moscow suburb estate of their relatives the Pashkovs – Krekshino and from there often exchange letters and notes with Tolstoy. In the beginning of November Tolstoy received a telegram from Vladimir Grigorievich and Anna Konstantinovna that their daughter was born and he answered with a letter:

"I am glad for your joy, sweet dear friends, very, very glad. Masha and Ilyusha ran to me with shining faces and your telegram and all my relatives are glad for me, for you and for her. What will you call her? I am writing nothing more, I want you only to know that I am with you."[16]

The Chertkovs named their daughter Olga but absolutely refused to baptize her despite the insistence of those close relatives convincing them to do as others do.

The child brought with her much joy into the Chertkov family and required much attention: feeding came with difficulty, it was necessary to think about a wet nurse and Chertkov wrote to Tolstoy about their difficulties in detail, announcing that he and Anna Konstantinovna considered it possible to take only such a wet nurse who had no living children since they don't want to deprive the infant of its mother's milk. Tolstoy, for his part, gives advice, expressing his conviction that it is necessary, however possible, to try to feed the child mother's milk, even though it would be little at first, continually sharing his experience as father of a large family. When the difficulty with feeding continues, he himself participates in the search for a wet nurse, carrying out negotiations for possible candidates with an acquainted doctor, specialist in preserving the health of infants.

At the same time Tolstoy writes Chertkov about the work in which he is involved: about the correction and reworking of the article "About Life", which was typeset for the magazine *Questions of Philosophy and Psychology* and was sent to him in galley proofs. Chertkov reads this article in manuscript form and writes Tolstoy:

"There is a lot I would like to tell you, especially about your article, but not all of it is approving... Still I know one thing: that this article is joyful and important for us, but I would like it if you expressed your discoveries of truth not in polemic form, which is less persuasive, but in the form most attractive for those who will disagree with you in the future and be accessible to all simple people."[17]

Tolstoy agrees with Chertkov and writes him:

"I felt this deficiency and corrected it as much as I could – in type it is less, but what can we do if it just comes out in such form. There are even a few excuses here. I write mainly for myself: those who I attack – who I try to convince – this is me. What can be done if I am still such an unpleasant person with whom it is necessary to speak in such a confusing language? God willing, I myself will become clearer and simpler, only than I will be able to talk simply with myself and through me with others – like you want. But to use the instructive tone – you yourself know this is not allowed."[18]

In November 1887 Tolstoy intensely worked on the article "About Life" and wrote Chertkov:

"I would very much like to be at your house, but I cannot finish the last chapter of my book, and not finishing, I cannot leave."[19]

In a few days, Tolstoy again writes Chertkov about his desire to visit him:

"I would so very much like to talk with you. If you don't come soon, I will come in the snow."[20]

Tolstoy arrived at the Chertkovs in Krekshino in the beginning of January 1888 and by the way, in this meeting told them about his intention to write a story about "how the husband killed his wife" which he fulfilled subsequently in "Kreutzer Sonata."

Still before Tolstoy's arrival at Krekshino, the Chertkovs made the decision in the meantime to return to the Voronezh region, and, living in the countryside, to continue their work on editing publications for people.

"We are everywhere on the necks of others, – Chertkov wrote Tolstoy about this situation, – but it is less so since monetary expenses are less and closer to that simplified situation, which, if we will be alive, we want to live on a small portion of my mother's estate given by her to me."[21]

Still earlier, when Chertkov thought more about acquainting himself with farming, his parents assigned the village of Rzhevsk with the land adjacent to it for his disposal. This land by itself was very attractive, hilly steppe, fields and ponds, and at the same time near the very village forest and river. A house was built on a high hill with four rooms, with a big terrace, simple but warm and comfortable, where the Chertkovs took up residence, and nearby stretched out little houses for their guests, assistants and workers of the village. This dwelling didn't have that opulence which was in the lordly house of Chertkov's parents in Lizinovka, but it had all that was necessary to live peacefully and comfortably.

Vladimir Grigorievich and Anna Konstantinovna lived in Rzhevsk in conditions much more simple than those which they had in Lizinovka, although even here, as Chertkov often wrote to Tolstoy with usual reproach of himself, a whole state of people serving them was created around them: a cook, a coachman and various other staff in one way or another working for the master of the village.

From Rzhevsk the nearest post office – the village of Rossosh – was nearly 18 versts, so letters arrived from Petersburg on the 4th or 5th day and from Yasnaya Polyana on the 3rd or 4th, but this did not prevent Chertkov from immediately starting a wide correspondence – business letters concerning the printing house and personal, continual and without stop, with his mother and with Tolstoy. The printing business continued to develop and soon after his return to the countryside he wrote his mother:

"It became more peaceful, and I took upon myself work in publishing with great joy. The business is very successful. By the way, the woman doctor Drenteln compiled a wonderful book for people about pregnancy, birth and medical care for women preparing to give birth and newborns."[22]

But fearing that business correspondence would take all his time, Chertkov searched for a co-worker who was able to write letters concerning the printing house and could carry out reworking of manuscripts, when it was necessary. With this goal, Chertkov invites

Ivan Ivanovich Gorbunov-Posadov, already working in the book warehouse of Mediator.

Correspondence between Tolstoy and Chertkov continues at this time with its former intensity. In 1888 Tolstoy wrote Chertkov 36 letters, just as in other years, on average one letter every ten days. Chertkov writes more often, and his letters, in which he endlessly tells Tolstoy about his internal life and shares thoughts about various questions of his life-understanding, often are very long.

Despite the fact that Chertkov's attention to a great degree is focused on business, concerned with the printing-house work, he intensely thinks about questions of world-outlook and faith, about prayers, about the essence of Christian learning, of free will, about the afterlife. These thoughts pour out of him in letters to Tolstoy and in entries in his diary, which he sends from time to time to Tolstoy.

At the same time, knowing that Tolstoy stopped carrying his diary, which he discontinued in 1884 and resumed in 1888, Chertkov wrote:

"It seems to me that you should certainly put down in a notebook all those thoughts which are appearing in your head in an unpolished form, and not with the purpose of giving them final form later, but only for people following in your path who are able to understand you with half a word and use these thoughts."[23]

In his turn, Tolstoy, receiving entries from Chertkov's diary wrote him:

"I always want to know all this, and am glad for people I love, that in them goes real internal work."[24]

Sharing his thoughts with Tolstoy, Chertkov often insistently puts those questions facing him that he himself thinks about. Response letters of Tolstoy hold the account of thoughts on themes that are of interest to Chertkov, while Tolstoy, not limiting his answers, begins to work on a formulary of these thoughts which he expressed in his letters to Chertkov, and sometimes, finally develops them in one or another work.

Tolstoy had no shortage of correspondents, who asked him questions about his views, but Chertkov's letters were of a different type: he did not wait for Tolstoy's prepared opinions, but opened for him his own mental work, the initial point of which they had in common, and Tolstoy answered him the same way.

Letters of this kind occupy a large part of the correspondence between Tolstoy and Chertkov. One can get an impression about the character of these letters just by taking a look at the correspondence between Tolstoy and Chertkov on the topic of human relation toward death and on a few other theoretical questions.

Thinking a lot about the meaning of death and the afterlife, Chertkov asks Tolstoy to express his opinion and tell him about his reflections on this theme:

"I would like it if you told me, in a few words *how* you understand this afterlife, this continuance of life. I only need this for myself and you know, that I indeed know you to be quick on the uptake; and therefore I ask you, if you answer me for me, not demanding from you serious work for the expression of this in words. For me, this question is decided such that the condition of space and time, the most comprehensible of these questions, fully conditional and results from the limitations of our earthly world outlook. In reality there is no space and time. It is like to a person going along a river on a boat seems that the shore and everything on it is moving, but this seems to him only because he cannot give up the idea of the movement forward of his own boat. In reality, the shore and everything on it stay in place, and for his life, it is not at all necessary, and does not at all take part in such movement in which all is carried along in the eyes of the traveler on the boat. Such is life for us, while we are in fleshy caging, it seems one thing happens before, one after; one is here, the other there. And as the development in us of understanding of truthful life – these limitations gradually vanish and we peacefully mix with each other and unite out of space and time."[25]

Tolstoy does not immediately answer Chertkov's question. In a short time Chertkov writes him two letters in one day – one in the morning and the other in the evening of 24 August 1889.

In the first of these letters, analyzing his relations toward death and expressing his convictions that "the essence of everything living is the only reality – out of time and space and therefore not knowing death", Chertkov writes that he internally is still not ready toward death:

"I am disturbed that the thoughts of death don't encourage me. When I think about death, all my interests indeed lose their

112

meaning; but what disturbs me is that toward impersonal goodness I also feel indifferent. I somehow lose consciousness of the necessity of work for God and other human beings. God doesn't need anything in me, and to my neighbor and to his earthly existence, nevertheless, as to me, one end."

The evening of the same day Chertkov writes that in his morning letter he imprecisely expressed his thoughts and from that could appear a wrong impression, that he is depressed or questions the afterlife. Again stating his views and analyzing his experiences concerned with death, Chertkov writes in conclusion: "I expressed to you what is in my soul, because I am used to and have the need always to express this to you."

Tolstoy answered Chertkov with a long letter in which he formulated his thoughts on death:

"Yesterday, in one day, I received both your letters, dear friend, the first and the additional, which gave me more joy than the first of depression. I know this feeling, dear friend, to loose heart during thoughts of death: I don't need God, he can go on without me, and people even more so; that which I can do for them, is so insignificant.

Everything material is insignificant and spiritually I am helpless; the thought still comes that if the laws of God ought to be implanted in people, that it will take place without me. And I am giving up and want to do nothing. Yes, I knew this before, and now with difficulty I can restore such a mood in imagination. The difference came for me from that I better understood my relation to God, as I wrote to you or Gorbunov, and not that I *better* understood, but simply for the first time clearly understood this relationship. Firstly, to say that I don't need God and he can go on without me is like if my hands or eyes or nerves said that they don't need me, that I would go on without them. No, I cannot go on without hands, eyes, organs of my life, just like God cannot go on (if to express such, although this expression is incorrect, because the question is put incorrectly) without me, without you, without people – one of his organs. God made cliffs, stars and me just because he needs me and cliffs and stars. And therefore it is ridiculous to say that He doesn't need me. If He did not need me, I would not exist; but I am needed, I am His organ or his servant. My relationship to him is not love only, as

Moses expressed, but of realization of unity with him. He is in me and I am in Him. So it is impossible to say that He needs me; but as it is said in John V, 19, 20 and in 26 and in all the Gospels of John, I am one with Him, I am His instrument. And my life consists of keeping everything that he gave me, not to loose anything to resurrect that in the last day – i.e. to keep the organ given me clean, purify it, working it and bringing it into the new life. If such is the meaning of my life, then what influence could death have on it? True, there are actions that don't go with this thing. One loses interest in such actions in view of death and it is better to avoid them entirely; but all kind actions – help your neighbor materially and spiritually, all these activities go into the maintenance and purification of that work which God gave me. Even those matters can come, or not come, considering how it is related to it. For example, it is possible to plough, write, such that it will not be in compliance with the maintenance and purification of the work of God's organ, in which is located in my life, but to plough and write for yourself and for people, and then the desire toward this fades in the view of death; and it is possible to do these things, only as maintenance and purification in the work of God's instrument, which makes up my life and then nothing disturbs the interest and joy until the last day and hour, for the meaning and value of my life grows with deprivation, suffering, illness and death.

If this is unclear, blame yourself. You promised to understand with a hint. For me this is not only clear, but this is experience, the joyful experience of life."[26]

Answering Chertkov, who was thinking a lot at this time about matrimonial relations and about sexual abstinence, Tolstoy writes him in 1888 a few letters, in which he formulated ideas more and more precisely expressed later in "Kreutzer's Sonata" and the afterward of "Kreutzer's Sonata", which was written to a certain degree in development of thoughts expressed in letters written to Chertkov:

"First, that it is necessary for me to say about this, it is that I, speaking about how one must live with a spouse, not only doesn't imply that I lived or live like I must, but to the contrary, I know hard as nails as I should only because I lived as I should *not* have." – Tolstoy wrote Chertkov on November 16, 1888. After outlining on several pages his thoughts, in part already thought through, in part still in the process of being formed, Tolstoy announces to Chertkov of his intention to express them in a new work:

"Read all this nonsense so as to guess what I wanted to say, and what I should say, but won't. These thoughts are not accidental, but grew from my consciousness and my life and I, if God allows, will try to express them brightly and clearly."

Settling in Rzhevsk, far from the city commotion, with its daily impatient procrastination, routine inquiries, Chertkov receives a great opportunity to devote his time to matters demanding unhurried and protracted work.

Besides editing publications for people, Chertkov's activity is divided into two other directions which permeates all his correspondence with Tolstoy: work on his articles and keeping and publishing of Tolstoy's manuscripts.

Chertkov did not consider himself a writer and did not strive to become one, but he felt the need to express his thoughts and it was difficult for him to confine himself to the role of editor of other authors' books. He not only constantly urges Tolstoy to write popular literature but he himself works in this direction.

Chertkov writes little and very slowly, persistently adding to the preciseness and clarity of statements, not hurrying to print what was written and not always carrying his work until completion because sometimes, new, more urgent demands and tasks tear him away from the manuscripts before he can successfully finish them. He writes the article about hunting "Evil Pastime", a book about Epictetus, whose thoughts were very close to him, a book about vegetarianism, at first called *Do Not Kill*, worked for a long time on the popular account of Tolstoy's *About Life* and tries to finish the book Tolstoy began about the life and teachings of the Buddha, on which, besides him, worked A.P. Barikov and A.I. Ertel.

Each manuscript is sent to Tolstoy, who, in his letters, gives not only his evaluation but also advice on literary technique, sometimes himself making changes and insertions.

Having read the manuscript of the book about Epictetus, Tolstoy writes Chertkov:

"Very, very good. I know him and nevertheless received a lot from yesterday's reading. I read with a pencil and corrected and marked what seemed necessary."[27]

Looking through the excerpts from the popular book about Buddha that Chertkov sent, Tolstoy gives him advice:

"It might come out very well. Only it is necessary, if possible, less descriptions and epithets."[28]

Tolstoy reads Chertkov's manuscripts about vegetarianism – "Don't Kill", aloud to his guests and writes Chertkov:

"I read it and I – and not the only one – liked it very much. Its deficiencies – fluffy literary language, some passages are too long, but others are clear and often strong. The quotations from other articles included in the introduction, it seems to me, are unnecessary and weak in comparison with the serious content of the article itself."[29]

And further, Tolstoy gives a detailed opinion about this manuscript, indicating all the noticed shortcomings.

In his turn, Chertkov also, like in the first years of the acquaintanceship with Tolstoy, very directly expressed his opinion about each of his new works with which he is acquainted in manuscript form, tirelessly repeating the argument that it is desirable to write in literary form and possibly more popular. Chertkov meets each new manuscript of Tolstoy with great joy and in time notes those parts which to him appear weak and Tolstoy often agrees with him.

Having received the manuscript of the "Kreutzer Sonata", Chertkov wrote Tolstoy:

"I am full and overfilled with you, dear friend and brother, Lev Nikolaevich... How strong and good are the impressions I got from this story, which I wouldn't tell you: it is clear without words. I will tell only about those moments, which, as it seems to me, still require some improvement; although I only read the manuscript version that you perhaps have already changed. It seems to me that discussions and thoughts about sexual questions are too intertwined in the narrative passage about how he killed his wife, and as a consequence it looses something in liveliness and naturalness; and the discussion itself is too ashamed of the necessity not to be too detailed, minute and bent in the form of speech, possibly

116

characteristic of the character and mood of the narrator. I say "possibly" because this goal, it seemed to me, was not achieved: there are parts where the character of the narrator is totally disregarded and his thoughts are presented in such a manner which he could not use talking about his past to a fellow traveler – the passenger on the railroad... It would be worth trying in conclusion to add in some kind of form, for example, from some kind of new person, or author, or in the form of a letter from the murderer, written, a few years later, add a more detailed view of the question."[30]

Tolstoy received the letter on one of those days when he felt especially sharply mental fatigue from those conditions in which he had to live, and wrote in his diary:

"Yesterday I received a long letter from Chertkov. He criticized "Kreutzer Sonata." Very truthfully, I desired to take his advice, but there is no inclination. Apathy, melancholy, depression..."[31]

But already the next day, on November 1, 1989, he writes Chertkov about his critical observations:

"Thank you for them, I want to use them. I even began to write the afterward, answer to the question: what does the author himself thinks about the subject of the story."

Tolstoy works on the afterward to the "Kreutzer Sonata" long and persistently and finishes this work only in April 1890.

Chertkov is very interested in the afterward and beforehand talks to translators. Tolstoy often writes him about how the work is going and even asks him to decide which of the two variations of the beginning of the afterward is more fitting.

As usual, being sure that theoretical articles of Tolstoy were less effective than his literary works, expressing those ideas, Chertkov makes use of a trick tested many times in the past, in order to convince Tolstoy to resume using his artistic creativity.

At the end of January 1890 Chertkov arrived at Tolstoy's for a few days at Yasnaya Polyana. Tolstoy was very glad and wrote in his diary:

"Chertkov is still more close to me."[32]

They talked a lot to each other. Tolstoy himself writes in his diary that he talks with Chertkov "all the time" and in one of the conversations Tolstoy told him about the concept of the story

"Father Sergei." Chertkov asks Tolstoy if it is possible to quickly write the story, drafting it, although in summary in the next letter to him. Tolstoy promised to do this, and soon after Chertkov's departure, wrote him a letter, the first words of which are clearly the echo of their conversation:

"Well here is the history for you. It is necessary to quickly tell, or I will forget. Served in the 40s in the cavalry regiment, graduate of the Corps of Pages of Prince Kasatsky-Rostovtsev. He was handsome, young, not poor and a favorite of friends and faculty."[33]

And further on several pages Tolstoy told the story of Father Sergei from that moment when a merry company, led by the 'divorced wife, the beautiful Makovkina", sledding in a troika, decides to go to Father Sergei:

"Coachmen were treated to wine for themselves. They had a trunk filled with pirozhki, wine and candy. Ladies were wrapped up in white dog fur coats. Coachman asked who is going ahead and one young man, turning his dashing side, hit the long whip handle, screamed, the bells rang and the sled runners screeched."

Chertkov received this letter and in a short time rewrote it with such calculation in order that between the lines were large blank spaces for insertions and corrections and at the end remained blank paper, sent this copy together with the original to Tolstoy. He hoped that Tolstoy, rereading his draft in rewritten form, would begin immediately to correct and add and is carried away by this work.

Chertkov's calculation to a certain degree proved to be correct. Having received the letter with the beginning of the story, Tolstoy wrote Chertkov:

"The tale of Father Sergei interested me very much. I finished the preface to Alekseyev's book and will start it. Perhaps it will be very interesting."[34]

Tolstoy began to work on "Father Sergei", but the artistic creativity demanded a lot of concentration and it was difficult to split time between the story and those religious-ethical works that Tolstoy mainly wrote during these years.

Not receiving news about work on the story of "Father Sergei" for a long time, Chertkov reminded Tolstoy of it:

"Well what, Lev Nikolaevich, is Father Sergei doing? He doesn't live far away: it takes a company too long to get to him on troikas, but the first coachman already had turned to the side, carried the whip handle, – gathered to drive fast."[35]

"Of "Sergei" – I began to write, – answered Tolstoy, – and I like him very much, i.e. that the subject was enlarged and I wanted to express my thoughts about him. I don't take to it because the road is blocked by the comments towards the declaration of Harrison and catechism of Ballou."[36]

Tolstoy's article about the declaration and catechism of American preachers of the study of non-resistance to evil by force of Harrison and Ballou, which stood in the way of work on the story "Father Sergei," grew into the book *The Kingdom of God Is Within You* on which Tolstoy worked intensely for nearly three years. In this book, it's as if Tolstoy concentrated all his negative opinions about governmental structure and the Orthodox Church, generously bringing examples of disgraceful actions of the Russian leadership for illustration of his thoughts and not sparing any words of the portrayal of church hierarchy. It wasn't conceivable to think about publication of this book in Russia, and when it was published in French translation and a copy was sent to Russia, the censorship withheld it.

N.N. Strahov wrote about this to Tolstoy:

"The censors announced that this is the most harmful book, of all those which have been banned by them so far."[37]

Chertkov followed Tolstoy's work on this manuscript with intense interest, and in order to make it easier and accelerate his work, sends him his copyist. When the work nears the end, Chertkov often sends couriers from Rzhevsk to Yasnaya Polyana who must bring back the manuscript version to him so that he could read them and copy them together with his assistants.

Tolstoy works on this book with great enthusiasm, many times changing his conclusion chapters and writing about it to Chertkov:

"Never have I worked so intensely as I did these past months. Because of this I haven't been able to do anything else."[38]

"Never has any effort cost me so much work or this just seems to me so. I would like to finish and at the same time it is a pity to part with this work. Don't blame me my friends, that I write so little, so seldom and so stupidly. I have a pile of shamefully unanswered letters. I cannot do anything, except this one work; all drops of water I conserve so as to let them go on this project."[39]

Chertkov wrote Tolstoy that he liked this book so much that he even has difficulty to find words in order to express his opinion about it, but nevertheless makes some critical observations.

He expresses his conviction that exposure is much more effective when it is done in a form which would not alienate the extreme sharpness of expressions of the people having the opposite point of view; and he thinks that there are parts in this book which can offend those who sincerely shared different views.

Tolstoy answers him first off that such softening can weaken the impression that the book brings to the reader:

"To soften, stipulating is not right. This breaks the whole tone, and the tone expresses the feeling, and the feeling infects (feelings sometimes of indignation) more than various arguments."[40]

But coming near to the end of the work, Tolstoy, like he did with a few other manuscripts, looks through this book trying to remove expressions which appeared to him excessively harsh and writes Chertkov that he is "weeding them out" of the conclusion.

The other theme, which Chertkov, living in Rzhevsk, devotes much space in his correspondence with Tolstoy, is gathering and storing of Tolstoy's manuscripts.

Already in June 1885 Chertkov wrote Tolstoy about how important it is to save all his manuscripts in complete order and asked him if he could entrust this job to some member of his family?

But the systematic gathering and preserving of everything written by Tolstoy was not begun in Yasnaya Polyana and Chertkov worried about this project for a long time.

At Chertkov's in Rzhevsk, in addition to his assistant from the printing house, a paid copyist almost continually lived, and beside them, people sympathizing with Tolstoy's views who could be entrusted with rewriting and putting in order Tolstoy's drafts and copies of letters to various people, often arrived there and lived for months. Chertkov begins this work and it gradually turns into one of his principal projects that he carries out with concentrated persistence.

Tolstoy wrote his works, painstakingly formulating his thoughts, many times reworking the initial drafts, and each of his articles in the final version strongly differed from the first variant; often in the sketches remained unused pages, not less powerful than those in the finished version, but rejected by Tolstoy because they diverted the attention of the reader from the fundamental ideas and complicated the structure of his work.

Chertkov began to gather and systematize the drafts of Tolstoy's manuscripts, often mixed together illegibly written, crossed out and re-corrected pages.

Sorting out these manuscripts, not included in final version, Chertkov made excerpts out of them, earmarked for an intended larger work – the systematic collection of Tolstoy's thoughts. At the same time Chertkov periodically reminded Tolstoy about these passages so that he could use them for his other works.

This project demanded an exceptional expenditure of time because manuscript drafts, taken together its volume usually many times surpassed the final editing – sufficient to say, that draft manuscripts toward one book – *The Kingdom of God* – all in all weighed almost one hundred pounds. Tolstoy sent them to Chertkov in the process of work and Chertkov quickly began to sort them.

Having received one of these packages, containing part of the draft manuscript of the book *The Kingdom of God*, Chertkov wrote Tolstoy:

"I received your drafts with lively interest, as you can imagine yourself, with interest, looked through them and made for my work excerpts from the crossed out parts."[41]

And Tolstoy, finishing, as it seemed to him this book on which he worked almost a whole year, wrote Chertkov:

"My writing, it *seems*, is finished. Today I again signed it. How much work and how little difference it seems, to an inattentive glance. But I think the difference in rewriting is great. You always help me in my writing. And in this you helped by gathering the drafts. Sometimes it is a pity to throw away those that are not in total character and weakens the whole, but it is necessary, and I would fiddle, desiring to hold them. But now I bolder throw them away, I know, that if there is what is necessary, that this won't get lost."[42]

At the same time in Rzhevsk Chertkov begins yet another project, tied to the preservation of Tolstoy's writings: gathering his letters and diary entries.

Tolstoy received a great deal of letters not only from personal acquaintances, but from the most varied people, reading his works, sympathizing with his views, or, just the opposite, decidedly against them, objecting, sharing their doubts and frequently appealing to him for the favor of advice on this or that matter. Therefore response letters of Tolstoy often went far away from the framework of his own personal relations with this or that person and held an account of his views on the most varied questions. During the course of many years, Tolstoy sent these letters, not saving copies. No one kept a list of these written letters and because of this, there was no way to know more or less how many, to whom or when Tolstoy wrote.

Chertkov begins to gather letters of Tolstoy to various people and tries to convince Tolstoy himself to assist in this project. He not only tries to copy already written letters of Tolstoy, constantly appealing with suitable favors to people with whom Tolstoy corresponded, but in every way possible insists that Tolstoy's letters be recopied before being sent.

Only a person, living under the same roof with Tolstoy and internally close to him, could fulfill this work. Tolstoy's sons, by all his accounts, were alien to him, his eldest daughter, Tatiana Lvovna, was close to him, but the closest of all in the family, Tolstoy was tied to his daughter Maria Lvovna.

Still a completely young girl, she was upset by the whole lifestyle her mother tried to establish, strove to comprehend her life, pulled toward her father, was glad to help him, to do anything. In 1887, Maria Lvovna wrote Anna Konstantinovna Chertkova:

"I live very vilely. I don't do anything good, and at the same time, I am busy all day. I study. And it is all such nonsense; it's not necessary for anything. Sometimes it becomes horribly disgusting and vile. You live, don't do anything, eat, sleep. But there is a lot of strength. And often envious of others who live well."

Chertkov understood that Maria Lvovna was closer than anyone else to Tolstoy, would be useful in the project of gathering letters. Beginning in 1889, he starts constantly and persistently writing her about this, persuading her to recopy as much as possible all the letters of her father, and in those cases, when she does not do this, at least note to whom and when Tolstoy wrote:

"Please record consistently all the people to whom he sends letters, marking the dates, – Chertkov wrote to Maria Lvovna. – It is unknown who will outlive whom, but certainly in their time people close by spirituality will carefully gather every line, written by your father, for this final time, and the detailed record of his letters completed by you will help them in a good and necessary deed."[43]

Tolstoy, on his side, agreed with Chertkov on this intended project:

"What you want to do with my letters is very desirous to me. This surprises you. I myself was surprised, but this is what's up: these days Maria Aleksandrovna sent Masha excerpts of my letters to Boulanger, and imagine... this was very necessary for me, and I read this, like we read things written by others but close to our hearts."[44]

Thanks to Tolstoy who entrusted Maria Lvovna to copy his letters, Chertkov wrote:

"Thank you that you remembered me and entrusted Masha to copy a few of your letters. I don't want to rush and act beforehand; but if you could only see, how, by the way it goes, how it is necessary for, in order to avoid omissions in compilation of my index of your thoughts; sometimes even the smallest of your observations, said in passing here or there, under various impressions and on various occasions, if you could only convince yourself of this, then you would certainly not only willingly, but with joy entrust Masha to copy out for me your letters, holding whatever meaningful."[45]

Gathering, copying and painstakingly saving everything written by Tolstoy, Chertkov intends to copy Tolstoy's diaries. Already in the first months of his acquaintance with Tolstoy, Chertkov showed him his diary, in which he wrote his thoughts and experiences, and soon after Tolstoy did the same, having given Chertkov his diary for 1884. Then this diary was rewritten and the copy saved at Chertkov's. From 1885 to the fall of 1888, Tolstoy apparently did not keep a diary and Chertkov wrote him about how significant it would be to have his diaries:

"I still one more time reread your old letters and I again found a lot necessary to me in them. Do you know that you should really keep a continual record, something like a diary of your thoughts and feelings... I noticed that your thoughts, your words are much more forceful when they are expressed immediately under the impression of the minute – "for real" and not worked into an article. It seems to me, that in our time, "articles" are not necessary. This form is already obsolete... In the past, true, people took books, read, reread, and studied them. Now people are more captured by immediate impressions and acts. And therefore it is more interesting, attracting and convincing all those words which lend themselves more to personal conversation, personal appeal, spontaneous announcements of their feelings and thoughts for the sake of joining with people, and not thinking about calculated discussions, denials and the like."[46]

In 1888 Tolstoy again began to keep a diary and, with a few breaks, kept it until his very death. The diary served foremost for recording his reflections, but at the same time he wrote there about the internal side of his life and about his relations with other people, including his own family.

In the beginning of April 1890, Tolstoy himself wrote Chertkov that he would send him his diaries so he could copy out his thoughts from there. But Sofia Andreyevna, having found out about this, rose up against this plan, not wishing that other people knew about their family life, which was found in his reflections in these writings. Tolstoy changed his mind and wrote Chertkov about his diaries:

"I decided not to send them to you. Believe one thing, that I didn't only think about it but felt it with all my soul. This is, so far, not allowed. But I promise you and will fulfill it if I will live. I will from the beginning to the end mark with blue pencil in the diaries everything, having common interest, and my daughters will copy them and I will send them to you."[47]

In one of the following letters – 23 May, 1890 – Tolstoy announced to Chertkov that he is sending him excerpts from his diary and explained that he cannot yet send the whole diary, not only because he would not be able to do this, behind his wife's back, but also because he felt that the decision to send these diaries breaks that mood in which he writes them for him, and how the thought that they will be recopied and read by others paralyzes that internal work which is tied to these writings.

At the same time, Maria Lvovna who at the instruction of her father, rewrote his diaries and letters for Chertkov, began to experience unpleasant feelings, during the time of this work, feeling, that copying the diaries and letters of Tolstoy interferes with his expression of that spontaneity with which he would write, not thinking about others who will read this.

Maria Lvovna wrote about this herself to Chertkov:

"I must confess, that I had a bad feeling against you. It seemed to me that you pull things from under papa's pen too much. I believe that he does not want others to read his diaries, while he is still living... Nothing would give me more joy than excerpts of his diaries, but I think it is unpleasant for him. I know that you, as do I, don't want to do anything unpleasant to him, and therefore, I will do what is better."[48]

In addition to these apprehensions Maria Lvovna had other feelings in which she confessed to Chertkov later with great sincerity:

"It was always difficult for me, that in me was some kind of bad feeling concerning you. I thought about it and know that its seed was in me. I like you and appreciate and mainly respect you for your love toward papa and for your understanding of him, and from this, in me rises an embarrassing feeling of jealousy. Forgive me."[49]

Already before the receipt of Maria Lvovna's letter about the recopying of diaries and letters, Chertkov answered Tolstoy that he fully understands his motives and only asks of Tolstoy that he give those letters to be copied that lacked intimate nuances and hold an account of his thoughts.

Tolstoy answered that he already instructed Maria Lvovna to copy out a few of his written letters and send them to Chertkov. In one of the following letters Tolstoy sent Chertkov was a large excerpt from his diary and in a few years began to give and send him for copying whole diaries in their entirety.

For her side, Maria Lvovna continued the project of recopying her father's letters and from time to time sent finished copies to Chertkov.

An exceptional collection of Tolstoy's manuscripts, including drafts of his works as well as letters begins to be created in Rzhevsk.

Chertkov gathers Tolstoy's drafts and letters of with constant persistence, trying to have every written line, if not in the original, then at least in copy. Chertkov sorts the manuscripts received from Tolstoy with pedantic thoroughness, copies them himself or checks the correctness of their recopy, if this is done by others, and follows up such that they are preserved in complete order.

Chertkov's life in Rzhevsk develops differently than Tolstoy's in Yasnaya Polyana, but between them exists a strong bond not only in the sphere of conviction and common work: telling each other about their difficulties and about those sides of their lives which give birth to feelings of discontent, they also feel a point of contact.

Tolstoy lives, as before in these years, surrounded by his family, but internally he is almost totally immersed in his work.

By custom, created a long time ago and made stronger still in the years of enthusiasm of life as a landowner-farmer, Tolstoy gets up early. Having drunk coffee with homemade cookies and a light breakfast, he usually has a short and always solitary morning walk. In these minutes, alone with himself, just as then when he changed the walk for work in the ploughed field or hayfield, Tolstoy sometimes experiences strong and immediate feeling of joy in life, judging by his diaries of these years, seldom experienced in other hours of the day:

"I walk on the hard road, some colorfully dressed women walk nearby from the work with a merry song. Short intervals in singing – and one can hear the measured thump of their legs on the road. And the song grows again, and again it dies down, and the thumps of the steps. It's good. In youth, it was often that something was singing inside you without the women's song. And everything – the sound of steps, shine of the sun, and the vibration of hanging branches of birches and everything, everything is if was completed under the song."[50]

"It's totally summer. Ivan and Maria*, the smell of rotten honey from chamomile, cornflower, and in the forest is quiet, only on the tops of trees humming bees do not stop. Insects. Yesterday I cut. It was good."[51]

Then, returning home, he goes to his study and for whole hours sits and works, covering sheets in handwriting thin and without pressure, looking through what was written earlier, stubbornly again and again rewriting a paragraph which does not satisfy him; changes, crosses out, writes one word over another so many times that sometimes he himself can only read with difficulty and many times returns to formulation of those thoughts, which he seems were expressed insufficiently clearly. This work, persistent and stubborn, fills most of his days, and when it is interrupted and does not go well, Tolstoy gets depressed and continually writes in his diary about this feeling of depression, which possesses him during such periods. In one of his letters to Chertkov, Tolstoy writes about his work:

"There is no desire, no energy to write, and without intense writing work, life is idle, the one I lead is to me torturous, disgusting."[52]

But this work does not give him satisfaction, strong enough to suppress the unhappiness of life, and looking back, he writes in his diary:

"Everything is the same: the stubbornness of work, the slow movement, and the unhappiness with myself."[53]

The second half of the day and evening, Tolstoy reads, interested, as always, in a variety of topics, from philosophical works to booklets of fat magazines, from following Buddhism or Confucius to popular books about hygiene for Mediator, writes letters, accumulated sometimes by the tens, or conversing with one of his guests – both at Yasnaya Polyana and in the Moscow house are many of the most varied visitors.

Among the guests at Tolstoy's from time to time appear people sharing his views. Tolstoy's relatives ironically called them "dark" – opposite of the high-society guests of Sofia Andreyevna, and the hostess related to them with open hostility.

By Tolstoy's diary entries and by his correspondence it is possible to judge that relations with these people was often pleasing to him, but usually did not turn into long friendship especially necessary for him.

He related to the attempts to create agricultural communes with interest and sympathy, which at the end of the 80s and the beginning of the 90s sprang up in various places and invariably ended more or less with quick breakdown, but not feeling any enthusiasm about these attempts. Having listened to stories of one of the more energetic members of the association, A.V. Alyehin, about how quickly and staunchly members founded their commune to carry out their principles in life, Tolstoy writes N.N. Ge, that after this story he was left with a "heavy impression", although he himself does not know fully from what:

"I recognize their loftiness and am joyful as though it is mine, but still something is not right."[54]

The prospective of having followers, united in some kind of a sect does not gladden Tolstoy. Having mentioned in a letter to Chertkov, that to Yasnaya Polyana arrived one of their like-thinkers, Tolstoy writes:

"Here are some thoughts related to this. A person comes from Kharkov, from Alekhin or Poltava, or even from you to me or further to Novoselov, comes tens of millions of people, considering themselves alien, such that in order to come to the like-believers in Tver, Tula, or Voronezh. It's like in the city, gentlemen drive as guests from Morskoi Street to Konyushennaya Street, and all these people, among whom they push through, are not people, but obstacles, but people real for them only there on Morskoi or somewhere else. There is no more non-Christian attitude toward people. But for high-society people this is excusable, this is logical. But for people wanting to follow Christ – there are not more anti-Christian relations – this is denial of something that makes up the essence of teaching. And as any current hour is the only real one, like that of a person who is in front of me, is the real person, a most important brother. I sinned having such attitude and therefore I noticed and will try to sin less."[55]

Tolstoy's life goes on its own path as if without any sharp turns. He does not make attempts to break the forms of life established in his home and understands that it is hopeless to try to convince his wife of his views, who is totally absorbed in the busy and intense life of hostess, trying not to let go of the field of vision not one insignificance and elicit for her family, as much as possible, profit from their assets. Even those events of family life which call for the usual feelings of joy, he experiences differently than his wife, and writes to Chertkov about the wedding of his son Ilya:

"The wedding in the coattails and with chorus and thunder. Surprisingly how on earth it is easy to do everything that is complicated, luxurious, stupid, immoral, everything is done by itself, but if you try not to do anything unnecessary it would require a great effort."[56]

His life in his family Tolstoy does not feel painted completely with black color. There were things making it easier for him: the friendship with Maria Lvovna, fatherly feelings toward his small son Vanechka, who grew into an attractive and affectionate child and minute personal attachment still did not disappear from his relationship with his wife, despite the whole depth of their divergence. But as usual he felt sharp pain from the contradictions between the conditions of his life and his views, and after one of the conversations with his wife, made an entry in his diary:

"She doesn't understand and the children don't understand, spending money, that every ruble, they live on and acquired from books is suffering, my disgrace. Let there be disgrace but what is upsetting: the weakening of influence which could have the sermon of truth."[57]

Oppressed by the conditions of his life, Tolstoy writes Chertkov on July 5, 1892 about his mental condition:

"I was very sad all day. Very, very sad. It seems that I got lost, I don't live like I should (this I certainly know) and I don't know how to extricate myself: on the right is bad and the left is bad and to stay where I am is also bad. One relief, when you think and feel that it is a cross and one has to bear it. It is difficult to say what this cross is: my weaknesses and the consequences of sins? And sometimes it feels so hard."

Many relations form Chertkov's life in the years while in Rzhevsk, internally more favorably than Tolstoy's. Chertkov not only did not have to experience constant disagreement with his wife about the very basics of his life-understanding, but he could always depend on her for support on her side, and he himself wrote about this in one of his letters:

"I was always ashamed that the fortune which somehow fell on my lot – fortune of cohabitation with my wife – sister by soul – friend and helper in everything that I see as the essence of life, even if I don't fulfill it."[58]

His little daughter Olya – Lucya as they called her in the family, – was an original, lively and tender girl, and the notes about her life, which her mother wrote shows how firmly attached to her were not only her parents and grandmother but all the inhabitants of Rzhevsk, among whom she grew up. In April 1889, the Chertkovs had still another child – this time a boy – and Tolstoy again wrote letters in which he thoughtfully gave advice to Anna Konstantinovna about feeding her son:

"I am glad that the feeding goes well. Scary too: what if it is getting worse when I am writing this? The main thing: don't be afraid and then don't worry."[59]

But in three months after the birth of their son, a tragedy fell upon the Chertkovs: in two days their daughter died from dysentery.

"We are deprived not only of our favorite child, we were deprived of the small connecting link and softening strength between all of us,"[60] – Chertkov wrote Tolstoy:

This death presented itself as a very heavy blow and for many years damaged the strength of Anna Konstantinovna, who besides that was physically weak. After the death of their daughter, she, for many years felt such a sharp loss in life force, almost uninterruptedly is sick and it was necessary for many weeks for her to stay in bed.

In the fall of 1889, Chertkov leaves Rzhevsk for Petersburg, the summer of the following year in the hope that the change in conditions of life will help Anna Konstantinovna, they go to the Caucuses and only in the end of August 1890 return to Rzhevsk. On the surface their life there goes as usual, although the sharp loss of strength in Anna Konstantinovna interferes with her active participation in editorial work of the printing house.

Chertkov continues to carry on the work in Rzhevsk in such conditions that could be found envious by many. But his constant dissatisfaction with himself and his life does not leave him and he writes a lot about this in letters to Tolstoy.

Trying in his way to build his life, Chertkov left that environment in which his childhood and youth were spent a long time ago already. Even the closest friends of his youth were as if they remained on the other side of the grain across which he stepped and he almost totally does not correspond with them.

One of the Chertkov's relatives, moving in those high-society circles that he left, confessed to him candidly that she had nothing about which to write him:

"We are living in the old style, like you don't live for a long time, so there is nothing to talk about."[61]

Instead of those people, with whom Chertkov was connected in youth, new ones appeared, to one or another degree sharing his views and participating in his work.

In Rzhevsk, often, besides Chertkov's permanent coworker connected with the printing house, people stay for a long time, considering themselves like-thinkers of Tolstoy, helping Chertkov in the rewriting of Tolstoy's manuscripts and other projects. But Chertkov, just as Tolstoy, not only did not strive to create a sect of people, "Tolstoyans", but often decidedly underlines that he does not feel especially close to these people since new teaching often does not change their essence:

"Like I wrote to Pavel Ivanovich these days, – Chertkov tells Tolstoy about one of his letters to P.I. Biryukov, – I see more love and Christianity in, how to say, pagans like Repin and Garshin, relations with whom encourage me in a good sense of the word, than in our, how to say, followers."[62]

In another letter Chertkov, in his usual directness, shares with Tolstoy his observations of himself and other people sharing one and the same teaching:

"The main thing that strikes me is that our understanding of life does not call, does not even enforce in many of us (including myself) truthful direct kindness, love, good will toward people. The person who is himself kind, remains kind and he who is less kind will not become, apparently, more kind."[63]

Already in early youth, in his letters to his mother, and to the extent of all his future life, Chertkov constantly expressed his conviction that certainly truthfulness must be one of the basic demands shown toward every person:

"One thing I crave for every minute, search for one, appreciate one – truth. It is the one that saves when everything is unsteady. Truth – strict toward itself, loving toward people, soft toward people."[64]

Truth, strict toward itself was undoubtedly was used a lot in all of Chertkov's expressions, but the second condition – to make truth soft toward people – to him was more difficult to fulfill.

Tolstoy wrote Chertkov about this on November 17, 1888, answering one of his letters:

"There is much there good and joyful – the main thing – that you strictly judge yourself: but it is sad that you don't get on with people. I know this and am the same myself, am familiar with this matter and therefore can offer knowledgeable advice: the main thing, don't be depressed, judge yourself, be guilty, repent, break yourself again and again and some time will pass, glance back and you will see, it will be better."

Anna Konstantinovna, in one of her letters to Tolstoy, said of her husband that he could usually talk to people all about what he thinks of them "with relentless candor." In relations with his like-thinkers, Chertkov considered it necessary to express his opinion with special precision, and often wrote, that those of them who had new views get on with hypocrisy and lie to themselves and others, although they "dressed" their words with "feelings, thoughts and words from unpublished compositions of Tolstoy", much more alien to him than ideological opponents. Dealing with such people and talking about them, Chertkov did not worry about how to deliberately soften his expressions and artificially encircle the corners:

"Some kind of drunkard, steeling for the feeding of his family, or even stupid old metropolitan, from his carriage on rubber wheels blessing passersby – in his ignorance is higher than those who have ears in order to listen and plug them up."[65]

Straight-line truthfulness combined with great persistence which Chertkov displayed, so that those who work with him, completed their projects, namely as it seemed to him to be right, created total lack of flexibility in his relations with these people, and he was much more solitary in his work than one would think. But the tie with Tolstoy had continued to be strong and he himself wrote about this to Tolstoy:

"My love toward you constantly reveals itself in that special character, probably, love in general that is capable of continuing to grow even after that moment, when, so it seemed, it couldn't grow anymore."[66]

"How I feel so joyous, when I write you, that between us there cannot be a disconnection and that you understand even that which I don't finish saying or not exactly say. It is surprising how without love, even the most intelligent person becomes stupid and makes a fool of himself and the other way around."[67]

Despite that, in the end of the 1880's and beginning of the 90s in society and in print, a lot of attention was devoted to the so-called Tolstoy movement, it did not attract too many followers. In Chertkov's papers, saved during 1890 and 1891, is a list entitled "List of People, Sometimes Mistakenly Called "Tolstoyans" – the term used to designate people, not existing or at least not having the right to exist." On this list are included like-thinkers of Tolstoy, living in Petersburg, Moscow and in the whole country, and however, it numbers in total only 60 names; and the inclusion of some is more or less unfounded. Chertkov himself ascertained the small number of people identical with him in views, but, looking negatively at the possibility of creating some kind of a sect, writes about this in one of his letters to A.I. Ertel:

"For me, beginning 15 years ago, to break my life and take on totally new activities, following the explanation of my internal conscious of new relations to life, then, when, I was in this relation absolutely alone, not knowing one person, thinking the same way as I do, what for me would have meaning, could a lot be found in a modern group of people ready to share my life-understanding? I understand life this way, and not differently, not because I thought it would be quicker to influence people, but simply because I cannot understand it any other way than how I understand it."[68]

In his letters to Tolstoy from Rzhevsk, Chertkov continues to tell about everything that troubles him and for that he reproaches himself. Especially often he is concerned with one side of his life, appearing for him as a constant cause of unpleasant experiences, and especially understandable to Tolstoy in his own life at Yasnaya Polyana, – the contradiction between convictions and material wealth, in the basis of which, in the final analysis, lay the use of land, although, not belonging to him personally.

Already when settling in Rzhevsk, Chertkov decided that half of the money that he received every year from his mother – 10,000 rubles – would be assigned to peasants: partially for the expenses of the trade school established by him, partially for a people's publishing enterprise, and part of the money went to help needy families. Also at Chertkov's in Rzhevsk was his friend and helper, N.D. Rostovtsev, whose responsibility was the administration of the farm plus material help to poor families in the neighboring villages: by distributing money, by buying clothes, horses, etc. for those in need. But Chertkov realized that this charity would change nothing in reality. Already in the first years of his life in Rzhevsk, he wrote to a teacher of one of the neighboring village schools, N.D. Kivshenko:

"I am not playing the role of benefactor since I consider and feel the surrounding population as my benefactors and not the other way around. But this role, by virtue of circumstance, outwardly thrusts itself on me and represents the most difficult side of the present conditions."[69]

In a period of time this acknowledgement of the removal of the contradiction between his convictions and conditions of life became more and more burdensome. Chertkov often writes Tolstoy, how torturous is this created situation:

"The condition of our life and relations, master to hireling, which poisons my relations toward those surrounding us, working for us, – all the more and more burdens me. Sometimes it seems to me that I fell into some kind of vicious circle, from which there is no exit beside carnal death, and this is very torturous."[70]

This disparity between convictions and the way of life creates discord in Chertkov's life, about which A.I. Ertel wrote to him in one of his letters:

"Your unhappiness is based in the fact that your way of life is doomed to contradict those logical conclusions which flow from your way of thought."[71]

Chertkov himself experienced this discord all the more and more sharply in the beginning of 1893, this feeling occupied more and more space in his life. He writes about this to Tolstoy:

"Denying property, I use this for my family. Here is this principle contradiction, which does not give me peace. Beside which all my situation, my relations with surrounding people, grates on me, and founded on the purchase of somebody's labor by stolen money."[72]

Tolstoy follows the experience of Chertkov with great sympathy, but holds back from interference with one or another specific advice. He feels, that some kind of change must come in Chertkov's life, but still does not know what form it will take, just as Chertkov himself does not know. And reading the diaries in which Chertkov makes entries about experiencing his emotional condition, Tolstoy writes him:

"I read your diary, and the reading, as always, very much touches and worries me. I also keenly understand and experience myself... How I would desire to help you in your spiritual work not through strength which I don't have but my love which is just as weak."[73]

VI
At The Crossroads

1893 found Chertkov in a condition of sharp unhappiness with himself, his way of life and this mood permeates all his correspondence with Tolstoy for the first months of this year.

On the external side of Chertkov's life, much was successfully accomplished. His publishing work continued to develop and Mediator little by little began to work on the basis of becoming self-sufficient.

Chertkov intended to broaden the publishing program by releasing a new series of books, earmarked for intellectual readers, and a series of reproductions with pictures that were close to him in his idea, "Life Everywhere" by Yaroshenko, "Division" by Maximov, etc. He energetically promoted both of these beginnings.

Tolstoy looked through books and manuscripts, earmarked for the new series with interest and for one of the first books "Ethics of Food" by H. Williams – wrote a big preface, transformed later into a separate article "The First Step."

Life in Rzhevsk externally was made more and more attractive – young trees which were planted on the estate grew up, the village continued slowly to be built up, and for various arriving guests rooms in one or another house were located where they could settle, not being a burden to the Chertkovs. But at the basis of this well-being lay the means, in the final analysis, was received from ownership of land belonging to Chertkov's mother and Chertkov was very upset by this fact. He himself defined his mental condition as a crisis, and talks about this in his diary:

"I know that my present difficulties are not accidental or easily eliminated, but the most serious, such, that to find a way out of them will call for the overturn of my whole way of life. In my life brewed a crisis. In the past I experienced an emotional crisis one day; now apparently comes the second."[1]

Chertkov writes about the same thing in letters to Tolstoy:

"I am in a crisis of my whole life: I look around, I look at myself and feel that something I will undertake soon, that some kind of overturn in my life is coming; but what specifically I do not know."[2]

Chertkov writes his mother that he has more determination to make the decision not to take more money for life from her, but he still does not know how to build his life on new foundations:

"The condition of my life and, in general, all my activities still have not changed and I still feel the necessity to peacefully understand myself and anything decidedly to undertake such that my practical life would be somewhat close in conforming to my beliefs and not contradict them, like now, beginning with the most important and ending with the most insignificant things... And for this I persistently free myself from the necessity to be day by day, almost all day, absorbed in the current business of Mediator."[3]

But to accomplish this goal, to change in root the material side of his life, was very difficult, since these conditions in which his life was channeled were in very close ties with the whole economical and social system creating them.

To refuse the money received from his mother meant not only to create family discord with her, without direct use for peasants, since her estate nevertheless would be run on a former basis, but also to face a difficult question: from where to take the means in order to carry on, without interruption, the work of preserving and spreading the works of Tolstoy, and how to support his family. **To go to** government service, which was a common source of income for people who received an education, had no property, would certainly contradict Chertkov's convictions not in less degree than using his mother's money. Occupation in one or another so-called free professions were not accessible because he had no special training and that this path was tied for him to a row of compromises. To leave everything and become a simple farmer was excessively difficult not only because it would mean refusing to spend his time and strength on the work tied to the works of Tolstoy, but there was no conforming skill, and even if he managed to acquire these skills, Anna Konstantinovna's constant illness wouldn't permit her to perform the chores which falls to a woman in a peasant household.

Persistently thinking about the situation, Chertkov often at this time expresses in his letters and diary the hope that it would be easier for him to change the conditions of his life if he frees himself from the current business at Mediator and will be able to concentrate on searching for an exit.

At first he thought about giving a big part of the business to his coworkers, but had no intentions of giving up the printing house itself. Political and censure oppression which he begins especially sharply to feel in these years, carried him at one time even to the thought of putting his name on covers, as editor, so that no one could imagine that he acts not so quite openly. Chertkov shares this project with his mother:

"Circumstances now on all sides are so imminent that I see in myself the need to sign under my business Mediator, and reveal this is my penname and in print show that Mediator is nothing other than Vladimir Chertkov."[4]

At the same time a sharp desire grows in him to leave for a time from all current matters of the printing house, take a "vacation" from himself, in order to return after he manages one way or another to escape from this current condition.

Chertkov writes Tolstoy about this decision on April 18, 1893:

"I decided to give the business, which I belonged to for 8 years, up for a time, since I am on the verge, and I must immediately free myself from various enslavements and belong only to me."

Tolstoy follows Chertkov's search with great sympathy, sending him I.M. Tregubov in the capacity of aide in the matters of Mediator, in place of I.I. Gorbunov, who left at this time from Rzhevsk and writes him:

"Let God help you have a rest, with new energy take on again the business of Mediator which became more dear to me and find what you want for yourself."[5]

But the simple passing of current work to the new aide did not change the situation since Chertkov feels the aspiration not only to part with this work temporarily but also to direct his strength in some other direction. More and more often, in his letters to Tolstoy, he talks about how he feels the need to decidedly and openly express those thoughts about government power and about the predominant church, which not only could not be expressed in a form acceptable to the censors, but must sooner or later call for one or another repression. He begins to consider even the presentation of the manuscript to the censors an intolerable compromise for him and writes to Tolstoy:

"It seems to me that such things as presenting the literary works to censors should not be done, since it means to participate and, probably, to acknowledge and use such evil, which should not be."[6]

At the end of the summer of 1893, Chertkov makes a decision, which must, to a known degree, put his life in new conditions. Considering those circumstances that the printing house Mediator already had reached such a state that is able to function without subsidies, Chertkov decides to give it to other people, adding to that sum of money which would allow the business to develop in the coming few years. At the same time, he plans to try to earn a living by means of translations, compilations and other literary work that he could do for this printing house after it would be given over to ownership of others and becomes materially independent.

At the same time Chertkov made the decision to direct all of his strength to the open expression of his views concerning the current social system, based on the exploitation of labor. He wants to do this, spreading corresponding compositions of Tolstoy. Concurrently, he decides to protest against the persecution of those not agreeable to the teachings of the Orthodox Church. He clearly understands what kind of consequences this path can carry and writes Tolstoy:

"I want to give more and more to make an effort in me towards that which can so easily result in forced departure."[7]

Tolstoy disapprovingly viewed Chertkov's intention to abandon the printing house Mediator. Fearing that his intention will lead to the closing of the printing house, Tolstoy wrote:

"Concerning your intention to close Mediator, I only think one definite thing, this is, that it is always dangerous and wrong to undertake something. *Le non agir (not doing anything)* it is necessary to observe. And *le non agir* in this case – not closing, but stopping publishing activities. And another dangerous thing is to make yourself a wide space for literary activities: this is such –

when it is real – activity not dependent on us, that it is difficult to foresee it."[8]

Chertkov fulfilled his decision to give the printing house Mediator to other people, convinced that it could exist independently in financial terms.

In August 1893 he called Biryukov to Rzhevsk and announced that he wanted to give him Mediator. It was decided that he would work with a close friend I.I. Gorbunov and that the business would be transferred to Moscow. Chertkov left only the choice of works for the recently created series for intellectual readers for himself.

Biryukov, after checking the administrative matters of Mediator in detail, wrote Chertkov that he found them in good condition and accepted the printing house from Chertkov.

Anna Konstantinovna wrote about this to Tolstoy:

"It's a pity and sad, like someone in the house died: everything was taken away, carried away, sad, true."[9]

Tolstoy answered her that it was sad for him to learn of this:

"I am also sad that Vladimir Grigorievich gave away Mediator. And not as much for Mediator but as much as for him. They were born together and merged such that they could not be separated. I wrote about "not doing anything" but this is necessary mainly, when a special importance is given to *doing*. Such was Mediator – this was only the best occupation in unnatural position condemned by himself in which he found himself. It was the best usage of unlawful leisure already existing."[10]

In October Chertkov decided to take the next step and wrote Biryukov that, thinking about refusing money received from his mother, he desired to have constant paid work in Mediator through translations, adaptations of literary works, etc. But Biryukov answered that work of this type, in such a small publishing house as Mediator, cannot give sufficient paid work, and therefore he referred to the offer of Chertkov "almost unfavorably." Further Biryukov wrote that in accordance with the insignificant compensation which coworkers of Mediator receive, he can offer Chertkov 25 rubles a month for four hours daily work on translations and adaptations of foreign literary works and the remaining time Chertkov can write for the publishing house on a per sheet payment.

At the same time Biryukov reminded Chertkov that he wanted to receive from him money for Mediator, since not all the money promised by Chertkov during the transfer of the business was paid:

"I am waiting for help, not only literary but monetarily, namely from you, because book sales still do not complete that turn, which can give revenue. How can I promise you constant work? ... If you allow me to state my opinion, that I would advise you to use all the strength of will and mind to organize your life independently of literary work, remembering that from wherever money came, it is always foul, and therefore the only solution to the question, as long as we cannot go on without money, will be to spend as least as possible, and from where it comes – this doesn't matter."[11]

Chertkov considered the question of where the money comes as not an insignificant thing, but he must have acknowledged for himself that the thought of living on literary pay was impractical. Desiring to fulfill his promise and not having money at his disposal due to the past winter, in hunger of 1892, he already had to spend nearly 5000 rubles on help for peasants in the neighboring villages, from the account of the next year, Chertkov borrowed under a promissory note written by his mother and transferred 2000 rubles to Biryukov.

Chertkov accomplished another intention to a certain degree – that of decidedly expressing his opinion about the general organization and about the existence of the government and church powers. It was prompted by the situation where Tolstoy and Chertkov had witnessed such facts that called for their deep indignation and made them both express their protest in one way or another.

In the beginning of July 1893 Chertkov found out that in the Voronezh penal battalion a prisoner E.N. Drozhin, sharing the same views as Tolstoy, was held in extremely harsh conditions. Chertkov quickly inquired and asked E.I. Popov, living at his house and helping him in correspondence and other work, to travel to Voronezh.

Information, received about Drozhin and what goes on in the penal battalion, demanded immediate interference in this matter.

E.N. Drozhin, born among peasants, was a rural teacher in the Kursk province. Still in early youth, thanks to the acquaintanceship of political exiles, he adopted revolutionary views and often was reprimanded by the school administration for open expression of his convictions, for non-observance of fasts and his liberal approach to education of students.

In 1889, he became acquainted with Prince D.A. Hilkov, who lived 25 versts from his village. Prince Hilkov shared many views of Tolstoy, and Drozhin also began to sympathize with his convictions, especially with his criticism of the church and denunciation of government power.

In a year, Drozhin was arrested with the charge that he gave one of the peasants a revolutionary book "The Tale of Four Brothers", fired from his position of teacher, deprived the postponement of serving compulsory military service and after release from prison in 1891, was called up for military service. Drozhin refused oaths of allegiance of military service, was arrested and after repeated confinement in lockup, was brought to military trial and sentenced to two years detention in a penal battalion.

The penal battalion represented a distinctive combination of military prison and the military unit in which the most severe discipline was maintained by use of corporal punishment. Continuing to categorically refuse to submit to the orders of his superiors, Drozhin systematically underwent confinement in damp and dark cells, food deprivation and finally new judicial processes, each of which ended in the extension of confinement in the battalion, such that in July 1893, this period extended to six years and at the end of 1893 – to ten years. Almost continuous stay in the cell ruined Drozhin's health and he quickly began to develop tuberculosis.

Having found out about Drozhin's condition, Chertkov went to Voronezh, had a meeting with Drozhin, sitting at that time in the cell, and wrote about this matter to Tolstoy.

In the response letter, Tolstoy wrote Chertkov:

"What's with Drozhin? It's horrible to read. It's exactly like Circassians torturing the captives. It is worth remembering that cruelty of his torturers is to a certain degree only a reflection of cruelty of various gendarmes, governors, military officers and that every official can become like that."[12]

Chertkov began to correspond with Drozhin and began to gather material about his case. In the search for a way out - for relief of Drozhin's situation, he came up with the idea of writing about his situation to the tsar.

Tolstoy approved of this idea, having become familiar with the draft of the letter, made a few critical observations, but accepted the correctness of it's basic tone, far from the usual petition of the highest name.

Chertkov hoped for the mediation of his mother and this calculation proved to be correct. Chertkova was well acquainted with Adjutant-General Richter, the head of the chancellery of Alexander III and he agreed to present Chertkov's letter to the tsar. As a result, an order was given to carry out the examination of Drozhin's health, and if he seemed unfit for military service, transfer him to the civilian prison immediately.

But this "kindness" was late: in the beginning of January 1894, Drozhin was sent from the penal battalion to the province prison, and on January 27, died in the prison hospital of tuberculosis.

Chertkov intended to write a book about the Drozhin case, which could be published abroad, but then, being busy with other things, on Tolstoy's advice, gave this work to E.I. Popov, free at the time from other projects, and entrusted him with his correspondence with Drozhin.

Tolstoy agreed to write a preface for this book, which grew into a rather large article.[13]

At the same time as the Drozhin matter, Tolstoy and Chertkov collided with other displays of administrative arbitrariness, not only with knowledge but also by direct order of the tsar.

Prince Hilkov, giving up almost all of his land to the peasants and striving to live by his labor in a small village, was sent in 1892 for five years to the Caucuses as a result of reports from the local priesthood and the police chief, charging him with instigation of peasants toward disobedience of the local authority. He was married, but refused to be wed in a church. His marriage was declared illegal, and the two small children from this union were declared illegitimate. His wife and two children, five and three, followed him to the Caucuses, and here, in October 1893, by command of Alexander III, the local police took away their children and gave them to Hilkov's mother, declaring that she wanted to take them away from their parents in order to give them a suitable upbringing, position and title, which they would be lacking if they stayed with their parents.

Tolstoy found out about this from a letter of Hilkov's at the time, when he answered Chertkov's letter concerning the book *The Kingdom of God*. Chertkov wrote that in condemning the representatives of the government and church powers for their actions, it is necessary, nevertheless, to remember that they are sometimes sincere in their own way in their motives.

Answering Chertkov, Tolstoy announced in passing to him what happened to Hilkov:

"I just received a letter from Hilkov. His mother arrived at his house with the police inspector from Tbilisi and took the children from him and his wife (on the highest command) and drove them away. Really, don't you see how she and all those who are participants in this senseless cruel matter, explain all this as good intentions? Who can find out to what degree they are sincere and unselfish. One thing is left for us: to try not to be connected with any part of their dealings and not become participants of theirs."[14]

Chertkov leaned of the situation with great indignation:

"I don't want to write about my life now, – wrote Chertkov to Tolstoy, – because I live tensely, like a volcano, and concerning the current situation in Russia, as if with a bomb in hand, and I don't know when to let it go: tomorrow or in a short time. And perhaps there won't be necessity in it. And I don't want to be distracted now with words about what I do, want or can do."[15]

Chertkov began to gather material related to the Hilkov case. He addressed Hilkov with the request of compiling memoirs of his life and write in detail about the kidnapping of the children, wrote to Tolstoy and his daughter so that they sent letters Tolstoy had of Hilkov's and began correspondence with Hilkov's wife, Cecily Vladimirovna Weiner.

Chertkov had the idea of compiling a report about the Hilkov case, giving it to the tsar through the help of his mother's acquaintances and, in case of refusal of the return of the children, publishing the gathered material abroad.

He wrote about this to Tolstoy and received a sympathetic response:

"I just wrote Hilkov about what you want to write that happened to him. Its wonderful and you will do this wonderfully. Only it is necessary to do this as soon as possible. But extensively as you have seized it, this perhaps won't be fulfilled that soon."[16]

At the same time Chertkov wrote his mother and asked to help Weiner in her attempts in returning the children.

Chertkova treated Weiner with great sympathy and in conversations with General Richter tried to test the water, desiring to explore how much hope there was for a favorable result of her petitioning. But inasmuch as the children were taken away on the basis of the tsar's order, his retinue did not permit even a shadow of criticism of his decision. Chertkova understood that this matter was hopeless and wrote her son:

"But, my dear, don't lash out as a fish about ice, so that Petersburg knows the whole truth about this matter. In Petersburg, and in other places, no one will learn anything that one does not want to know."[17]

Tolstoy, on his side, tried to help Hilkov and his wife in their efforts. He wrote a letter to Alexander III that in receiving the news of the children taken from the Hilkov's, wanted to publish an announcement about this matter in the English press, but decided first to try to appeal directly to the tsar, in the hope that he will change his command.[18]

The Minister of the Imperial Court, Count I.I. Vorontsov-Dashkov, agreed to give this letter to the tsar, but it did nothing to change the situation.

Nevertheless, Chertkov continued to gather material for his intended report.

At the same time Chertkov conceives another project, also connected with the gathering of manuscript materials. The intensifying reaction in the sphere of internal politics and activities in the synod, led by Pobedonostsev, called in the beginning of the 1890s of the persecution of people leaving the Orthodox Church. These persecutions took on various forms – from administrative deportation to pogroms of sects in Ukraine. Chertkov writes Tolstoy in December 1893 about his intention to gather all material about sect movements and asks him to compile a program of this work.

Tolstoy answers Chertkov on this offering:

"You have undertaken a difficult project, but a good one. The harvest is great, but not enough workers. The program is not needed. It somehow humbles the work."[19]

Chertkov begins this work, having concentrated it in the hands of his aide, I.M. Tregubov. Gradually it occupies one of the first places in his list of projects: from year to year gathers material, compiling in the end a considerable archive.

Statements in connection with the Drozhin and Hilkov cases appeared to a certain degree as new impetus in the common activities of Tolstoy and Chertkov. They put the beginning of that path, going on which, Chertkov inevitably sooner or later had to call out against himself repressions from the authorities. But at the same time Chertkov continued to develop his activities connected with Tolstoy's works, carrying them in the same manner that had formed and firmed up already in the first years of his acquaintance with Tolstoy.

Having finished *The Kingdom of God*, Tolstoy, with his usual persistence, begins work on new articles. In the fall of 1893, he set to work on an article about the festivities in the city of Tulon in connection with the visit of a Russian squadron to France, and this article, just as *The Kingdom of God*, having no chance of being published in Russia due to censorship, becomes the object of his efforts for some time. Intense and tedious work on this article, which does not satisfy Tolstoy for a long time, causes him for a moment the desire to discard this theme and he writes Chertkov:

"But what happened with Tulon was that I got sick of it. Some kind of very certain voice tells me that this is not a proper topic, that not so much of life is left and there is no sense to spend it on such trifles."[20]

But already in two days he takes his words back:

"I wrote you, that the article about Tulon alienated me, and I accepted this as my internal voice. This was very stupid on my part. I am again very busy with it, although there is not much good in it."[21]

Chertkov answered Tolstoy that he understands Tolstoy's relation to this work and shared with him thoughts of his articles:

"How I was pleased that in your letter you thought as though you were being with yourself. I understand everything that you think so well, when I know what you think. Just as now, I understand why the internal voice alienated you from the article about Tulon, and then why you wanted to finish the article. And it seems to me that both impulses were justified. I think that in your situation, it is worth always to try to express *everything* that is bursting from your soul, because I know and see how important this is for people. But there is no need to linger too long on the less essential, but state it as if in passing, almost not rereading so as to economize time and labor, for thorough treatment of the more important. And this, in your case, is more feasible, that your initial raw statement of your thoughts distinguishes itself in character and for you, one characteristic is individual spontaneity, freshness and strength, which for many readers is still more fascinating and your infectiousness more persuasive, even sometimes more than your polished writings."[22]

But Tolstoy continues with his former persistence to work, many times reworking one or another passage. M.L. Tolstaya wrote Chertkov in the beginning of December 1893:

"Tulon is high pressure work all the time. Today father signed it and said that he finished, but I don't believe this since he has said this many times and I will now cleanse the text of it for work tomorrow."[23]

Disbelief of Tolstaya seemed totally founded: this article, receiving its final editing, called "Christianity and Patriotism" was finished only in March 1894.

In other letters, Tolstaya announced to Chertkov that she continues to rewrite letters for him, which her father writes and that she is sending to Rzhevsk his draft manuscripts.

Living in Rzhevsk, Chertkov, as before, continues to actively participate in the organization of Tolstoy's works being translated into foreign languages. By his persistent advice, Tolstoy takes steps to help *The Kingdom of God* appear simultaneously in French, English and German and with this goal, sends the manuscript to translators of these languages at the same time. Chertkov translates "Christianity and Patriotism" himself into English, as well as a few other articles of Tolstoy's and constantly corresponds with him about business connected with the translations of his works.

Living almost continually in Rzhevsk, Chertkov almost completely does not see Tolstoy from 1891 to 1893 and intensive correspondence replaces their personal contact.

In 1893, despite the list of common projects, they did not see each other at all. In the beginning of 1894 Chertkov prepares to go to Petersburg in order to personally participate in the efforts connected to the Hilkov case and on the way intended to stay in Moscow in order to see Tolstoy. But this plan did not come to fruition because Anna Konstantinovna felt a sharp loss of strength, constant dizziness, heart attack and at one time her condition called for fear for her life. Chertkov asks Tolstoy to come to him in Rzhevsk.

Tolstoy decides to go to Chertkov's in mid-March, but was held up for a short time by his son Lev Lvovich's return to Moscow, who was suffering from nervous indisposition and receiving treatment abroad.

Tolstoy wrote Chertkov about this postponement:

"I cannot express to you, dear friend, how much I like you and would desire to be with you now. Now it is impossible for me to go, Leva only yesterday arrived and is very weak and pitiful: says that he feels that everything is finished, that he will not get healthy and is glad only that he will die at home among his own. I think that this is to a large degree following four nights in a train car, but nevertheless, I cannot leave him now, more so, that everyone objects to my trip. But despite their objections, in two or three days, when he, as I hope, will get a bit stronger, I will go, if I will live, and will have the joy of sharing your sorrow, hope and joy with you."[24]

At the end of March, Tolstoy left for Rzhevsk together with his daughter Maria Lvovna and spent five days at the Chertkovs.

Tolstoy wrote about these days to his wife from Rzhevsk:

"I am very glad I came; and he, and mainly she are so sincerely glad that we are so close to them physically, that together we are very well. She is very pitiful and kind and firm in soul. I now talk with her for half an hour and see that she is already tired. She already cannot sit on the bed herself. Elizaveta Ivanovna just came; I still did not see her. I was embarrassed by the thought that so many of us suddenly arrived all at once, but here are so many houses that everyone fits, and everyone, it seems, is comfortable and we have it too good. The place is very beautiful, built on a half-hill, goes down a steep ravine and lifts on the other side, covered by a large forest. I just walked alone and gathered snowdrops..."[25]

Returning to Moscow, Tolstoy wrote a letter to Vladimir Grigorievich and Anna Konstantinovna in which he stated that this trip remains for him one of the dearest reminiscences. At the same time, bringing up his impressions, Tolstoy wrote:

"Everything was good – and tender and nice Elizaveta Ivanovna (to whom I send my greeting and gratitude), and the unspoiled and natural, healthy boy, and kind-souled happy members of the household, but most of all for me was the new, more sincere acquaintance with you, Anna Konstantinovna, and joy to find out how close you are to your husband and me. You only have three things which are not good: 1) that you are unhappy with your life; 2) that you are sick; and 3) that you, Vladimir Grigorievich, are restless."

And on his side, Tolstoy gave the Chertkovs advice:

"You, Anna Konstantinovna, as little as possible, remember your illness and be sure it cannot interfere with your life, and you, Vladimir Grigorievich, forgive people more, investigate what brings them to such actions, to that life that you condemn and which annoys you."[26]

During the time Tolstoy was in Rzhevsk, the decision was made to spend the next summer not far from one another, and Tolstoy offered to rent them a dacha not far from Yasnaya Polyana.

Toward the end of April, Anna Konstantinovna's health improved so much that it allowed her the possibility to travel to other places.

Tolstoy begins to thoroughly search for a dacha, and finding a suitable place in the village of Dyomenka, five versts from Yasnaya Polyana, wrote about it in a letter to Chertkov with the efficiency of an experienced landlord. Having made a sketch of the inspected dacha, Tolstoy enumerates its advantages:

"The house stands separately from the village, in the garden. In the courtyard is an old barn, hut where the gardener lives, i.e. the tenant of the garden. The house is brand new, only just finished. No one lived in it. The walls are logged from the new forest, the roof covered with tin. The site in terms of fresh air must be wonderful – from one side open fields, the other – a fruit orchard and big trees, birch, oak, it seems one alley. The place is beautiful, comfortable. In one hundred sazhens is *zaseka,* i.e. a huge delightful forest belonging to the Treasury. The cost is 125 rubles… No one except you and the gardener will live in courtyard."[27]

Knowing that a lot of people always lived near Chertkov, more so, that his lordly upbringing created a habit of having no fewer than 2-3 servants, Tolstoy supposed that four rooms would not be enough for them and offered to build an added hut. Then he changed his mind and called for buying a wooden framework, in order to put in a log cabin, which, in his opinion, should go for around 40 rubles, but finally decided to finish the added lodging in the barn.

Sofia Andreyevna looked at this preparation with vexation. Already earlier, having found out that her sister, T.A. Kuzminskaya and her children wouldn't be spending the summer at Yasnaya Polyana, wrote her:

"Without you, visitors are expected – dark ones. And they grow so hateful to me that sometimes I want to take on them some kind of pistol or arsenic."[28]

When Tolstoy left for the whole day in search of the framework, she wrote Chertkov an annoyed letter in which she reproached him that he makes Tolstoy spend time on his behalf.

Having found out about this letter, Tolstoy wrote Chertkov:

"Tatiana Andreyevna won't be living with us; she is apprehensive of you since you support those of my views which horrify her. She is also scared she will be lonely. I had the impudence to say that your Dima didn't have the toys like Vanechka has. And here Sofia Andreyevna wrote you a letter. If you ask me does she want you to come, I will say no; but if you ask do I think you should come? I think, yes. Like I told her, as I tell you: if there is something unkind between you, it is necessary to use all your strength so that it will not be and that there will be only love. And this is possible and I know that you can do this and that she can and is almost ready for this."[29]

Chertkov answered Tolstoy's wife with reserved courtesy and a few days later arrived with his family to Dyomenka.

Until 1894 Chertkov did not live for a long time in one place with Tolstoy. He was at his house in Moscow and at Yasnaya Polyana on short visits only for a period of a few days. Now the Chertkovs were situated in direct proximity to Tolstoy and his family and as the summer passed, they had close relations with one another: by short entries which Chertkov made in his notebook, in the first three weeks after their arrival to Dyomenka, it is possible to establish that they meet in the beginning of this summer on average more than once in two days, while often Tolstoy is at Dyomenka with his daughters.

The relations that Chertkov had with Sofia Andreyevna during this time of his life in Dyomenka took shape without any kind of sharp hostility. When Chertkov, a few weeks after his arrival, was seriously taken ill with malaria, and not believing in medicine, refused to undergo treatment, Sofia Andreyevna even got involved in this matter and as characteristic of her decisiveness and impetuousness, went herself to Tula and brought him a doctor. And although in letters from Sofia Andreyevna to her sister from this summer creep in notes of dislike of Chertkov, nevertheless they are not enemies.

Dyomenka remains the place of summer retreat for the Chertkovs; they come here in 1895 and 1896.

In the summer of 1894 Chertkov does the same in Dyomenka as in Rzhevsk – works on English translations of Tolstoy's articles concerning festivities in Tulon and copying his drafts. Tolstoy gives him his diary, and Chertkov copies excerpts of his reflections out of it. Tolstoy notes Chertkov's work in his diary:

"He gave me excerpts from my diary, very good…"[30]

Malaria, which Chertkov caught increased so much toward the end of the summer that he almost could not be at Yasnaya Polyana, and Tolstoy often drove or walked to them in Dyomenka. When they leave, Tolstoy writes to Anna Konstantinovna that he misses their company:

"I am very, to my embarrassment, sad without you, sincerely sad and terrified for Dima, not the *noble son*[31], but big. How is he? Only that he would be such, as always, and everything will be OK."[32]

Returning to Rzhevsk, Chertkov writes Tolstoy a letter in which he tells that he experiences a condition of great weakness and physical inertia and feels satisfaction only when he is occupied with copying thoughts from Tolstoy's diaries.

Then Chertkov again switches to his work on the translations and reports to Tolstoy:

"I live now a bit more cheerfully and actively. Translated and sent off your article about Maupassant to England. Yesterday I finished the translation of your article about the composition of Bondarev and I hope today to correct it and send it off. Then I want to start working on your article about Zola and Alexander Dumas. I already finished compiling part of the notes about the Hilkovs, as I wrote you. Its conclusion is not."[33]

In the same letter, Chertkov, announcing the receipt of news from his mother about the hopeless illness of Alexander III, wrote that apparently they would have to resume an appeal about the return of the Hilkov children before the new tsar.

This news was soon confirmed – the tsar passed away after a few days.

Following, in the whole country had to give the obligatory oath of allegiance to the new tsar. Tolstoy made an entry about this in his diary:

"They want to hold on and save the sinking autocracy and send the orthodox to rescue it, but the autocracy will drown orthodoxy and itself will drown still earlier."[34]

No one appealed to Tolstoy with the demand to take the oath. Chertkov was in different circumstances. The local authority laid the claim to take the oath and received categorical refusal. Chertkov wrote about this to Tolstoy:

"We have uninvited guests for three days. In the beginning, a police officer to inquire concerning the oath; the next day a priest – to administer the oath; and yesterday, the procurator of the district to ask why I refused. I expressed everything in a calm conversation with the procurator and the district police."[35]

Chertkov's refusal did not have any repercussions for him. But the servants in his village in Rzhevsk took the oath, from fear of persecution, and Chertkov was upset about it. He went with his family to Petersburg in December 1894, partly under the influence of this feeling, in order to attempt to begin efforts in the Hilkov matter in front of the new tsar, and stayed for a few days in Moscow in order to see Tolstoy.

In Petersburg, Chertkov had to register. Considering that the passport in which he appears as orthodox, gives untruthful information, giving out in registration residence permit, attached to it a declaration that he doesn't consider himself orthodox. They called Chertkov to the town governor, who told him that such declarations "confuse police officers", and asked in the future not to do this, but, taking into consideration his high-society connections, was totally polite and did not resort to any kind of administrative measures.

Chertkov renewed his efforts in the Hilkov matter. Tolstoy was interested, but considered that under the new tsar they were just as hopeless as under the old:

"What's new? It seems everything is dead there where you expect to see life."[36]

In another letter Tolstoy wrote that from Chertkov's report about the case he does not expect any consequences. Chertkov did not have to wait in Petersburg for the decision of his appeal, and in May, returning to Rzhevsk, he found out that Hilkov's wife received a denial.

Chertkov's former comrade in the Life Guard Cavalry Regiment, D.F. Trepov, to whom Chertkov appealed with the request of assistance, wrote him about this and added that he did not expect another decision:

"The outcome of the Hilkov matter did not surprise me at all, I predicted it. The tsar has no servants, he has only underlings."[37]

In Petersburg Chertkov received Tolstoy's new manuscript.

Already in September 1894 Tolstoy wrote in his diary:

"In the morning in bed after a terrible night, I thought through a very lively artistic story about a landlord and a worker."[38]

In January 1895 the story was finished and Chertkov could read it. As always, he quickly wrote Tolstoy about his impressions:

"Yesterday morning I read the story and since then I am under the freshest, sharpest impression. Later – as I know by experience how it goes with me and your writings – I will gradually penetrate deeper into the meaning of what you told and develop a more definite account of how it connects in relations to life in general and mine in particular."[39]

In the next letter, Chertkov, as usual, expressed to Tolstoy a few critical observations concerning this story, with which Tolstoy partially agreed.

At the end of February 1895, a sad event took place in the Tolstoy family which for a short time pushed all work and all matters to the side: Vanechka, their seven-year-old son, the favorite of the whole family, died after two days of scarlet fever.

Tolstoy wrote Chertkov about this the next day:

"We have a heavy ordeal, dear friend. Vanechka became ill with scarlet fever and in two days, yesterday evening, on the 23rd, passed away."[40]

Vladimir Grigorievich and Anna Konstantinovna sent a sympathetic telegram, but following that, Chertkov wrote him a letter, in which, carefully touching upon the grief experienced by the Tolstoys, wrote:

"Anya and I were completely struck by the unexpected news about the grief befallen you. Under the first impression, I sent you a long telegram; but then felt bad about this because it is impossible to define in words what one thinks and feels in such situations, and mainly because what happens in the soul of the closest to the deceased is much more deep and meaningful than anything that people farther away can say, even the most devoted friends."[41]

Tolstoy wrote in his response letter that Vanechka's death deeply shook Sofia Andreyevna and at the same time called in her an unusually soft mood, uniting the whole family in common grief. Maria Lvovna wrote Chertkov about the same thing:

"Vanechka joined and united us in such love like there never was before. Papa is worried for mama who suffers terribly, and is himself very sad about Vanechka. He was very attached to him, and loved him exceptionally. It seems to me that he got older and has become bent at this time and he himself is not well."[42]

Tolstoy himself at this time often writes that he feels the fall in life strength, as if in the approach to old age and work he has goes less intensively. In two months after Vanechka's death, he writes Chertkov:

"Mentally I am very – just mentally – I can't say spiritually – weak. There are no thoughts and no desire to express them. If this is old age – a new step toward it – or fatigue from an experienced intense condition, but I feel the change in me, and only try that such changes don't change the main foundations."[43]

Despite the fact that Tolstoy turned 66, he was still far from old age in the common sense of the word: in his letter he writes Chertkov that he is learning to ride a bicycle, visiting with this purpose a riding school, and even writes in his diary that this pursuit "amuses him in a sinless childish manner." But in his diaries and letters to Chertkov more often than earlier, appears references about inertia and weakness, incapacity to work, and although he still works a lot and persistently, it seems that his life begins to come to a turn from which old age is visible.

At this time – March 27, 1895 – Tolstoy makes the first draft of his will in his diary. He asks to be buried very simply, refraining from speeches and eulogies, and appeals to his family with the request of refusing the right of ownership of his works written before 1881. Tolstoy already announced publicly about the refusal of author's rights on everything written after this period. At the same time Tolstoy entrusted the sorting and revision of all his papers to Sofia Andreyevna, Chertkov and N.N. Strahov and especially concentrated on the instruction which he gave to Chertkov:

"The diaries of my former bachelor life, having taken from them whatever is of worth, I ask to be destroyed, and the same to those of my married life, everything that could be unpleasant to anyone if published. Chertkov promised me already during my life to do this. Considering his great love toward me, which I don't deserve, and great moral sensitivity, I am sure, that he will do this wonderfully. The diaries of my bachelor life I ask to be destroyed not because I want to hide my foolish life from people – my life was the usual worthless life of unprincipled young people – but because these diaries in which I wrote only what tortured me in confession of sin – carries a pseudo one-sided impression and represents... and by the way, let my diaries remain the way they are. At lease it is evident from them, that despite all the triviality and worthlessness of my youth, I however, was not abandoned by God and in old age become, a little, to understand and love Him."[44]

For a few months before that – October 19, 1894 – Tolstoy wrote Chertkov that he reread his diary of 1884, copied by Chertkov, and experienced a very heavy feeling, thinking about how many harsh opinions about people there were and how hurtful it would be for them to read. Tolstoy asked Chertkov to destroy this diary. Chertkov answered that this diary, along with other, more important documents are kept in Petersburg in conditions which precludes the possibility of outsiders reading them and asked permission to postpone the receipt of this diary for a short time. In November Chertkov wrote Tolstoy that he reread his diary and considers it not deserving of destruction, but, if this is necessary, he can cross out those passages that Tolstoy has in mind. Tolstoy responded to this letter:

"I am very thankful for the survey of diaries that you made. It is absolutely necessary to do as you said: to smear all these foul passages. And do the same to others. Please do this."[45]

In the summer of 1895 the Chertkovs again went to Dyomenka. Tolstoy, in expectation of their arrival, wrote Chertkov:

"You say that I have an encouraging, inspiring effect on you; your presence has the same influence on me ... I very much want to work and I do something insignificant. But already four months that I don't have that persistently concentrated work which took place for these past years."[46]

But toward the middle of June, when the Chertkovs went to Dyomenka, Tolstoy little by little settles down to the work usual for him, which the spring did not give him. He works a lot on *Resurrection* and writes a string of long letters in which he states his views.

Living in Dyomenka, and often being at Tolstoy's in the summer of 1895, Chertkov paid his attention to the fact that the drafts of Tolstoy's manuscripts, letters he received and his other papers were kept at Yasnaya Polyana not sufficiently carefully and in great disorder. Chertkov arranged with Tolstoy that he offer his assistant, I.M. Tregubov, who lived with him, to bring order to Tolstoy's archive. Tregubov lived at Yasnaya Polyana until the end of September, occupied with this work.

Chertkov specifically asked to make a separate file of his letters to Tolstoy and, returning to Rzhevsk, wrote about this to Tolstoy:

"At Yasnaya Polyana I used the occasion that Ivan Mikhailovich brought order to letters which you received for the last years, in order to ask him to take out for me my letters to you, which he did. I want to preserve them for my son, along with diaries in case, if he outlives me earlier than when he reaches such an age as to directly understand my life and me. I planned to bring all the diaries in full and leave them in full to him with an explanation of my life, those sides which could afterwards, without explanation, serve for him as temptation, or at least be incomprehensible to him. But I somehow can't consistently carry this diary and at the same time I want to write you constantly with everything that's in my soul. So I combined this and that part: save my letters and during meetings I will take them out and save them for Dimochka. When I want to make entries, as in the diary, I will send those pages to you for more communication with you, which is very dear to me, and you save them together with my letters in the same folder that I will send you in the mail. On the folder I signed a request that no one beside you read it's contents."[47]

Life close to Yasnaya Polyana in the summer months gave Chertkov the possibility of direct dealings with Tolstoy to enliven those projects about which they had to constantly correspond. Therefore, in the summer of 1895 he had the idea to acquire a piece of land the size of a peasant allotment near Yasnaya Polyana and to move there from Rzhevsk.

In September, returning to Rzhevsk, he carried on correspondence on this theme with Tolstoy and Maria Lvovna, but soon abandons this plan.

At the same time as he had the idea of settling near Yasnaya Polyana, the book of E.I. Popov, *Life and Death of E.N. Drozhin* is published abroad, in which letters of Drozhin's to Chertkov were included; the book exposed the cruelties occurring in penal battalions. Gendarmes already carried out searches of Popov's and Biryukov's apartments and Chertkov had reason to expect that soon his turn would come.

Thinking about his near future and looking at what was going on at this time in Russia, Chertkov could not but understand that the path he was on must sooner or later carry him into internal exile. Knowing this, organizing permanent residence near Yasnaya Polyana made no sense.

Expecting that the government will use some form of repression against him, Chertkov thinks at one time to emigrate from Russia and expand his publishing activities abroad, but soon abandons this idea.

In September 1895 he writes Tolstoy about this project, analyzing motives, expressing his desire to leave Russia. Sharing consideration that a lot could be done from abroad, having organized a printing house in England, free from the oppression the Russian censors created, Chertkov writes:

"I am ready to admit that my motive behind the idea of emigrating is simple faint-heartedness. But at the same time I feel that staying here and occupying myself with that publishing activity which must inevitably carry me off to jail, and from which, at the same time, I feel that I can no longer restrain myself – I would not feel just in front of my wife and son and all the time would be depressed in my soul. It is possible to object: why – instead of the whole family going abroad, not to abandon publishing activity without which I lived for many years before? The point is that, living here, among those holding the population in the dark, I already was *no longer able* to keep silent, to be idle. Even if I postponed my departure even for one winter, then I would now, immediately resume that publishing work, which, probably, in a few weeks or months would dissolve me with my family."

In the postscript to this letter Chertkov added:

"We would hardly go abroad of our own will. This, it seems, was the minute of faint-heartedness on my behalf."[48]

Answering to this, Tolstoy wrote Chertkov about his publishing plans:

"Concerning the matter, I will say this, that recognizing that it is good and obligatory to direct your main strength to the purpose of serving with your thoughts and words not to our brother, parasites, rotten with sin of eating his neighbor, but to the working people – I myself especially lively feel this in the past time, – recognizing this, I however do not sympathize with your plan, in the first place, because all my writings – I say sincerely – are not worth it – its not so simply and clearly written in order to spread them with great risk of suffering for you and people close to you, and – mainly – in the second place, that it would be horribly tortuous for me to think, that I, my writings were the cause or even incentive of suffering of people who are most close and dear to me. This is the main thing. Wait for my death and then do this. If I would sit in jail or was killed, then it would be OK, but I eat food and almond milk surrounded by those who I love, and at this time people dear to me will suffer for me."[49]

Chertkov answered Tolstoy that he cannot agree with his arguments and thinks decidedly to spread those of his works that are able to result in persecution from the authorities:

"Never refusing to fulfill one of your wishes, I now decidedly refuse to fulfill the request of waiting until your death, which I don't want and for which I cannot wait."[50]

At the same time, Chertkov had a plan to systematically publish in England those of Tolstoy's works that cannot appear in Russia.

Already in 1894 Tolstoy and Chertkov started correspondence with John Kenworthy, former pastor, who, in his letters, expressed complete sympathy with Tolstoy's doctrine. In his book, *The Anatomy of Poverty*, sent to Tolstoy, Kenworthy spoke out against the social system based on exploitation of labor. In his articles he stated his views, close to Tolstoy's, but at the same time did not

159

completely dismiss the heritage, passed on to him by the English church: the circle of like-thinkers he called "the brotherly church" and on Sundays they gathered in the small town of Croiden, where Kenworthy lived, externally reminiscent of religious gatherings in Protestant circles.

In 1895 Kenworthy intended to organize a publishing house and monthly magazine in which he offered to give Tolstoy a place for his articles. Chertkov had the idea to widely use this beginning. He wrote Kenworthy a letter to come to Russia and took on himself half of his traveling expenses.

At the end of December 1895 Kenworthy arrived in Moscow, at the same time as Chertkov.

In conversation with Tolstoy, they work out a plan for publishing Tolstoy's works in English and other books, close to his ideas, while Tolstoy expresses agreement for the expansion of publishing activities to give him and Chertkov the right of first publication of his new articles in English translation.

In 1896 the reactionary direction of government politics did not grow weak, but actually got stronger in comparison with previous years.

Tolstoy soon had to face the administrative persecution of people sympathetic to his views.

Dr. Holevinskaya, living in Tula received one of Tolstoy's manuscripts, banned by the censors, from Tatiana Lvovna, and gave it to one of Tula's workers to read.

As a result, a search was conducted of her house; she was arrested and in administrative order, sent to Astrakhan.

Even Sofia Andreyevna, who could not be suspected of sympathy with Tolstoy's ideas, was indignant over this matter and wrote her sister, T.A. Kuzminskaya, a letter, with some colorful twists:

"You know, Tanya, how I despise all these so-called Tolstoyans. Idle, weak people, always struggling against something, living in somebody's house (preferably rich), and eating somebody's bread. But this Holevinskaya – a worker, good girl, takes care of the sick, doesn't propagandize anything, the whole sin that she had

Levochkin's compositions. And they grabbed her, sat her in prison, held under surveillance of the police, treated her rudely."[51]

Tolstoy wrote letters to the Minister of Internal Affairs, Goremykin, and the Minister of Justice, Muravyov, in which he announced that the writings found at Holevinskaya's were received by her from Yasnaya Polyana, and if they contain anything criminal, then he himself should be made to answer, as the author of the writings, and not those who might be found in possession of copies of his manuscripts.

This letter remained without answer, and Sofia Andreyevna wrote about this in the very same letter to her sister:

"Not one of the ministers answered him, but Davydov said that Muravyov expressed that Levochka, personally, wont be touched, but let the persecutions suffered by his followers serve as a punishment of him."

Chertkov was in another situation than Tolstoy. Still in the beginning of their friendship in 1885, Chertkov wrote Tolstoy:

"I received information that Pobedonostsev thinks about undertaking measures because I "on the right and left spread your manuscripts, acquired some kind of lithograph machine", etc. Pobedonostsev is looking at you, like a well-known lunatic, and I was told they don't want to touch you in view of your social and family position; but he considers me actively spreading your revolutionary doctrine and at the first chance is ready to place me in the lunatic asylum or exile me."[52]

During Chertkov's absence from Rzhevsk in July 1896, while living with his family in Dyomenka, searches were conducted of his, as well as his assistant, Tregubov's house, gathering materials about persecutions, which, in various places in Russia, were directed against people, leaving the Orthodox Church.

Tregubov remained free, but the police took a lot of manuscripts from him.

Chertkov had to expect that in the near future, his turn would come. The outcome came in connection with the movement among the Dukhobors, which occurred during these years in the Caucuses and which, for a long time already drew the attention not only of

Tolstoy and people sharing his views but also of more wide circles of society.

Already in the winter of 1894, E.I. Popov, visiting E.N. Drozhin's friend N.T. Izyumchenko, held in Butyrskaya Prison, sent their after being in a penal battalion in Siberia, saw another tsarist prisoner, P.V. Verigin, behind bars and paid attention to the three visitors in peculiar, half-peasant/half Caucasian clothes who came to him for a meeting. Having spoken to them, Popov found out that they were Dukhobors and came for a meeting with their leader Verigin, also held in Butyrskaya, on his way from the city of Shenkursk in the Archangel Province to Obdarsk in the Tobolsk Province, where they transferred him in order, to a great degree, to isolate him from followers communicating with him through the messengers. Popov asked for their address, told Tolstoy about them, and the next day, Tolstoy, Popov and Biryukov visited them in order to talk about their convictions.

The Dukhobor sect, or Dukhobors as they called themselves, were concentrated at that time in the Tbilisi Province and in the Elizavetapol and Kursk Regions, where they were sent in the 1840s from the Tavricheskaya Province, after experiencing a period of sharp surge of their religious activity at the end of 1880s and 1890s.

Dukhobors for a long time rejected rituals and sacraments of the Orthodox Church, related negatively to the authorities and there were among them, already at the beginning of the 19th century, individual cases of refusal to fulfill military service. The leader of the majority of the Dukhobors, P.V. Verigin, was sent in 1887 to the Archangel Province, became acquainted with political exiles there, received unpublished works of Tolstoy from them, and this reading furthered the fact that those elements of Dukhobor doctrine, which appeared close to Tolstoy's views were stressed by Verigin as the most important.

He wrote letters in appropriate spirit to his followers, not mentioning in them, however, about Tolstoy. Verigin was not acquainted with him personally, and on his behalf, Tolstoy, until this time knew little about the Dukhobor movement, although he was actively interested.

In conversation with the Dukhobors, Tolstoy discovered his like-mindedness with them on many points, but they didn't tell him directly that at the same time they received instructions from Verigin to prepare for general refusal from military service.

In May 1895, not long before Chertkov's departure from Rzhevsk to Dyomenka, he got a letter from Hilkov that in April, eleven soldier–Dukhobors – stationed in Elizavetapol, refused to march in an Easter parade and then announced that they didn't want to continue military service. Chertkov immediately wrote Tolstoy about this.

Hilkov's subsequent letters described how the movement of the Dukhobors developed: the number of soldiers refusing grew to forty people, they were sentenced by a military judge to imprisonment in a penal battalion and systematically underwent various punishments from lockup in special solitary cell to flogging with thorny branches of acacia.

In June 1895, Dukhobors, followers of Verigin, ceremonially burned their weapons and the reservists returned their military documents; in the Tiflis Province, after burning their weapons, Dukhobors were surrounded by Cossacks who drove them with whips to the Governor and beat them in front of him. Other measures followed – Cossack billeting in Dukhobor villages combined with various violence, arrest of prominent Dukhobors supporting Verigin.

With every new report about the persecution of the Dukhobors, Tolstoy felt the desire to get involved in this matter. In the beginning of August 1895, he writes in his diary:

"There was a letter from Hilkov with the account of persecution of the Dukhobors. I wrote a letter in the English newspapers."[53]

In September, Tolstoy announced to Chertkov that he is sending Biryukov's article about the persecution of the Dukhobors abroad for publication in English newspapers, having attached his letter to it and, asking Chertkov's opinion about the plan, adds: "I would wish very much to have you near me to get your advice."[54]

Chertkov on his behalf began to gather material about the persecutions that the Dukhobors underwent, preparing to use his connection for providing some relief of their sufferings.

The Dukhobor situation continued to worsen. Nearly four thousand Dukhobors of the Ahalkalak Uyezd of the Tiflis Province were evicted from their settlements, their houses and property were sold very cheaply and they themselves settled in mountain villages, where they were doomed to unemployment and hunger.

In the beginning of 1896, during his trip to Petersburg, Chertkov attempted to spread information about the situation of the Dukhobors in circles, near to the government, but these steps did not have any success.

In the fall of 1896, returning from Dyomenka to Rzhevsk, Chertkov, together with Tregubov composed an appeal of help for the Dukhobors, thinking to publish it in English newspapers and works on notes about the situation of the Dukhobors earmarked for distribution among government officials. He sends Tolstoy the project of the appeal to society about assistance for the Dukhobors and asks him to make corrections.

Tolstoy decided to join to this appeal by writing a letter, which Chertkov would be able to spread together with the appeal and transfer money to the Dukhobors, settled in the mountains, which he received from theaters, like pay-per-nights for his works and everything donated to charity.

"My participation in this matter, – wrote Tolstoy to Chertkov, – is that I will write to you the following: I sympathize very, very much with your appeal. I knew already before about the horrible situation of the Dukhobors, but did not know those terrifying details about the death of one of them in confinement and about the illness of all the Ahalkalak community. The fate of children is most pitiful. I have a thousand rubles earmarked for charity. It is doubtful one could find a better use. Write where to send it."[55]

In November Chertkov writes that he plans to go to Petersburg in order to continue his efforts. At the same time he finishes the book about the Hilkov case, earmarked for publication abroad, in the case if hope will be lost on the return of the children to their parents, but decides beforehand to try one more time to secure the return of the children, trying to give the manuscript of this book for reading by the tsar, although he doesn't hope for success.

Tolstoy writes Chertkov that he would like to see him and shares his mood:

"I am waiting for you and postpone writing you, hoping to talk – an there is a lot to discuss. It is necessary to discuss the appeal and the Dukhobors – this is the main thing. I rarely spent time so idly and so foolishly as in these last weeks and especially in Moscow, and idly not in merry mood, but melancholy, heavy. I stopped all my work and don't want to take it up again. Now it is better. Also experienced that which was difficult. And when it is difficult for me, I want to see you."[56]

Chertkov arrived with his family in Moscow on December 12 and lived there over a week. At this time the editing of the text of the appeal for help for the Dukhobors was completed, and Tolstoy wrote his postscript for it. The appeal was called *"Help!"*, signed by Biryukov, Tregubov and Chertkov and began with words, which immediately might cause irritation of the government officials.

"A horrible situation is now occurring in the Caucuses. More than 4000 people are suffering and dying of hunger, illness, exhaustion, beating, torture and other persecutions of the Russian government."[57]

In Petersburg, Chertkov immediately plunged into intense and burdensome work: he visits people, who he thinks he can use concerning the Dukhobor matter, and finishes the report about the situation of the Dukhobors which he considers necessary to present to members of the highest administration. He writes about himself to Tolstoy:

"From the first day of my arrival here I found myself intensely involved in the matter well-known to you, glad that I came, and I only remove this yoke in order to eat, sleep, and entertain my soul a little, so I to write you like I want to, concentrated about the most important of my internal life I could not and still cannot"[58]

Tolstoy didn't have any illusions concerning the final outcome of this effort, and he answered Chertkov:

"I know that you are moved, not by personal, but by Christian feelings, believe that what you do is good, but on the other hand, perhaps, from this vile pride which I passed on to you, I condemn all these demonstrations and don't expect anything good from them, I think that this energy would find a better goal."[59]

In a few days after Tolstoy wrote this letter, his fear came true in full measure.

On February 1, Chertkov received an invitation to appear at the office of the Minister of Internal Affairs, Goremykin, and planned the next day to use it, presupposing that he will be asked to provide additional information and explanation of the matter about which he endeavored in Petersburg. But the next morning gendarmes appeared in his Petersburg apartment, conducted a search, and took away his accrued material concerning the Hilkov matter and many other documents.

Chertkov decided to refuse Goremykin's invitation and answered him in a letter:

"Having received your invitation yesterday evening to appear before you, I planned to fulfill this today, presupposing that my personal meeting with you could further help the positive progress of a few matters in which I very actively participate. But this morning your subordinates intruded in my apartment, and, having rummaged through my papers, grabbed them and took many with them. Such methods of treatment of me too clearly show me on what kind of principals are based these relations in which you want to start with me. Not considering it to be morally correct on my behalf voluntarily to participate in relations, based on these grounds, I am sincerely sorry that I have to refuse this meeting with you in which I placed hope in the interest of the projects which could only inspire the approval of all those who support good and truth."[60]

The next day it was explained why the Minister of Internal Affairs invited Chertkov: Goremykin went to E.I. Chertkova and told her that according to the will of the tsar, her son must be exiled and he is offered a choice between banishment to the Baltics or exile abroad.

Chertkov chose exile abroad and received a deadline of 13 February for necessary preparations.

At the same the decision of Biryukov and Tregubov's exile took place – the first was sent to the city of Bausk in the Kurlyand

Province and the second to the city of Fenil in the Estlyand Province, both for five years.

Tolstoy, having found out about the Chertkov's exile, immediately left for Petersburg together with Sofia Andreyevna in order to see them off.

He made an entry in his diary that the meeting with Chertkov was joyous.[61]

In a letter to Hilkov, written from the Chertkov's, Tolstoy wrote about those days that he spent with them:

"Ashamed to be joyful during this separation with dear close people, but the joy of closeness spiritually, which came about following this affair, between many people, as much as exceeds personal grief of separation, that since then I can't call myself sad, which befits this case. They are so bright, joyful and simple that also does not arouse external feeling of despair. In them something happened more significant than that change of place which they are forcibly subjected."[62]

Sofia Andreyevna was also swept up by this mood and wrote T.A. Kuzminskaya:

"To my joy and surprise *all* Petersburg society in different stratum are indignant because of these exiles and completely understand the source of malice. But yes, God be with them, the place in history which Tolstoy and his followers will occupy, will be much more enviable than that which will fall the fate of various people the likes of Pobedonostsev and Ko...

The sendoff and farewell of the Chertkovs and Biryukov with friends was very touching and ceremonial. Every day almost forty people of the most varied conditions and situations would come: the highest aristocrats and peasants, writers, nobles, educators, musicians, students, soldiers, dark ones, various ladies and women who walked on the road, who ran errands, who, sitting on the floor, orated, who wrote, who, arriving at the train station, ate kasha or vegetarian broth."[63]

The Chertkovs left for England, not knowing if they could ever return to Russia.

Chertkov wrote his mother from England, bringing up the experience concerning exile abroad:

"This exile from Russia clearly showed me something specific, how sharply I parted from that "high" Russian society into which I was born and to which I add all government together with aristocracy which supports it due to faintheartedness or selfinterest."[64]

VII
L.N. Tolstoy and V.G. Chertkov 1897-1902

A new period in the relationship of Tolstoy and Chertkov began with the exile of Chertkov from Russia. That work of publishing Tolstoy's works and preserving his manuscripts which Chertkov carried out, living in Rzhevsk, continued to remain the basis of his work in England, but there indeed it had to take a little different form. External conditions of English life and new circles of people brought out new traits in Chertkov's life, reflected in his activities and showed in his correspondence with Tolstoy.

Vladimir Grigorievich and Anna Konstantinovna left for England with their whole house. Chertkov's mother went with them, wishing to see them off. They brought with them two servants, living with them for long time in Rzhevsk, – Annushka, serving in their house since early youth, and Katya – nurse to their son. Albert Shkarvan, an Austrian doctor, Slovak by nationality and sharing the same views as Tolstoy – refusing military service and, visiting them in Rzhevsk was invited to go with them.

In England they decided to settle far away from city commotion, in an isolated house, if possible in a country area, but not far from London, in order that neighboring with Kenworthy, it would be easier to develop publishing activities. This work would indeed be the continuation of the work Chertkov conducted in Russia.

Tolstoy was actively interested in all the aspects of their lives and wrote them:

"I would ask for more details of your life. What location? Where? Who is the owner? Who visits you? How do you pass the time? What do you do, Vladimir Grigorievich? What does Galya do? Dimochka? Shkarvan? Katya? Annushka? How does the day go?"[1]

Vladimir Grigorievich and Anna Konstantinovna gave detailed answers to Tolstoy's questions, and their letter gives the possibility to clearly see their new lifestyle.

The Chertkovs settled near London, in Croiden, a small and quiet city, where Kenworthy lived and had a circle of Englishmen, sharing views close to Tolstoy's teachings. They rented a small, but spacious two-story house with a garden here for half a year. The house stood in the outermost district of the city and directly in front of them ran a wide green meadow on which children ran and the youth played football.

There was much with which they were unacquainted in their new conditions of life, Annushka cried bitterly, looking at the gas stove and remembering the Russian oven and stove in which it was possible to stoke real firewood. The Chertkovs wrote Tolstoy that with sadness think about the simple house in Dyomenka, where they lived in the summer for the past three years before their exile from Russia. But, in general, life in England was said to be comfortable, and many circumstances were helpful to begin publishing work.

In the first letters from England, Chertkov tells Tolstoy about his plans for publishing Tolstoy's articles in Russian and English. At the same time Chertkov quickly takes measures for the publication of that appeal "Help" which served as the direct pretext for his exile from Russia.

Tolstoy maintains constant relations with Chertkov after his exile – from the day of Chertkov's departure until the end of 1897, Tolstoy wrote him thirty-four letters – but he sharply experienced his absence.

Maria Lvovna wrote Chertkov about her father:

"He feels your absence very much, and I feel that he is alone sometimes from the realization that you are far away. He always says that distance cannot break closeness and strength of spiritual relations, and this, of course, truthfully, he feels this in relation to you, but personally, however, he is melancholy. For example, yesterday, as an illustration of one of the cruelties of your exile, he said that if he died, he would like to see you and say goodbye before his death, that they would not let you come to him, and saying that, his voice wavered."[2]

Tolstoy, having left in the spring for Yasnaya Polyana, where Chertkov was so often in the past summer, especially sharply felt his absence and wrote him about this in his letters:

"In Yasnaya Polyana I incessantly think about you. I enter my room in the morning and remember the feeling that I felt, finding you on the sofa: minute unhappiness that I am not alone, and great joy that you are with me. I don't know how I helped you, but you helped me many times over and in various ways live better."[3]

"Incessantly now, I feel you in Yasnaya Polyana. If I go bathe, go horseback riding, sit and eat lunch on the terrace, and you either joke, or seriously, or very seriously talk about something with the boys. In general, I feel, how I like you and how much joy you added in my life."[4]

Tolstoy especially felt Chertkov's exile because at that time he felt himself more alone in his family than earlier.

Much had changed in the Tolstoy home during those fourteen years, beginning in 1883 when he met Chertkov. His three eldest sons already had their own families and lived their own lives with their own interests. The two youngest grew into useless sons of nobility, despite all the efforts of their teachers, they did not receive a good education and they did not have any interest in intellectual life, but then early on acquired a taste for light entertainment, distressing their father and mother.

The two eldest daughters – Tatiana Lvovna and especially Maria Lvovna – were close to Tolstoy and willingly helped him in his work. Tolstoy knew that in the heaviest moment he could meet in Maria Lvovna a total understanding and wrote her about this:

"Dear Masha, although when you are here, I rarely talk to you, now, when I feel very vile, I want your sympathy. Of all our family, you are the one who despite the strong demands of your personal life, you are the one who understands, feels me."[5]

But both his daughters experienced a strong awakening in an inclination toward their own personal lives at this time – the desire to have their own families – and Tolstoy clearly saw how this feeling pushed everything else aside for them and increased his loneliness. Chertkov knew about this and pointed it out to Tolstoy's daughters.

Maria Lvovna wrote him in reply:

"Thank you for telling us what papa said – that he alone is pulling the string. This was, for me, unexpected and horribly painful. This crept in so unnoticeably, but it is true. I talked a little with Galya about my emotional condition, about that personal life which I suddenly want, and the desire that grabbed me and from this spiritual life froze and I let myself go. It seems to me that all this came about because I stopped going on my path and wanted to go on another, more easy."[6]

Leaving abroad, Chertkov thought with alarm that Tolstoy's daughters, absorbed in their personal lives, would continue to leave him, and wrote about this to Tatiana Lvovna; Maria Lvovna responded to his letter:

"I feel in your letter to Tanya the fear that we can leave papa alone and this touched me a lot. True, we both currently live our own personal lives, but it seems to me, that for both of us papa always stands in first place, and knowing that this is our best part, we will never leave him such, that he would not feel our love and our whole spiritual sympathy toward him and our unity with him."[7]

Less than three months after this letter, Maria Lvovna married Prince N.L. Obolensky, despite the fact that her father and mother did not approve. And, although her relationship with her father remained close, her life went on its own course and she lived in her own home, visiting Yasnaya Polyana from time to time. Tatiana Lvovna married a bit later, but already in 1897, Tolstoy clearly saw that her relationship with M.S. Suhotin, attracted her attention more and more, leading up to marriage, and had a premonition that she would be leaving her home.

The youngest daughter, thirteen-year old Sasha, a lively and unruly girl with boyish manners, for which she constantly "got it" from Sofia Andreyevna who considered that she poorly adopted the manners of a well brought up girl from a good home, grew in constant opposition to her mother, but was still too young that she could replace her two older sisters for her father.

Sofia Andreyevna, as before, firmly held all the household matters of Yasnaya Polyana in her hands, talked with the management of the educational institutions in which her youngest sons studied poorly, made and accepted visits, proofread the collected compositions of Tolstoy, published under her supervision, and at the same time, looked into every insignificant household practice.

"In washing also thick linen is no good," – wrote Sofia Andreyevna to her sister, – "it tears sooner and uses more soap. I grasped this a long time ago. It is also necessary to buy linen for night shirts for forty kopeks, although I try for 38 kopeks."[8]

But she also, to a certain degree, carried all of this work totally on inertia, felt that her home will become empty and her efforts will loose a lot of their meaning.

Already in 1894 Tolstoy wrote in his diary:

"The situation of our children is very bad: there is no direct authority. Sonya destroys my authority diligently and instead of it puts her comic demands of propriety, and they disregard it easily. It is a pity for them and her. I feel especially sorry for her lately. She sees that everything she did was not right and came to no good."[9]

As before, filling her life with various efforts, Sofia Andreyevna felt after a while that it was a huge waste of energy and to a certain degree remains futile.

In the spring of 1897 she wrote her sister:

"How spring begins – my languor increases. I want again to wait for spring and your arrival – and instead of this you see emptiness, everything great around you and you feel like an old gnarled fallen tree, which, at some point, was magnificent with thick foliage and flowering, grew strongly and happily. To tell you the truth, beside grief, complications and various emptiness, life doesn't give me anything with years."[10]

But despite that, her life goes on the former course, and the feeling of dissatisfaction shows itself only in increasing irritability, of which she herself sometimes complained to her sister.

And, as if making a conclusion of what happens in the Tolstoy home, Maria Lvovna wrote A.K. Chertkova in the summer of 1897:

"It is melancholy at Yasnaya. Everyone experiences their personal difficulties separately and feels that they are alone and sad. Papa writes a lot, all articles about art, he promised to slow down, but, of course, continues to work, at one time he worked so much, that the three assistants – mama, Tania and Maria Vasilievna could not keep up with him. Papa is very sad at this time and it seems to me that he is lonely."[11]

And on the very same day that Maria Lvovna wrote this letter, Tolstoy, thinking about his life in the family these past years, came to the conclusion that it was impossible to live like that anymore it was necessary to leave his home.

Already on 12 January 1897 Tolstoy wrote Chertkov:

"I write you today especially because it is difficult and lonely for me. Masha is not here, and there is no one such as you and Posha, with whom I would like to pour out my soul, complain, to ask for sympathy, compassion. Life around me becomes crazier and crazier: food, attire, games of all sorts, vanity, jokes, wasting of money, living among poverty and oppression, and there is nothing more. And there is no such possibility to stop this, expose it, to be ashamed of it. The deaf sooner hear than those who shout non-stop. And it is horrible for me, terrible, difficult... In the good moments I say to myself that what is happening to me is necessary for me, that it is necessary to live until death, and then again, protest and desire and reproach, why isn't it given to me before death to live at least a year, at least a month, the life which is natural for me, outside of those lies in which I not only live, but participate and wallow."

On July 8th Tolstoy wrote Sofia Andreyevna a long letter, after his death often reproduced in print[12] in which he wrote that for years it was becoming more and more difficult for him to endure the disparity between the life he had to lead and his convictions and the increasing necessity for seclusion. Explaining his intention to leave, he wrote his wife that he does not blame her since she could not change her life for the sake of something that is alien and incomprehensible to her, but he himself could not and cannot think differently than his convictions demand. And expressing gratitude to Sofia Andreyevna for this selflessness with which she devoted her efforts to her family, Tolstoy wrote, that he asks to reconcile with his departure, not to search for him and not condemn him.

Tolstoy did not fulfill his intention and remained facing a crucial gap. He sealed the envelope and gave it to his son-in-law N.L. Obolensky with the request of delivering it to Sofia Andreyevna after his death.

Remaining in the family, he resorted to that resource which he increasingly used in the last years and about which not long before he wrote his brother Sergei Nikolaevich:

"Living this disgraceful life, the only way to reach some tranquility is to throw myself into work 4-5 hours a day which you consider not quite useless."[13]

He intensely works every day, conducting several hours at his desk; Tolstoy considered, that regular labor is necessary in order not to add depression and the weakened influence of idleness. Two months after Chertkov's exile, Tolstoy wrote him:

"I am terribly afraid that all your relatives have little occupation or none at all, and I allow myself to advise, as much as possible to try to organize themselves into a yoke, and not to be too choosy what kind of yoke. This is especially important in a foreign country."

Soon after the Chertkov's departure, Tolstoy expressed other fears:

"I am very afraid that you will deteriorate in England. I just received *Review of Review;* I read and felt an atmosphere of this incredible English smug dullness, that transmigrated myself into you and thought about how you will become friends with them. I think this about everybody, except the small circle of free people among whom you live or can live. When you collide and find out about the wildness of thoughts and feelings in our country, you explain it by our regime, but when you see the same in England you get lost and ask yourself: why?"[14]

Chertkov answered Tolstoy's letter:

"I am not scared of English social sophistry: I don't feel in myself any shortcomings in scrupulousness in this relation... but I am terribly afraid that this permanent life in total contradiction with my convictions in the sphere of material life, equally in Rzhevsk, and in Petersburg, Dyomenka and Croiden did not dull my need to somehow or another get out of my criminal situation."[15]

In the first weeks after his arrival in England, Chertkov began to prepare the basis for those activities that he wanted to start. In his youth – in 1879 – Chertkov, having arrived in England, stayed in the home of a Russian ambassador and started an acquaintance with a tight circle of English aristocrats. Now he becomes acquainted, on one side, with Russian political émigrés, who could give him a string of useful advice about the organization of publications in Russian, works, which were not allowed to be published in Russia, and on the other side, with a circle of Englishmen, united around Kenworthy to a more or less degree, sympathizing with the views of Tolstoy. He visits the colony, organized by them in Essex, two hours from London, where a few people settled, striving toward the simplification of life and toward working on the land, and shares his impressions with Tolstoy.

In one of his first letters to Tolstoy from England, Chertkov announces his acquaintance with Felix Volhovsky, editor of the revolutionary publication "Flying Pages", in another – the acquaintance with P.A. Kropotkin.

As it was expected with new acquaintances, Chertkov carried on not only conversations about how to produce Russian publications in England, but arguments on the principal themes.

The echo of these arguments were saved in a letter which Kropotkin wrote to Chertkov after one of these conversations:

"If you would manage to unite a large number of people – absolutely large – who in the name of the whole of mankind in solidarity (religion *separates* people, only the feeling of solidarity, common to all mankind, can unite them), will risk their place in society, peace, freedom and life, and if it will be necessary (again such a necessary precondition), raised their voices against *all forms* of violent oppression from the top – economic, political, moral – then the violence from below, as selfless protest against the forces on top, would become less and less necessary. While this is not happening, the violence from the bottom remains a factor of moral progress... Mankind always was moved only by *actual* forces that you try to create. Will you be able to unite these forces – I don't know; I don't think so."[16]

Resending this letter, Chertkov announced to Tolstoy his impressions of the acquaintance with Kropotkin:

"He is a very sympathetic, sincere and warm person and I am touched by his spontaneous kindness which comes from him."[17]

Tolstoy answered that he liked Kropotkin's letter to him very much, but certainly did not agree with his argument:

"His argument of the use of force did not seem to me an expression of conviction, but only truthfulness to that banner, under which he honestly served his life."[18]

With the assistance of new acquaintances, Chertkov started the publication of a string of works in Russian. First released was an article of Chertkov's, written in 1896, "Unnecessary Cruelty: About Whether It Is Necessary or Worth It for the Government to Make Martyrs out of People Who Cannot Participate in Military Service Due to Their Religious Convictions," after which followed other books. Altogether, nine books were released in Russian in 1897, among them, *The Kingdom of God*, and the next year was already published the new catalog of the new printing house.[19]

At the same time, in the first months after his arrival in England, Chertkov intended to publish a periodical.

Already in 1894, like-thinkers of Tolstoy from time to time began to retype and spread among their circle a collection of texts under the title "Archives of L.N. Tolstoy," every new issue appearing as soon as there was enough material. In it they placed letters having general interest, received by Tolstoy from people sharing his views, a few articles, news about the spreading of views of Tolstoy abroad and other similar information.

Settling in England, Chertkov already on April 16, 1897, writes to Tolstoy that he thinks about releasing this publication abroad and asks to send him material. But he had to postpone fulfilling this intention due to other projects, and it only came to fruition in 1898 in the form of the publication *Pages of Free Word*, and then in the form of a magazine *Free Word*.

Concurrently with the Russian publications, Chertkov began work on the release of English publications.

Chertkov carried out this work in two directions: he himself translated a few articles of Tolstoy's, in part, soon after his arrival in England, begins to work on the translation of "Christian Teachings", and at the same time participates in the organization of the English publishing house which was to release Tolstoy's works and other books, corresponding to the views of Tolstoy.

Already in December 1895, organizing Kenworthy's trip to Russia, Chertkov had in mind a plan of creating a publishing house abroad, which he, in correspondence with Tolstoy, called "International Mediator" and assisted Kenworthy in obtaining permission from Tolstoy to publish his works in English first. Now, Chertkov, together with Kenworthy and a few other people became staff of the printing house "Brotherhood Publishing Company."

In the beginning of May 1897 Chertkov writes Tolstoy about this, asking to mail the first copy of the new articles to him, not giving them to other translators until they are published in English, as promised to Kenworthy. At this time, Chertkov asked Tolstoy's permission to publish "Christian Teachings" in English, which Tolstoy himself considered unfinished. Not receiving an answer to this letter, Chertkov repeated his questions:

"I asked you if you would give permission to publish your "Christian Teachings" which all of our friends are asking about here. It would be cruel to deny them the possibility of a more attentive study and spread of this book necessary to everyone. For this I offered to write a preface from the publisher, a proviso that you consider this work unsatisfactory and wish to rewrite it, but, for the present time, you agreed to allow publication of this version, responding to the requests of your friends. I asked, will you give me "carte blanche" to publish parts of "Collection of Your Thoughts", gathered from various sources and diaries, trusting my tact? Do you agree to send me a copy of each of your new writings and are ready to send them here to us and to direct all the translators here? I also explained how important this is for the support of our enterprise "International Mediator."

At the same time Chertkov persistently asked Tolstoy to answer his letters timely:

"I cannot express to you, how terribly and hurtfully to feel that the thread of our written relations could be broken, and having written you a letter, I will never know if you received it, as if I dropped it in the bottomless barrel. And beside that, without exact answers to all these questions, which might seem to you insignificant, it breaks off various mechanical possibilities for me to bring those of my and my friend's work on your writings, which we devoted so much time, labor and mainly souls, to fruition."[20]

Having received this letter, Tolstoy rushed to answer Chertkov's questions:

"It is understood: Yes, Yes, Yes. Spread "Christian Teachings" with the preface you offered, publish excerpts from letters and diaries. You know that I always relate to my writings this way regardless who handles them; but in relation to you, you know that I trust you, and I am happy when you do this, because I know that you do this with exaggerated attention and respect, and mainly, not exaggeration but precious love, so that there is good in all of this. Everything that I will write will absolutely send first of all to you."[21]

For the English publishing company in which Chertkov participated with Kenworthy and other people, Tolstoy's promise to give his articles first of all to Chertkov had special meaning; it not only provided thorough work for translation, but also had to give some material support. The publishing house did not have any means and his publishing program in and of itself was not in such order as to provide conducting work while not entailing loss. According to Tolstoy's wish, all his works immediately after publication became public domain, any publisher could translate and republish them and new small publishers could not, it is understandable, compete in this relationship with large publishers. It could receive some income from the first release of Tolstoy's new works. Also, commercial printing houses worked much quicker, often producing an inaccurate translation, demanding painstaking work, but just free narration of Tolstoy's articles, which could be prepared sometimes in a few days. Therefore Chertkov could depend on the fact he would be given Tolstoy's new articles in translation to publish, releasing them under his supervision, in the case, if he received Tolstoy's articles before their publication in Russian, in order that they could be released simultaneously in Russia and England.

But fulfilling this plan of publishing translations of Tolstoy's works proved harder than was imagined. Chertkov realized it in his first experience – during the publication of the translation of Tolstoy's work "What is Art."

Tolstoy intensely worked on this article in the beginning of 1897 and in his letters told about this work, how it was coming along.

As it usually was with Tolstoy, in the beginning, the work did not develop satisfactorily to him, but as he delved more deeply into it, it grabbed him more and more.

In a letter to his brother, S.N. Tolstoy of February 22, 1897, he wrote:

"I am writing about art and the work is going badly, but the work is interesting and of which you probably approve because you will find many of your ideas in it."

But already after a month, he was so absorbed in it that it began to captivate him and bring joy. M.L. Tolstaya wrote Chertkov about this:

"Papa is healthy, cheerful and is writing a lot of his article about art, he says he feels that he is coming to the end of this article and is glad about it. In recent days after writing, he comes out very happy, jokes, jumps up, – and this is always a sign that he worked well and that there will be a lot of copying which I am always glad about. He says that there is a lot that is necessary and still wants to say, and is afraid that he will not succeed, there is little time and strength."[22]

At the end of April, Tolstoy, telling Chertkov about his oppressive mood, which he experienced at this time, mentioned that this work is moving forward and is coming to an end:

"I will not say that there was depression, because when I ask myself: who am I? Why am I? – I answer myself positively, but there is no energy. I feel that Lilliputian ropes tie me and all less and less enterprise and activity. I work – am ashamed to say such a word – spend time on the article about art, and not only see the end but only *lacunes* – empty places that are necessary to fill. Without false modesty, I think that it will not be good, that is, not that it will be foolish, but noting good will come of it, although I am not repenting, that I wrote, and think that it is necessary to do it. I have not written letters or diary for a month now."[23]

In a few days Tolstoy wrote Chertkov, explaining why he abandoned his diary and correspondence:

"I don't answer letters and don't write in the diary because I felt all last winter and now – spring – especially now, very weak. There is only enough energy for morning work about art. I cannot break away from it and think that I am ending. Nothing of special import will come of it, but without modesty I will say that something new and negative, denunciatory, and favorable will be."[24]

The closer the end of the work came, the stronger it grabbed hold of Tolstoy. Despite the painful experience, pouring out in his letter Sofia Andreyevna on 8 July in which he wrote to her that he must leave their home, Tolstoy continues to intensely work on his article and on the 12th of July, writes Chertkov:

"I don't know what happened to me, I can't keep busy with anything as much as my article about art. Since it is finished and now only make the last *coup de main**, I can't think about anything else. I want to free myself as soon as possible. Sometimes it seems to me that it is very good, but more often it seems that it is worthless and I do not have the right to put my last strength on such an unimportant project, I want to do something else, but I can't tear myself away from it."

Having received this letter, Chertkov announced to Tolstoy that everything is ready for immediate translation of his article into English and reminded him one more time that the success of the work organized in England depends on if he will grant the right of first publication of all his new articles:

"If this article will be printed in full or in part in Russia in Russian, then put an indispensable stipulation on it in order that the publisher did not give proofs to *anyone*, until the release of the article. Otherwise they could, as already happened to me, fall into the hands of an enterprise and transient translator who might succeed to release his hurried translation, which though being not accurate will close all the doors for our thorough and accurate one. In any case, in the interest of projects of our International Mediator, it is desirous, in order that, as I already wrote you, *all* translators appealing to you, be directed to me here and that not one be given a page without me. And in addition, that I receive a manuscript for the translation, at least *three weeks,* not only before it's publication, but even it's distribution by private persons."[25]

Tolstoy confirmed his decision to direct his manuscripts, earmarked for translation, first of all to Chertkov:

"That my writings first of all be received by you and you will be in charge of translation and publication cannot be a doubt."[26]

It was decided that English translations be left to the translator A.F. Maude, who at that time, together with Chertkov and Kenworthy, was one of the participants in the organization of the publishing house and agreed to translate this article for it.

But Chertkov and Tolstoy himself insufficiently took into account the habit, characteristic of Tolstoy, to insert various corrections into his writings, already after he considered them finished, and expose them to essential changes even in editing. Therefore, even sending manuscripts of his articles for translation earlier than it was given for publication in Russia, Tolstoy continued to change it and inevitably slowed the progress of translation. The Russian publisher received the possibility of releasing it sooner, since he could more quickly insert the corrections than the English, who were not able to start publication until in the translation was made of those corrections which Tolstoy made even in the editing of the Russian text. On this basis, inevitably misunderstandings must have arisen.

Tolstoy sent the first part of his article to Maude, who began to intensely work on its translation, writing Tolstoy concerning individual unclear expressions and finishing off the accurate presentation of the original.

The first Russian publication of this article was left to N.Ya. Grot, who had to publish it in his magazine *Questions of Philosophy and Psychology.*

Having begun to insert the corrections into his article, Tolstoy stopped sending further chapters to Maude, having offered Grot to send the proofs with the author's corrections to England. But this measure called for the delay in publication of this article in Russia and at the same time did not give the necessary period for its advance translation in England.

Grot, not having received permission for publication of chapters of the article for the November-December edition of the magazine already typeset, so that the rest of the chapters could be published in the first edition of the following year, sent Tolstoy a sharp letter in which he wrote:

"I offered to divide the article from the point of view of "literature" and you write me about some English translator with whom I have no business. Indeed you don't have a contract with him?"[27]

Chertkov, on his side, wrote Tolstoy that the delay in sending the continuance of this article to Maude makes a simultaneous translation of the article in Russia and abroad impossible and undermines all the calculations concerning its publication:

"We, counting on your promise to grant us the possibility of first publication of all your *new* writings in the interests of our publishing business, hoped that this book proves to us assistance in material relations; but on this side, until now, leaves one loss and following a deficit in the kassa, we cannot publish anything that we would like, or what is necessary in the interest of our business... In such a case, it turns out, that this whole plan of our initial publishing of your new writings was only a dream, but in reality those who are closer to you, who at this time turns out to be available and suit you continue to receive this profit. If you knew how much labor and time we had to waste here with the publication of your writings and how at a loss all this was since."[28]

Sofia Andreyevna, unhappy that Tolstoy does not publish his new works first in her publishing house, reproached him for this.

Tolstoy found himself between several fires and wrote Chertkov:

"I just received your angry letter, dear friend, Vladimir Grigorievich. I totally understand you, but I regret that you don't trust me, that I do everything so it will be more advantageous for your – our – business. In the beginning I wanted to publish the whole book immediately and then organized that it would simultaneously be released in Russia and England, now having decided to give the first chapters to "Questions of Philosophy", I however, will do such that the first chapters (probably the 5th included) would be released simultaneously in England and Russia. I wrote Maude about this and am waiting for an answer.

The most surprising of all is that here they are angry with me because I placed the indispensable stipulation of publication in Russia that it first be released in England. (Grot is going out of his mind and wrote unpleasantness) and you are angry with me because it is being published here, as it seems to you, to the detriment of your publishing house. How much easier to act, like everyone, not trying to act better. Until I published for money, publishing different compositions was joy; since I stopped taking money, publishing different compositions is similar to suffering. I am expecting it all the time from family, friends and different publishers."

And in the end of the letter, softening his words, Tolstoy wrote:

"But you, please don't be angry; I remember your interests – our printing house and jealously guard work for it. Tomorrow I will write more. You let me know soon: do you agree to give five chapters to the magazine and when they are released, so I can determine the release of the Russian. Very, very much yours, affectionately, always thinking about you, L. Tolstoy."[29]

This letter clearly showed Chertkov what a difficult situation Tolstoy found himself in.

Reproaching himself, Chertkov answered Tolstoy:

"Forgive me, dear friend, forgive my inattentiveness to you. Exactly inattentiveness. In connection with this event, horrifying for me, that *I*, liking you and appreciating you the way I like and appreciate you, could magnify those unpleasantness and grief, which you undergo, – in connection with this I think about myself all evening... I will not forget this lesson and it will serve me well... One creates projects, undertakings, plans, devoting to them all one's soul and because of them, doesn't see that there is only one reality in life – the soul of that person with whom you have dealings, you forget that soul who you love more than your own."[30]

At the same time Chertkov wrote that he wants to carry the publication of Tolstoy's book about art to fruition, then leave from the number of members of the printing house, organizing in the future editing translations of Tolstoy's works, since the practical business, tied to material difficulties, could again put him in such an unpleasant position.

The first five chapters of Tolstoy's article appeared in Russian earlier than in English, and Tolstoy, having written about how he was annoyed that he could not fulfill his promise to release the text in both languages simultaneously, offered Chertkov to publish it in English, together with the second half of the book, which by his assumption, could not be released without changes of the Russian censors. In addition, he offered to write a preface for the English publication, explaining that it is more complete than the Russian.

At the same time Tolstoy could see just how well-founded Chertkov's fears were, that the translators, using the fact that Tolstoy's works were declared free property, would translate his article quickly and carelessly.

In the middle of February Tolstoy wrote Chertkov:

"Yesterday I wrote a letter in *Journal des Debats* that *Revue Blanche* published a disgraceful translation of two chapters torn away from everything and lacking any sense. And this is not important and would not be necessary, but it became so annoying when I saw this translation, that I could not relax until I wrote."[31]

Following that, Tolstoy signed a declaration authorizing Chertkov to spread the publication of his works abroad as well as dealings with translators. In this way Chertkov formally became a plenipotentiary of Tolstoy abroad in literary-publishing activities.

In the spring of 1898 the English publication of Tolstoy's book about art finally was released, but before that came out, Chertkov fulfilled his intention of resigning from the board of participants of the Brotherhood Publishing Company, which soon after folded. He himself decided to continue releasing his publications not only in Russian but also in English as long as circumstances allowed.

External conditions, it seemed, came together favorably enough so that Chertkov could occupy himself with peaceful and unhurried work on editing and translating Tolstoy's writings.

In the fall of 1897, Chertkov and his family moved to Essex, and having settled there near the city of Purleigh, a two-hour trip from London, rented in a house with an apple orchard and plot of land in the countryside. His Russian typography, still in embryo, but for which he gradually acquired everything necessary was located not far from there.

A small colony of Englishmen sharing many views of Tolstoy and desiring to simplify their lives and be occupied with physical labor was located nearby.

Already in Croiden, Chertkov began to organize a small meeting at his house weekly, in which participated people of various views, listening sometimes to readings of Tolstoy's works, sometimes lectures on one theme or another, after which lively discussions always started. Apart from that, Chertkov took part in the meetings organized on Sundays by Kenworthy and other people, explaining views of Tolstoy and entering into debates.

He wrote Tolstoy about these meetings, telling him about people agreeing with his views, sometimes sending him letters received from them and excerpts from their speeches at the meetings and Tolstoy answered him on this:

"What a joy to know that what I live for, that my real *I* is not limited by me alone, but lives outside, in people totally far away in time and place, whom I never saw. And why see? It would be worse."[32]

In Essex Chertkov continued the same relationship with the Englishmen that he held in Croiden. Already in the beginning of 1898 he writes Tolstoy, that from time to time he receives invitations to join various meetings in which he gives his usual speeches about Tolstoy and his teachings, about the Dukhobors and other themes of that type.

At the same time Chertkov works on the big article "Where Is Your Brother"[33], concerning the refusal of military service, containing information about the Dukhobor movement and giving critical evaluation of the actions of the government authorities in

Russia concerning the refusal of military service in general and of the Dukhobors in particular.

As in past years, Chertkov sends his manuscripts to Tolstoy. Very much approving of this article in its entirety, Tolstoy subjects it to attentive analysis, giving advice on literary technique:

"The main thing: don't be afraid to cross out. It is necessary, like with equalization, to be forthcoming, carrying it to the simplest form. You have a lot of good there, so that the exclusion of everything that overloads an article only makes it better. With me it is always such – remove the weak, of little importance, and unintentionally add something significant, and what was high before now goes down, and something completely different goes up, new, and gradually less fat remains and a lot more muscle."[34]

At the same time Chertkov continues the work on Tolstoy's writings, which he did in Rzhevsk, still persistently asks if Tolstoy's letters are being copied and asks to send him copies of these letters and various drafts for preservation in the archive which he brought with him to England. From time to time the papers prepared for him are delivered by mail or by people traveling to England from Yasnaya Polyana. In his turn, Chertkov, from England, just as from Rzhevsk, sends Tolstoy excerpts of his drafts and a few versions of already finished manuscripts that could be used in new work.

Conditions of correspondence from abroad, with secret, but permanent mail censorship of the letters, were, it is understood, very much unfavorable, however, in general, letters usually go by destination, sometimes lying too long on the way. Receiving from Tolstoy an announcement that this or that letter was apparently held, Chertkov uses a special trick - putting text earmarked for those outside eyes who read his letters in his letter to Tolstoy.

"I suppose, however," – wrote Chertkov, – "that if my letters, sent by mail are read by those poor people who serve the authorities, demanding the secret reading of private letters and similar actions then they prefer that our correspondence continue by mail and be read, then, if it completely passed their hands. Therefore, I think, my letters will be reaching you by mail."[35]

It is unknown if these arguments had any effect or for some other reasons, but Tolstoy's letters went, apparently without interruption, and Chertkov's letters, although coming less regularly, but not so much as to create some kind of break in correspondence. Certainly, it did not stop Tolstoy and Chertkov from using traveling acquaintances, sometimes that would be more pleasant, although they were not always more reliable.

Continual relations with Tolstoy through correspondence, the receipt of his articles and manuscripts before they were published in Russia must have created favorable conditions for that editing and translating work, which Chertkov planned for himself. But two projects, begun in 1898 and closely linked to one another in a period of a short time did not give him the possibility to concentrate on his work, demanding a great expenditure of strength and took up considerable space in his correspondence with Tolstoy: the emigration of the Dukhobors from Russia and the publication of *Resurrection* in foreign languages, which in the initial project had to give part of the means necessary for the emigration of the Dukhobors.

In February 1897, the Dukhobors, repeatedly submitting applications with the request of permitting them to leave Russia, received permission to resettle abroad with the obligation of never returning to the homeland. At that time Biryukov also received permission to go abroad, as well as others who were sent to the Baltics for helping the Dukhobors.

To organize the emigration abroad of 8000 people, expressing the desire to leave Russia, not knowing foreign languages, practically completely ravaged and emaciated by illness, was very difficult and without help on behalf of the Dukhobors, probably, would not have brought this task to fruition satisfactorily. Tolstoy decided to help them, participating in the emigration and assisting in the receipt of means necessary for this.

In March 1898 Tolstoy wrote Chertkov about this:

"The main and most important thing are these Dukhobors. They write me here already the third letter, that they are permitted to emigrate abroad and ask for help..." Having mentioned further that the Dukhobors must have a conference to decide where they want to go and how many people will emigrate, Tolstoy continues: "But not waiting for this, I will compose and put an appeal into one of the English and American newspapers, asking for help of all sincere Christians – help and leadership with direction for a place, methods of travel and money. I will send this appeal to you, probably tomorrow. If you find it unsatisfactory – as always I give you carte blanch to correct it – send it as the letter which you will put on the enclosed blank with my signature to the editor of one of the largest newspapers; if not *Times* than *Daily News* or *Daily Chronical*.[36]

Chertkov not only fulfilled Tolstoy's request but also appealed to the Quakers with the request of help for the Dukhobors and became a member of the committee created by the Quakers for the organization of the emigration. The Quakers began to gather money for the Dukhobor emigration and proved in many ways essential to the support of this venture.

The matter of the Dukhobor emigration was difficult in and of itself, proved especially difficult in that all the organizational work had to be carried out in England and Russia, while the participants in this work were located in various countries and did not have the possibility, not only to timely personally talk to one another, but also with the Dukhobors themselves.

These complicated circumstances produced the inevitable misunderstandings, arguments and friction among individual participants. First of all, a group of the Dukhobors waiting for a steamship in Batumi had to be transported to Cyprus island; then, only after the first wave of Dukhobors were transported, it became clear that Cyprus was not suitable and Canada would be a better choice because there was more free land and better climate conditions.

Besides the efforts of organizing the Dukhobor emigration the negotiations about the publication of "Resurrection" abroad were taking place.

In mid 1898 Tolstoy wrote Chertkov a letter in which he announced that he decided to publish three stories in his possession – unpublished and as of yet, unfinished: "Resurrection", "Devil", which at that point Tolstoy called "Irtenev", and "Father Sergei", and as an exception - take the fees for their first publication and donate them for the Dukhobor emigration. The right of further future publications of these works would not be anyone's property.

Later Tolstoy changed his mind about his intention to publish the last two stories having explained to Chertkov that the reason for this was "some displeasure risen at home"[37], but "Resurrection", by Tolstoy's estimate, could give a considerable sum, which could cover expenses incurred by the Dukhobor emigration for payment of which there was no money.

Calculating the estimate of the Dukhobor emigration and still not refusing the idea of publishing the tale of "Father Sergei", Tolstoy wrote:

"Here in Russia I earn 30,000 for two stories; abroad – the English, Germans and French it is necessary to receive as much from each nationality, and we will do fundraising, asking the rich, so lets hope that there will be enough money."[38]

Chertkov had to organize the publication of translations and entered into negotiations with publishers and translators, and Tolstoy at that time began to reread "Resurrection." As this was his habit in such cases, the work captivated him and he began to insert corrections.

On August 30, 1898 Tolstoy wrote Chertkov:

"I am now correcting "Resurrection." I am going through it for the second time, am changing a lot, and it seems to me that this will not be a bad work. At the very least, work on it makes me happy. It is so ready that I can send the first portions of the manuscript for translation."

The American publishers with whom Chertkov began negotiations for the publication of "Resurrection" were lively interested in this work, but in order to determine the fee, they persistently expressed their desire to know its content, at least to receive a short synopsis. Chertkov wrote Tolstoy asking to send a summary. At the same time Chertkov, responding to the demands of the Quakers, requesting that the sum be deposited, necessary for the payment of the steamship companies for transportation of the Dukhobors, because they already invested much of their own means in this matter, partially given them in the form of loans, asked quickly to send money Tolstoy already had at this time gathered for the Dukhobor emigration. Tolstoy decidedly declined both Chertkov's requests:

"It was unpleasant for me and confess, insulting, your demand to give the first chapters to the publishers to read. I would never have agreed and am surprised you agreed to this. And the summary for me represents something unimaginable. They want it or don't want it, but to give it for their approval, I am surprised that you, liking me, agreed. I remember that the American publishers wrote me letters many times with offers of very large payments and I supposed that would be the case, but if it is necessary to show the goods and wait for le bon plaisir*, good mood, of the buyer, then as much as I want to gather money for the Dukhobors, I cannot agree to this because it is not practical and beside humiliation for no reason, it also could result in selling the goods too cheaply."

Further, expressing readiness himself to carry on all negotiations, Tolstoy wrote that he cannot produce summaries since he wants to save himself the possibility, as long as the story still is not published, to change it, and explained the reasons for his indignation:

"So my indignation against summaries and preliminary reading is not from pride, but is some realization of my writer's vocation, which cannot subordinate my inner activity of writing for some kind of different practical consideration. Here is something repulsive and troubling to the soul. In general I am sorry that I agreed to make that step, all the more that you don't make it easier for me, as in many cases, liking me, you did; but now you make to feel disappointed."[39]

At the same time Tolstoy wrote that he cannot transfer money, gathered for the Dukhobors, to Chertkov, since, for the success of matters, it is necessary to know ahead of time how much, what for and when it is necessary, and that, being in Russia, he is closer to the center of action and can more easily direct this money there, where it is most necessary.

The next day, Tolstoy sent Chertkov a different letter, in which he wrote:

"Yesterday I wrote you a letter, dear friend, and couldn't get out of my head the letter itself and what kind of impression it would make on you. Please, cover everything that is not good there with love."

At the same time, returning to Chertkov's letter, Tolstoy wrote that he did not fulfill his wish since he did not believe in its practicality:

"It seems to me, that you always gather too many projects, not by your own strength, and they do not move from this. You, from this exaggerated accuracy, are slow, sluggish, then you look at everything condescendingly, like a big baron, and from this you don't see a lot, and beside that, already for psychological reasons, changing in mood, sometimes feverously active, sometimes apathetic. To this whole thing I think, that you, following the good in your character, are a very precious coworker, but if left on your own, turn out not to be a very practical entrepreneur. That is why I would like to know, what and how this is done and participate in decisions. About this final point, perhaps, here is a bad feeling of pride, but the point is that it is not possible since I continually change. The main thing is not to be angry with me and if I made a mistake about your practicality, then it is better."[40]

Chertkov decided not to undertake further steps in the matter of the emigration or the matter of publishing stories, until Tolstoy, having found out the motives of his actions, made his final judgment about these matters. He sent Tolstoy his coworker the Englishman Archer to Russia to tell him in detail about the business side of these negotiations which Chertkov had to carry on concerning the emigration of the Dukhobors and the publication of "Resurrection." At the same time, in a postscript to A.K. Chertkova's letter to Tolstoy of November 1, Chertkov explained the motives leading him to ask Tolstoy to send summaries of "Resurrection":

"I myself *did not think* that *you* would give them summaries of what you write, and am surprised that you could suspect me of this. I only wanted that someone else, not you, wrote a summary of what was already written, in which I see nothing humiliating for anyone, namely because these are not goods. I recognize the desire of publishers to know beforehand, whether a venture they invest money in will bring them revenue or loss, as completely justified. The Americans offer 8000 rubles for this story, not reading one chapter and not knowing its contents. If they find out the contents, then I hoped to receive 20-30 thousand rubles. I already know that the contents are not dangerous for them, but to convince them of this could only be done by having shown them the summary and first chapters. But if this is not allowed, it is possible now to receive 8000 rubles without anything. The big sums which the publishers offer to give you personally, immediately become comparatively inconsiderable when they find out that you do not agree to give them copyright."

Archer acquainted Tolstoy with the situation and Tolstoy wrote Chertkov:

"Thanks for your kindness, I consider our sad misunderstanding finished, so now we can forget about it."[41]

He dictated the contents of "*Resurrection*" to Archer and made an entry in his diary:

"I was not pleased with Chertkov and saw that I was to blame."[42]

Tolstoy sent Chertkov his diary with Archer. Chertkov, with great joy, having received this package, began to make excerpts of thoughts for inclusion in the index and wrote Tolstoy:

"The work which you gave me the possibility to resume, was always the most joyful of my projects even then, when I used personal contact with you; now during the separation, it gives me still more sincere satisfaction and joy."[43]

Having received from Tolstoy the account, dictated to Archer, of the contents of "*Resurrection*", Chertkov could resume negotiations with foreign publishers. On his side, Tolstoy finished negotiations with the publisher of "Niva", A.F. Marks, proposing to publish the novel in his magazine, giving out the fee in advance that could be used quickly for the Dukhobor emigration.

Since Tolstoy's works, in agreement with his will, became public property after their publication, and those foreign publishers, naturally, could agree to pay a fee for their first publication - under the condition that "*Resurrection*" did not appear earlier in the Russian magazine than in their own publications: after publication in Russia, everyone could translate and publish it free of charge.

But in order to timely translate and publish the novel abroad, it was necessary that the manuscript be sent earlier, meanwhile Tolstoy wanted to have the possibility to rework it in editing. Marks agreed to publish *"Resurrection"* with such calculation in order that foreign publishers could simultaneously publish it in their publication, but insisted that a fixed number of chapters appear in each issue of *Niva*.

Thus the publication of translations of *"Resurrection"* abroad created the same situation as the publication of *"What Is Art?"*, and inevitably the same misunderstandings and difficulties appeared. The difference was that *"Resurrection"*, as an artistic work attracted still more attention than *"What Is Art?"* Various foreign publishers and translators interested in it materially participated in the project, but the publisher of *Niva*, Marks, putting the commercial interests of his publishing house first, was still less inclined to consider the interests of foreign publishers, than N.Ya. Grot.

There is no necessity to describe all the upheavals of this business, which takes up a lot of space in the correspondence of Tolstoy and Chertkov for 1898 and 1899.

Tolstoy, already on September 12, 1989, writing Chertkov that he can send him *"Resurrection"* piecemeal with the calculation that in two months perhaps he can send the whole thing, immersing himself in work, began intensely to insert corrections into the manuscript.

In three months – 13 December 1898 – he wrote Chertkov:

"I now decidedly cannot work on anything other than *"Resurrection."* As a cannonball coming closer to the ground all the more quickly, as with me now, when the end is almost near. I cannot think about anything else, no, not only "cannot" even think, but don't want to think about anything else as I do this."

But the end of this work could not be reached until the release of the published book, meanwhile abroad it was necessary to give the translation of the last version of the novel with all its inserted corrections.

The beginning of *"Resurrection"* was sent to Chertkov before it was published in *Niva*, but the manuscript that he received required a great expenditure of time reworking before it could be given to translators.

Maria Lvovna wrote Chertkov:

"In a few days I hope to send you still another 20 chapters of *"Resurrection."* Are those we were sending you clear enough? We must confess, we send you the most dirty and illegible copies, hoping for your experience."[44]

Chertkov, after receiving the manuscripts and making clear copies from them, gave the text to translators and the beginning of the process went successfully enough. However, it immediately became clear that publishing *"Resurrection"* in a *weekly* publication in Russia significantly worsened those conditions on which the work could be published abroad: monthly magazines could not publish it, since *Niva*, released weekly, would leave them behind by several chapters which could be translated faster by any weekly publication and appear in print earlier than theirs. Weekly publications that could sign an agreement were comparatively few and their publications usually preferred to receive material for free, translating and reprinting them following their release in issues of *Niva*.

Nonetheless, Chertkov made the agreements with American and French publishers. But when the novel began to be published in *Niva*, it soon became clear that the proofs with Tolstoy's final corrections got to England too late. Marks did not demonstrate the desire to take the interests of foreign publishers into consideration and began to leave them behind, although Chertkov, in the beginning of publishing abroad, when the French publisher started to leave *Niva* behind, stopped it resolutely. As a result foreign publishers and translators began to blame Chertkov for breaking their agreements.

Tolstoy expressed his desire that Marks would slacken the pace of publishing *"Resurrection"*, but did this in an insufficiently categorical form, about which he himself wrote to A.K. Chertkova:

"It is so unpleasant for me to hear the expressions of various dissatisfaction from other people, even from Marks, that I hurry to hide from them, and meanwhile I forget that hiding myself I readdress them to Dima, who is so overloaded and in more difficult conditions than I."[45]

Tolstoy wrote about this in still more energetic expressions to Chertkov:

"I cannot express to you, dear friend, Vladimir Grigorievich, how I it is painful to me, that in so many aspects I was the cause of that disgraceful unpleasantness which you had to go through. Please don't be angry with me."[46]

But Tolstoy could not back away from his habit of correcting the manuscript until the last moment, and the delay in sending galley proofs continued.

Finally Tolstoy offered Chertkov to completely cancel agreements with translators and publishers, having explained the reasons that caused the delay in delivery of the original. But in order to avoid paying for forfeit it was necessary to wait so that the publishers did this themselves.

The American publisher, by the way, himself gave the possibility of breaking relations with him, having begun to redo the text of *"Resurrection"* his way. Chertkov wrote Tolstoy about this:

"My agent Reynolds (in America) exceeded his authorization, agreeing to corruption of the novel, and I therefore immediately stopped all further delivery of the manuscript, and all other business dealings with this agent to whom I returned 2000 dollars, *refusing to accept it.*"[47]

In the final analysis, monetary gain from the publication of *"Resurrection"* in foreign languages proved totally insignificant, and the estimates that this would render vital material support for the Dukhobor emigration did not come to fruition.

Simultaneously with the publication of *"Resurrection"* in foreign languages, Chertkov decided to set to work on publishing this book in his publishing house in Russian, with the reinstatement of all parts omitted in *Niva* following the demands of the censors.

This publication, released in circulation of 2000 copies, rendered support for the printing house which Chertkov organized, since it attracted public attention, but the material effect was insignificant; the manufacturing cost per copy for such a small print run and expenses of publishing in England proved to be so high, that when it was deducted from the sales figure very little was left.

Meanwhile the printing business begun by Chertkov was in great need of financial support, since it was intensively developed and consumed more and more attention of Vladimir Grigorievich and Anna Konstantinovna.

Already in the first months after their arrival in England, Chertkov began to gather material for a periodical publication which should, in his mind, appear as the continuation of the manuscript collection "Archives of L.N. Tolstoy" released in Russia.

In 1898 this project began to come to fruition in two forms – Chertkov's published "*Free Word*", under the editorship of P.I. Biryukov to whom Chertkov gave material, and "*Pages of the Free Word*", released under Chertkov's own editorship. "*Pages*" would respond more quickly to the events occurring in Russia, placing announcements among the small articles, which could become obsolete if their publication had to wait until the next issue of the collection saw the light.

Biryukov, having released the first issue of the collection "*Free Word*", in which, by the way, Chertkov's large article "The Kidnapping of Hilkov's Children" was published based on the materials which survived the police search in Russia, and the second release having been prepared for printing, left together with his family to Switzerland, where, after a short time, began to publish a magazine "*Free Thought.*" The publication of "*Pages of the Free Word*" remained in England.

The first release of these "*Pages*", seeing the light in November 1898, but prepared for printing already in the spring, presented itself as a small brochure with 68 pages, typeset in the small but very precise brevier. Beside small articles of Tolstoy, "Two Wars", it contained the following sections: "Information

About Dukhobors", where, by the way, many Dukhobor letters about the persecutions they suffered were published, "Lev Nikolaevich Tolstoy (information about him and excerpts from his personal writings)", "From Modern Life", articles and announcements of P.A. Kropotkin, D.P. Makovitsky and A. Shkarvan and other materials.

Tolstoy, having read the first release, wrote:

"I just read *Pages of the Free Word*", everything is wonderful except the last page – Appeal for Donations. This appeal will not bring any donations and discredits the merits of the publication. It seems to me that donations should be called for in a private manner and is not good in print. Everything remaining, the whole tone – everything is wonderful. Only it should have a little less Tolstoy and some kind of information about governmental sins in general and not religious persecution exclusively. Read and think all the time: what can I do that there would be the possibility of increasing the number of readers. It seems, probably, that I made a mistake, - that for the various unprejudiced, not totally broken person this reading must have an irresistible impression. And I liked the letters of Dukhobors and Shkarvan and Kropotkin articles very much."[48]

Chertkov, already before the receipt of this letter, announced to Tolstoy that he intends to include the "Denunciatory Section" in *Pages of the Free Word*." He wrote about this in the preface of the first release:

"People living within the boundaries of our Fatherland can be especially useful, announcing to us such facts of modern life which government servants of darkness and deception are afraid to admit publicly in Russia, but acquaintance to which is desirous in the interest of all Russian people."[49]

In the next release of *Pages of the Free Word*", arranged basically in the same scheme as in the first release, information appeared about displays of administrative arbitrary rule in Russia, not only in the sphere of persecution for religious conviction, but also for social activities. In a short time, Vladimir Grigorievich and Anna Konstantinovna set to work on preparation of material for a special release of *Pages of the Free Word*", having a subtitle "Information about Modern Life in Russia" and containing material about the workers movement, student unrest, administrative actions during the suppression of peasant uprisings, etc."[50]

Editing-publishing work all the more grabbed Chertkov's attention, as well as his wife's, who participated in it more, devoting especially a lot of her efforts to the preparation for publication of *"Pages of the Free Word."*

Chertkov wrote Tolstoy about this on December 2, 1898:

"Galya and I more and more are drawn into our publishing business and all the more feel, that this is truly our business at this time and during real circumstances."

And Chertkov often wrote Tolstoy about this in almost the same expressions, noticing that this work can more than anything give meaning for his stay abroad.

There had to be monetary means for the development of publishing activities and there was very little, since it was impossible in Russia to organize a large collection of money from those people sympathetic to publishing and who could share money for this goal money from their paycheck. Well-to-do people, liberally minded and critical of government powers in their discussions, for rare exceptions, limited themselves to more sympathy than material support.

At the same time those means that Chertkov's mother gave him were considerably reduced; the estate of E.I. Chertkova was at this time in disorder and its income fell sharply. Thus Chertkov could not continually put large sums into the printing house from his own means.

Considering it necessary to regularly announce information about income and expenses of the printing house, Chertkov began to publish detailed accounts. Studying them, one could see that the influx of means from outside supporters was completely insufficient to widely expand publishing work.[51]

Due to insufficient means they had to somehow delay publication of material concerning events in which it was necessary to respond to as soon as possible.

Tolstoy, not knowing that the routine release of *"Pages of the Free Word"* which gave information about events in Russian life, not subject to publication in censored Russian press, was held back due to insufficient means, wrote Chertkov on 8 August, 1899:

"You write that you have ready or are preparing articles about hunger, students, Finland. All this should have appeared six months ago. Now it is all old, new events are happening. It is necessary to write quickly and boldly, Gertzen-like, magazine-like about current events. But you meticulously investigate them, as one has to examine eternal questions."

Having found out from Chertkov's response letter that the reason for the delay was lack of funds for publication, Tolstoy hurried to take back his reproach. But to put collected material in "*Pages of the Free Word*" was, indeed late, and they were released in individual publications, in the form of special collections.

That coverage of Russian life provided by "*Pages of the Free Word*", attracted the sympathetic response from various circles. P.A. Kropotkin wrote Chertkov that he is glad about the success of these "Pages", and then, having found out about monetary difficulty of the printing house wrote:

"Have you found the means for the continuance of "*Pages*"? You prove a huge service at this time in them. It is necessary to continue by all means."[53]

Despite the material difficulties of "*Pages of the Free Word*", it continued to be released until 1902 when they were converted into a magazine which Chertkov called by the same name as the collection published in 1899 – "*Free Word*." The new magazine came out under Chertkov's editing as soon as the accumulation of material allowed and included among the articles the announcements about events occurring in Russia.

Parallel to the publication of "*Pages of the Free Word*", work was carried out concerning publishing individual works.

In his publishing activities, Chertkov did not limit it to the release of Tolstoy's writings, but they occupied the first place among his publications, meanwhile, it was understood that, for the most part, were released those works that could not be published in Russia. Beside individual works of Tolstoy, Chertkov intended to publish a complete collection of his compositions, barred by Russian censure. This publication was initially expected to be

200

twenty-five volumes, and so that it could be completely realized, it demanded huge means, which the printing house did not have available. But Chertkov, regardless, started this project, and, in the beginning of 1902, began gradually to release individual volumes, having planned first to publish ten volumes.

Less successful came the realization of another of Chertkov's projects – publication of the *"Collection of Tolstoy's Thoughts"*, on which Chertkov, together with his wife and various coworkers worked in 1899.

In May 1897, soon after his exile from Russia, Chertkov wrote Tolstoy:

"At the present time our work on systematically arranging your thoughts moves forward; Galya, her aides and I were working on it for a few years and came to such a situation that it is now possible to start to share with people its results, that is, gradually publish individual releases, finally putting into order its chapters. Do you allow me to start this? You know, that the contents of this index gathered from all your writings, having them in my hands, in the number of letters to different people, drafts, excerpts from diaries and other similar items, and the exception, of course, of those works about which you warned me, that you don't want their publication."

But only a few works from this project were published: "Thoughts About God", "About The Meaning of Life", "About Upbringing and Instruction", "About The Sex Question."

Tolstoy wrote Chertkov about these publications:

"In general, all your collections, like "About The Sex Question", were done with surprising tact and mastery, good, because it was filled with love which I feel and for which I am always touchingly thankful."[54]

But the publication of the entire index of thoughts had to demand great expense and this work remained in manuscript form.

At the same time of the publication of Tolstoy's works in Russian, Chertkov continued their publication in English.

In particular, Chertkov closely participated in the organization of the English printing house "The Free Age Press" which released works of Tolstoy at the most inexpensive cost, making them the most popular. This publishing house had considerable success, since, thanks to the energetic work of Chertkov's coworker, the Englishman Fifield, the publications were priced reasonably and became available to the widest circle of readers.

At the same time, Chertkov continues himself to work on the translation of a few works of Tolstoy in English. Using the right, which Tolstoy granted him, he carries on negotiations with translators of different languages.

Tolstoy, having finished work on the editing of *"Resurrection"*, quickly takes on the next theme and writes about it to Chertkov:

"Change and addition to *"Resurrection"* I will not, yes, I think, I cannot make: the umbilical cord is cut... Two themes are next: one is a letter to the Canadian Dukhobors about their life, about the deception of ownership. I began to write, but nothing came of it. But I want to clearly show the youth, the enthusiastic people among them what a tricky and rude deception it is – the desire for property and security. The other theme: about Afanasii Kaznachievsky, remember, who now serves as the checkweighman on the Kazan' railroad, told me that stevedores work thirty-six hours straight. I went there and saw these people and this work and want to tell what thoughts I had about this."[55]

The latter of these themes lays the groundwork for Tolstoy's article "Slavery of Our Time."

Starting to print this article, which came out as an individual brochure from the publishing house *"Free Word"*, Chertkov asked Tolstoy if he could make timely corrections so that it did not have to be changed later, when the article would be compiled, and received an answer:

"I did not want to make corrections, but your call made me review it and I am sending you a few changes. In no case do I intend to make more, hoping that you can correct some vagueness, and inaccuracies coming from me, and sometimes from the copiers, yourself, and that I give you, as always, carte blanche."[56]

Following that, Chertkov began negotiations with translators, appealing to them as Tolstoy's representative in publication of his works abroad. Despite the fact that the right of translations and publications was granted to translators and publishing houses for free, relations with them caused a lot of unpleasantness.

Chertkov wrote Tolstoy about the conditions in which he had to conduct this business:

"As you know, we don't receive decidedly any monetary advantages from placement of translations of your writings in various countries. I insist that all publishers knew definitely that your writings are granted them free of charge, and they have to pay the translators only for the translations."

In other letters, Chertkov wrote about the same subject:

"French translators appealed to us a lot, and we, not guaranteeing any of them a future monopoly on the first publication of the translation done from our proof sheets, conduct relations with them such as to give preference to the publishers who agree then to publish the cheapest for the working class."[58]

Chertkov wrote Tolstoy that the publishers and translators, knowing that Tolstoy's works are given them free of charge, could not show any displeasure. But in these relations, he was mistaken – some were indignant because they were not granted the right of first translation, others found those demands that Chertkov showed in relation to the accuracy of the translation to be excessive. The majority of publishers couldn't comprehend those principles on which they were denied the rights to possession of Tolstoy's works that they published.

Chertkov wrote about this to Tolstoy:

"In general, my position between you and those who don't understand you and disapprove of something or another, is very ambiguous: not daring to condemn you, they blame me for everything that they can't accept in your conduct, and in these cases, the more devoted and more faithfully I adhere to your views and desires, which are mine as well, the more resolutely I act in your moral interest, the more I am condemned by the people not sympathetic to your line of action."[59]

On his side, Tolstoy wrote Chertkov:

"I know how important for business and, mainly, for your peace I steadfastly held to the prescribed manner, so that abroad all my writings percolated only through you and that is why I strictly hold and will hold this."[60]

Continual relations with translators allow Chertkov, sometimes very quickly, to fulfill simultaneous publication of Tolstoy's new articles in various countries. Thus Tolstoy, working on articles and knowing that they cannot be published in Russia, could be sure, that soon he will see his writing translated into many languages.

In July, 1901, having finished "The Only Means", Tolstoy wrote Chertkov:

"I am sending you, dear friend, the article "The Only Means." I don't totally like it, although I reworked it innumerable times. I think, however, it can be useful."[61]

In less than two months – 12 September – Chertkov announced to Tolstoy:

"The Only Means" already appeared in Russian and English. In a few days it will appear in German and French."

The possibility to publish new articles quickly and without any kind of negotiations and effort abroad had special meaning for Tolstoy - when he had to write on one or another event in which it was desirous to respond without delay and about which it was totally not allowed to write in Russia.

So, when Tolstoy, concerning the decision of the Synod about his excommunication from the church, began to receive innumerable letters, in which some greeted him, others attacked him and Sofia Andreyevna, found it necessary to write a personal letter of protest to Metropolitan Antonii, Tolstoy felt the necessity to speak out about the decision of the Synod, creating his "Answer To the Synod." He announced to Chertkov:

"These days, I wrote, it seems, finished. First of all I will send it to you."[62]

And Chertkov immediately took measures for the publication of the article.

In the winter of 1901, Tolstoy began to take ill, periodically, experiencing a decline of physical strength. On January 18th he wrote Chertkov:

"I am sick and weak. Gradually I am becoming free of my body. In spirit I am OK."

Chertkov also received information that Tolstoy's health was getting worse from people living in Moscow who were close to Tolstoy in their views.

Chertkov decided to make an effort to see Tolstoy. He wrote a letter to the tsar, in which, reminding, that for him it was impossible from a moral standpoint to use the standard in such cases - expressions of loyalty to a monarch which would be in his situation insincere, asked to be permitted to go to Russia for a meeting with Tolstoy, expressing hope that this unusual form of appeal does not appear as an obstacle for satisfaction of this request:

"Here already four years," – wrote Chertkov – "that I am living abroad, lacking the possibility to freely live in my homeland and being separated from all of my friends who are close to me. Of them is one with whom I am closer than all tied by heart and soul and the separation from whom is more painful than anything to me – Lev Nikolaevich Tolstoy – at this time considerably weakened in health and a few times was sick. In the period of the last few weeks, especially, his strength has noticeably decreased, various new bouts of illness have affected him much more seriously, than was before, and in general, highly possible, that he will not still long live on earth. Therefore, I am experiencing a burning desire, if only still one time in life to see him and to say goodbye while further progression of his illness does not block the possibility of peaceful personal contact with him."[63]

As it could be expected, this request was denied.

In the beginning of March Tolstoy wrote that he feels a lot better, but from time to time the illness reappeared, which the doctors explained as fits of fever.

At the end of June Tolstoy became seriously ill: sharp fits of fever accompanied such a strong weakening of heart function, that for the period of a few days, his life was in danger.

Barely recovering, Tolstoy began to work intensely on articles begun earlier. Trying to concentrate on one of them, "What Is Religion and What Is It's Essence", he explained to Chertkov:

"It is necessary to hurry."[64]

But the bouts of illness continued and caused alarm in those around him. Doctors advised to go to the Crimea for the winter. Countess S.V. Panina offered Tolstoy and his family a wonderful home on her estate in Gaspra on the southern shore of the Crimea, not far from Koreiza, and the Tolstoys accepted her offer.

Tolstoy wrote Chertkov about this in a letter of 12 August 1901:

"There are plans to go to the Crimea. I, thank God, am almost completely indifferent to this – but somehow it is pleasant for me. I so lively feel a great journey, which I am completing and in which I am passing the last station, that these changes in method of travel concern me little."

On the way to the Crimea, Tolstoy experienced great weakness, but for the first time on his arrival in Gaspra he began to feel considerably better. Maria Lvovna wrote Chertkov from Gaspra:

"Father feels very well here, enjoying the warmth, beauty and quiet. How happy to see this. I am sure that the Crimea must help him and am glad that we managed to bring him here all right."[65]

In the two-story mansion of Countess Panina in Gaspra it was possible to live comfortably with a large family. Beside Tolstoy himself, his wife and youngest daughter Alexandra Lvovna, came Maria Lvovna with her husband N.L. Obolensky, Olga Konstantinovna Tolstaya, Anna Konstantinovna Chertkova's sister, married to Tolstoy's son Andrei Lvovich, and then following a few other members of Tolstoy's family.

Tolstoy continued intensely to work here and Alexandra Lvovna, who already turned seventeen, began more and more to substitute Maria Lvovna who was often sick, for him as copier. Maria Lvovna's husband, Obolensky wrote about this to Chertkov:

"Sasha does all the recopying of his work with great effort and willingness."[66]

Tolstoy, having finished the article "What Is Religion and What Is It's Essence", wrote Chertkov:

"I am reading Polenz's new novel "Der Grabenhager", it is worse than "Buttnerbauer", but the chapter I read today gave me a strong incentive to write fiction. Now especially, after I finished a one-sided work about religion which tired me out."[67]

But bouts of illness, as before, periodically gave warning and Tolstoy continued to get sick.

In January 1902 Tolstoy became seriously ill: pneumonia began, which, during the weakening of heart function, made the condition of the patient, to a high degree, dangerous. Doctors came to Gaspra, daily bulletins were published in newspapers about the course of his illness and one could expect his death any day.

Chertkov had to stay far away and, receiving news that the condition of the sick one was getting worse, wrote him:

"Dear Lev Nikolaevich, I don't know, if you will read this letter, I don't know if this is the last time in my life I am writing "Dear Lev Nikolaevich", and I am sad, inexpressibly sad and melancholy that I cannot be near you in these minutes."[68]

Letters from Olga Konstantinovna Tolstaya, P.A. Bulange and N.L. Obolensky, helping in tending to the sick, allowed Chertkov to follow Tolstoy's condition, providing information not fitting into telegrams.

Bulange wrote Chertkov:

"He has minutes of depression, physical depression, when he gasps, and in one of these moments he called me and said: "Only just woke up, having heard two voices: one says – OK, OK, but the other – I am dying."[69]

Bulletins, which doctors created daily, while the danger did not pass, were announced daily to Chertkov, and a fat folder of telegrams sent from Gaspra is preserved in his archive.

The editors of foreign newspapers, already accustomed to consider Chertkov as Tolstoy's official representative abroad, bombarded him with questions and he organized the appropriate transmissions, passing the bulletins to news agencies which telegraphed them to hundreds of newspapers in America and Europe.

For more than a month the condition remained serious, then, the illness began little by little to pass.

On March 2, Tolstoy dictated a letter to Chertkov, first, after his illness:

"My health, in the words of the doctors, is getting better, but to my sense it is all the same: I cannot roll over from my back to my side and am very weak. But this doesn't interfere with my interest in matters…"

And having posed a few questions concerning how the publishing of articles, written before his illness is going, Tolstoy wrote in conclusion:

"I am doing very little, writing something and unintentionally thinking about the most varied begun things, which, probably, will never be finished. In spirit I am very good and peaceful and everything around me is good and joyful."

Health returned very slowly, his body was so weak that for a long time Tolstoy still could not stand on his feet, but on March 23 was already able to write letters in his own hand and wrote Chertkov:

"Apparently I have to live."

In April came a new danger: Tolstoy got sick with typhoid fever. But his organism endured this attack.

Nonetheless, those close to Tolstoy considered that the illness could not pass completely: it had to become the border where his old age began.

VIII
L.N. Tolstoy & V.G. Chertkov 1902-1906

At the end of June 1902 Tolstoy returned from the Crimea to Yasnaya Polyana and his life began to settle down.

In order to better understand much of the correspondence between Tolstoy and Chertkov, it is necessary to know how Tolstoy's life took shape during this time at Yasnaya Polyana and Chertkov's in England.

The proximity to death, experienced at the time of illness, left its mark on Tolstoy, and studying his letters and diaries at that time, it is impossible not to see how, having coped with illness, he clearly understood that the thread of his life could break at any minute.

Tolstoy himself writes about this to Chertkov in the beginning of July 1902:

"In secret I will tell you, that, despite the fact that I am getting better, I feel that I will soon step out from this life. And not that this thought doesn't leave me, but that I don't leave this thought, and I feel in this relation very good. Perhaps, I am mistaken, but I wanted to tell you this."

And in his diary Tolstoy writes about this recovery:

"My recovery is like dragging a carriage out of a quagmire where it is stuck, not in the direction in which one must to go, but in the opposite one. There is no avoiding going through the quagmire."[1]

But his health quickly began to be restored and became firmer to a much higher degree than his doctors and family expected.

During Tolstoy's illness Sofia Andreyevna wrote A.B. Goldenweiser:

"In any case, Lev Nikolaevich will live still a few more years, his life will be that of a senile old man, of whom it is necessary to take care, to whom it will not be allowed various worries, movement, excessive relations with people, etc. He, like a small baby, will go to sleep early, eat kasha and milk, stroll with an escort, will not converse, not listen to music, and in general, must take care of his heart, which became easily excitable and therefore dangerous for life."[2]

But Tolstoy's exceptionally strong organism overcame not only illness but also the danger of senility. Already in the summer of 1902 Tolstoy began again to take long walks on foot and on horseback, and doctors noted his endurance with surprise.

Despite the full recovery, the illness appeared for Tolstoy as if it was some introduction into the rights of old age. This was most apparent in Sofia Andreyevna's agreement not to insist on life in Moscow in the winter.

Before his illness, Tolstoy delayed their annual fall move to Moscow in every way possible, which oppressed and irritated him. But Sofia Andreyevna persistently demanded that he share life with her in Moscow. In the fall of 1898, she herself wrote about this to her sister:

"I don't know when he will move to Moscow. He does not want to very much, but for me he will move, when I want. I still think about this, I don't know, if I am emotionally strong enough to live by myself already almost two months. Without him, my usual anxiety and madness overwhelm me, but around him I, like around a nanny – peaceful and reasonable, and therefore much more happy."[3]

Now Sofia Andreyevna agreed with the doctors' opinion that for Tolstoy most important was the necessity for peace, and after the project to travel again to the Crimea for fall and winter was cancelled, she decided to remain for the winter in the countryside.

Thus for Tolstoy it was possible to live at Yasnaya Polyana, almost without leaving, carrying on his years of old age far away from city commotion.

Tolstoy's younger sons by this time were already grown, married, and settled in their own estates, and of all the family who were continual inhabitants of Yasnaya Polyana beside Tolstoy himself were his wife and daughter Alexandra Lvovna, all more and more helping him with rewriting his manuscripts and letters. But they were almost never there alone: there were always many guests at Yasnaya Polyana, especially in the summer.

Tolstoy finds himself, thus, in relations with the most varied people.

Sofia Andreyevna filled her life while in the countryside with continuous efforts and matters, – from the editing new publications of Tolstoy's collected compositions to the supervision of new construction in the farmyard, – as before holding all the housekeeping of the home in her hands and, although sometimes weighed down by too numerous visitors, at the same time, is bored, if they were not there, tries then to quickly invent some kind of project for herself.

"I decidedly do not invite anyone," – Sofia Andreyevna wrote to her sister, – "and all the time are guests, guests without end and I sometimes simply want to cry from fatigue. Already not speaking of children and grandchildren – this is natural and pleasant, – but relatives, strangers, foreigners – various people are crowding Yasnaya continuously. Work for placement, food, horses and carriages, beds take so much time and consideration, that there is no time to live."[4]

But in the winter, when guests more seldom arrive, she complains to Tatiana Andreyevna that her loneliness oppresses her:

"It is difficult to live in the country in old age; very lonely, monotonous. All day you are quiet. Levochka is almost not seen until lunch, visitors are few, and not ones preferred but those who arrive themselves and are very unpleasant sometimes."[5]

Tolstoy tries to use this life in one place without external change and city noise in order to concentrate on his thoughts and his work.

And Sofia Andreyevna writes about him to her sister:

"Levochka is healthy, cheerful, walks a lot, unfortunately often rides horseback feverishly, hurriedly works his mental work, absolutely hurries in life to do the most possible."[6]

Correspondence with Chertkov as usual takes up first place among letters which Tolstoy writes at this time: after his return from the Crimea, to the second half of 1902, Tolstoy writes Chertkov twenty letters – on average one every eight days, telling of his work and thoughts that occupy him.

In conversation with his daughter-in-law, Olga Konstantinovna, Tolstoy says about Chertkov:

"He and I live in one tempo."[7]

Chertkov's letters to Tolstoy, in his turn, as usual continually tell him about his internal and external life, shares with him his plans, reports how the matter of translating and publishing his articles is going, and in his usual directness gives his opinion of Tolstoy's new writings.

In the first years of being in England, the Chertkovs, settling first in Croiden, then in Purleigh, busy with a string of projects, lived there like temporary inhabitants, always considering the possibility of moving to another place.

Within a period of time they felt the demand more and more to choose a permanent place to live, and to get their external life going, occupying themselves with their main work.

Chertkov wrote about this to Tolstoy already in the spring of 1900:

"The main thing I want is internal peace, in which you don't get upset namely about what to take on, but wait for clear and undoubted internal assuredness that you take on namely what is necessary and not something else. Taking on one thing or another is not to fuss, afraid to be late for the next thing, but to do so purposefully and not rush, this same thing persistently and intensely until fruition."[8]

In the fall of 1900 they found a very comfortable mansion, 150 kilometers to the south of London, in an agricultural area near the small town of Christchurch. The house was situated not far from the seashore, before it was a plot of land with a fruit garden, and here it was possible to live peacefully and work. Chertkov's mother, spending the summer and fall in England, decided to acquire this home for him and his family. The Chertkovs moved their printing house to Christchurch and here began to release one publication after another.

Chertkov's efforts to organize his life such that it would not be rushed, but persistently to do and complete his projects, in considerable measure were successful in the time of his life in Christchurch.

His work develops in those directions which were already defined in the previous six years: the magazine "Free Word" is being published, the release of which depends on the assimilation of material and the amount of monetary means; from December 1901 to September 1905 eighteen issues were published. The publication of the complete collection of Tolstoy's works, not allowed in Russia, was continued and by 1904 Chertkov managed to realize a large part of the first series of this publication, released seven volumes.

They continue to release Tolstoy's new articles in individual brochures and a few other books, through the "Free Word" and developed the project of cheap publication in English of Tolstoy's books and others close to him in that direction.

Setting in Christchurch, Chertkov, together with a few Englishmen, regularly organize open meetings in the neighboring town of Bournemouth, – "The Progress Meetings For the Consideration of the Problems of Life", in which they discuss various questions of life-understanding, moreover, people of various views participate while in debate. The local newspaper, "The Bournemouth Guardian", which ran for four years from 1901-1904 constantly placed announcements about these meetings.

At this time, Chertkov gladly accepts invitations to appear for lectures about Tolstoy and his world-outlook at different types of gatherings – from discussions in a small circle to speeches at the Congress of Unitarians in London and lectures to Oxford University students.

Chertkov sends Tolstoy excerpts of a few of his lectures and writes him about his appearances:

"Already when I only just arrived, dear Kropotkin told me that it is impossible and one should not live in a country absorbed only by the interest in his own country, that from this you only get weak and loose ground under you. I didn't have a chance to experience the fairness of the last part of his observation; because instinctively I always searched for relations with Englishmen and always found refreshment in these and strengthening my pursuits at home."[9]

Living in his home, without fear of encroachment of Russian gendarmes, and not intending to move somewhere away from there, Chertkov continues to gather Tolstoy's manuscripts in his archives with special persistence, taking care in receiving drafts of his new articles, originals and copies of his letters to various people and recopied copies of his diaries. At the same time he continues the matter of gathering material about the sect movement, begun already in Rzhevsk with I.M. Tregubov. And the publication "Free Word" release of a series entitled "Material For the History and Study of Russian Sectarianism" appears in the form of small brochures.

Chertkov continually asks Maria Lvovna, her husband, N.L. Obolensky and Alexandra Lvovna to copy Tolstoy's letters for him, send him drafts, and they, from time to time send him these manuscripts by mail or with people going abroad.

In January 1901, Maria Lvovna sends Chertkov a considerable amount of drafts of Tolstoy's works and copies of his letters with A.M. Hiryakov and writes:

"I am sending you, dear Vladimir Grigorievich, much good and am glad in your joy and that all of this, finally, will be preserved by you. With love all this was gathered and with love it will be arranged in order by you. This is very good."[10]

In the beginning of 1903 Chertkov sends a list of materials in his archive, in order to clear up, if they have at Yasnaya Polyana such letters and manuscripts which he did not, neither in original nor copy.

N.L. Obolensky answers Chertkov that all drafts which were at that time neat; almost all the copies of letters, lists that were preserved at Yasnaya Polyana were sent with Hiryakov, and it turned out that Chertkov already had them, it remained only to make copies of a few of Tolstoy's still unfinished works, drafts of which were still not allowed to be sent, since they could be necessary to Tolstoy in future work.

In order to preserve these materials in total safety, Chertkov intended to build a place in his home completely inaccessible to fire equipped in accordance with the latest in fireproof technology.

In 1906, this depository was finished. It was a separate dwelling with thick concrete walls which were covered from within by blue tiles and from the outside with red fireproof brick, and was separated from the rest of the house by a system of doors, beginning from the outside iron-cast doors of special construction and ending with the inner doors. In accordance with archival technology, a constant temperature was maintained in the room where manuscripts were preserved with the help of a gas oven and ventilation. Unauthorized people were not allowed there – a special room was attached for work on manuscripts, bright and comfortable, where one could obtain manuscripts for some work or another - with Chertkov's permission.

In close connection with Chertkov's work in the gathering of Tolstoy' letters and manuscripts, was the question posed of what would be the future fate of these materials. Chertkov, preparing for the publication of Tolstoy's writings continues to take steps, to a certain measure, necessary so that the project could be fulfilled as completely as possible. Taking into consideration this circumstance, that Tolstoy's letters to various people formally were property of the addressees, and possibly, that some of their owners, desiring in their time to sell autographs for money, could oppose their publication, Chertkov in August 1902 asks Tolstoy to confirm in writing his permission to use copies of these letters for publication.

Tolstoy does not immediately agree to fulfill this request and writes Chertkov:

"This has such an appearance that I write letters to people, having the reading public in mind, but I don't want this, and this is not the case. I think, that one can write to those who have letters. And in general this is not worth it."[11]

Chertkov answered Tolstoy that he does not "complain" about this answer, always feels thankful for this trust, which Tolstoy continually showed him and continues to show, entrusting him in all matters of publication of his writings.

But in April 1903, Chertkov again returns to this matter and writes Tolstoy a long letter, in which he argues that if this declaration will not be made, it would create a very undesired situation: not recognizing the right of literary property of all his writings for himself, Tolstoy, factually appoints literary property of his writings to various people, among whom could prove to be the person, alien in view, desiring to use the letters for extraction of material advantage. At the same time, in the time of publication of Tolstoy's letters proves impossible to receive agreement from all addressees; copies of letters which Chertkov has in his archives often don't contain the addresses, many probably not among the living, thus creating insurmountable obstacles in the matter of "deprivatization of thoughts" of Tolstoy. At the same time Chertkov pointed out that during the publication of these letters, he, it is understood, takes measures so that their parts somehow or another touching on the intimate lives of people with whom Tolstoy corresponded would not be published, if this would be unpleasant for them. Therefore, Chertkov offered Tolstoy, giving his permission, to make appropriate provisos.

Tolstoy answered to this letter with agreement:

"Dear friend, Vladimir Grigorievich, I received your long letter about my letters. I feel sorry that my expression of apprehension does not cause the unhappiness of my correspondents left you with much worry. I totally agree with your offer: to do as you propose. This is all."[12]

In the next year, Tolstoy in one of his letters to Chertkov himself returned to the question of the future fate of his writings. The will, set forth by Tolstoy in his diary of 1895 in which he instructed that after his death the preparation of all his writings for publication go to Chertkov, N.N. Strahov and his wife and expressed the desire that his heirs renounced ownership of his works, recopied by M.L. Tolstaya in 1901, with the exception of N.N. Strahov, who was deceased by that time, and signed by Tolstoy. But Sofia Andreyevna, having found out about this, decidedly demanded that this paper be given to her. Tolstoy finally ceded to her insistence.

Sofia Andreyevna decided at this time not to fulfill Tolstoy's desire concerning the renunciation of ownership of his works:

"To make Lev Nikolaevich's works *common* property I consider foolish and senseless", - she wrote in her diary on October 10, 1902. "I love my family and want the best for it's welfare, by making his works public property we only line the pockets of the rich publishing companies like Marx, Tsetlin and others. I told Lev Nikolaevich that if he dies before me, I would not carry out his wishes and not renounce the copyright on his works; and if I thought that was the right and proper thing to do, I would give him the pleasure of renouncing it *during his lifetime*, but there was no point at all of doing so after his death."[13]

In a letter of 13-26 May, 1904[14], Tolstoy, returning to his will, written in his 1895 diary, asks Chertkov to review and sort out the remainder of his papers and together with Sofia Andreyevna deal with them as they see fit.

At this time Tolstoy again instructed Chertkov to review his diaries and publish them, excluding "everything accidental, unclear or excessive."

Finishing the letter, Tolstoy wrote Chertkov:

"Thank you for all your past work on my writings and in advance for what you will do with the papers remaining after me. Unity with you was one of the biggest joys in the last years of my life."

Fulfilling the accepted role of Tolstoy's representative abroad, Chertkov continues to receive manuscripts of Tolstoy's new articles earlier than anyone else, sharing with him his critical observations, organizes simultaneous publications of his writings in different countries. Tolstoy in his letters to Chertkov always lets him know what is going on with his work.

Barely recovering from illness, Tolstoy begins to work on the article "Appeal To the Working Class".

He first announced to Chertkov about this article in a letter, in which, answering Chertkov's question about what is happening in Russia, explains why he considered it necessary to work on this theme:

"I received, kind friend, Vladimir Grigorievich, your last letter, where you ask what we think about the current situation of events in Russia. I, in any case, although I live in Russia, cannot create for myself any kind of definite opinion about how this will end. You completely truthfully write that Russian people have awakened. This – undoubtedly new fact, and in addition to the fact that our dear Bulygin writes me these days absolutely correctly, that the current government reminds him of a drunk, who says: "to drink is to die, and not to drink is to die, then it is better to drink!" These two main phenomenon: that Russian people, and people as a whole even, woke up or are waking up and therefore are beginning to act; the government already more deeply retreats into its shell and wants not only to preserve the current situation, but also return to the older and more backward one. From the joining of these two phenomena, certainly will come something new, but what it will be, I can't even guess, yes, I think no one can predict, since history cannot repeat itself. The only thing that we can know, that the situation is very intense and all people, desiring to bring it to a good conclusion, more than whenever, similarly, energetically act. I lively feel this and while I am not sick, am occupied with the article "Appeal To the Working Class", which I have almost finished these days and hope to send to you."[15]

Having finished the article and sending it to Chertkov, Tolstoy wrote:

"I, as always, corrected it many times, but perhaps from this correcting appeared something awkward, absurd which you will correct."[16]

Chertkov, having received the article, as usual, offers Tolstoy a few corrections, elaborating on specific parts. At the same time he tells of his observations, pointing out that finding groundless condemnation of strikes is unjust, since strikes, without use of force, in his opinion, do not deserve any kind of censure. A.K. Chertkova, on her side, wrote Tolstoy concerning the negative opinion of revolutionaries presented in this article, that it is necessary to remember ideological content, and even, not agreeing with them, not to forget that they don't have bad motives.

Tolstoy accepted part of the corrections and responded with a letter in which he himself underlined that he expressed the point of view of the Russian "beaten" peasantry:

"As you, dear Galya, carefully appealing to my conscience - this is not necessary; I see your soul as the source of what you are talking about. You are certainly right. But not so much in your condemnation or justification of me, but, in order to point out the reason for a few of our various points of view, I will say, that you, living in Europe, you see the factory workers, they seem to you all the people, I see 99% of the Russian beaten peasantry, to which, as means to an end, to rescue the class struggle is offered spiritual evil, and material good, and cannot, without disappointment (I am guilty) see and hear this. And therefore I get excited and that's not right.

Please don't condemn me very much, but also, make allowances for me."[17]

In the postscript to this letter, earmarked for Chertkov, Tolstoy wrote that he sends more corrections for the article "To The Working Class" and added:

"In general, do what you think best. As in trust one writes: I wont argue over everything or contradict. And with this it will be finished. There is a lot about which to write, but I can't now. There are more and more matters and strength is less and less, although I can't complain about my health."

In one of the letters following, Tolstoy announced what he was working on at the time:

"I am healthy and write "Hadji Murat" – I am indulging. Brought to the same stage as "Father Sergei" and others, as what is connected and consistent. But I want to finish. And there are many demands more important, as it seems to me."[18]

The desire to express his thoughts finally overpowered the aspiration to work on the artistic polishing of the tale, and Tolstoy wrote Chertkov:

"I finished *Hadji Murat*, which I will not publish in unfinished form and postponed during my life. Very difficult to write "To The Priesthood" and in the evenings a little fiction."[19]

Following the small article "To The Priesthood", which Tolstoy finished in the beginning of November and sent to Chertkov with the request to express his "always necessary" judgment, he writes a new work, getting the title "The Destruction of Hell and its Restoration"

In the beginning of 1903 prolonged influenza resulted in Tolstoy's significant weakening. And still not recovering from illness, Tolstoy dictates a letter to Chertkov in which he writes about his work:

"I am still weak: one day is better, one worse, but, in general, however, everything is moving toward the better, although this does not always mean...I sent you an addition to the legend, if it is in time, OK, if not, then it is not necessary. This is very unimportant. Yes, by the way, how to entitle it: "The Legend of The Destruction of Hell and its Restoration", or just simply "About The Destruction of Hell and its Restoration"? Do whatever you think best."[20]

In the postscript of this letter, Tolstoy wrote about his future artistic plans:

"During the time of my illness it is good to think, the only thing that is not alright is that new and fascinating works unintentionally present themselves and it is necessary not to forget the years and illness carry one closer to death. What especially occupied me in this illness (reading of Kropotkin's wonderful memoirs contributed to this) were reminiscences for autobiographical notes, promised to Posha*, especially joyful were childhood, and especially painful were the senseless years of nasty life of youth. I would like to tell you everything."[22]

But Tolstoy's indisposition dragged on and until spring, 1903, he continues to experience weakness and he cannot work.

Chertkov, having found out about this, writes to Tolstoy:

"I have a serious request for you or offer: when you cannot write those serious things that you want to write, in order that your writer's "talent" did not remain unproductive, write such, for example, small tales or parables for illustration of one or another moral or religious truth. Write only as if for children. This is very necessary, these small fruits, if only you put fingers to them, they would fall from you absolutely ripe and prepared for us as food. And in order that you don't get excited about this, ie) don't be involved in painstaking reworking of these things, so that your attention and strength could be drawn to other work, which you consider more important, send these drafts, writing, when other work does not get on well, send them to me in a personal letter in the form of a very initial draft. I will recopy them and preserve them, and when a sufficient amount will be collected, then sometime I will send them to you for final revision, and if this cannot be done, it's OK, readers will know that these are only drafts... You can't even imagine, what a *huge* help for persuasiveness of your other writings your various artistic works would serve, even not works, but simply artistic form, comparison, parable."[23]

But Tolstoy knew that artistic work, even in such a primitive form, demands much mental intensity and answered Chertkov, that he couldn't fulfill this request:

"To your advice first about writing artistically, when I cannot work, I cannot follow. If there is not great sincere enthusiasm, it is impossible to write artistically. To write just anything embarrasses me, especially at my age. But I don't miss not writing, which now, by the way, is retreating. I always try to apply my definition of life in the diary. I will send you a few pages from the diary…"[24]

Following that, receiving news that Tolstoy feels better and is making drafts of his reminiscences at the request of Biryukov, writing his biography, Chertkov writes him about what kind of meaning this work can have.

Already in July 1902, Chertkov, announcing that he gave Biryukov material from his archive for this intended work, wrote Tolstoy about how important it would be for him to write his reminiscences. Now Chertkov again returned to this idea and in a letter of 31 March 1903 writes Tolstoy:

"I am so glad about the news that you are better. I am also glad that you are occupied with writing your reminiscences. I am afraid only, that since this involves your personal self, that this will seem to you unimportant. Meanwhile, such an assumption would be a big mistake. The idea, rise of conscience, tied to a definite person, yes still with the person of the writer and clearly such a writer as you, - has a *huge* significance for people of our time and for future generations; in some sense it is even more significant than the most painstakingly applied abstract thoughts. If this depended on me, then before the death of every person, in whom took place the increase in spiritual consciousness, I would separate him in a special room and would lengthen his life so much that he could succeed, although in general outline, in writing, communicate to people the highlights in his conception, outlines of all the periods of his lived life. It would create such a library, which would excel in comparison in the idea of usefulness that all others; for me, in any case, nothing would be so instructive as such autobiographical reminiscence. And therefore you can imagine how desirous I would be if you wrote out your reminiscences. There is no demand for consistency and there is no demand to dwell on that, which is unpleasant or difficult to reminisce. The best of all is to simply write in general terms, meaningful and sincerely, characteristic of that epoch of life, *illustrating* this with examples of factual reminiscences, some detailed, some not detailed, however God puts them on your soul."

But Tolstoy, involved in other themes, did not use this advice - reminiscences remained in the form of an unfinished draft.

Now, as in previous years, Chertkov sends Tolstoy manuscripts of his articles.

In March 1903, Chertkov finished a big article: "Violent Revolution or Christian Liberation"[25], in which he opposes the revolutionary movement and passive resistance, the path of refusal of the fulfillment of governmental orders.

Having received and read this article, Tolstoy writes Chertkov:

"Set out two days, that is, work hours to reading and thinking about your article. I changed some things, excluded some, in one place put an "A". The article, extremely important in content and inclusive of much necessary good, and therefore studied it with joy and an awareness of the importance of the matter."

After listing the proposed corrections for each chapter, Tolstoy summed up his observations:

"The correction must consist of that which is not only to compress, omitting everything irrelevant to the main topic, but also to compress the sentences, cutting the words without fear of not being clear enough. Also to soften all expressions aimed both at the government and at the revolutionaries. And to weaken the praise of the revolutionaries for their selflessness."

In conclusion, Tolstoy wrote that he will try to write a preface for this article and finished with a request:

"Don't be angry with me that I so boldly corrected not only the language, but in some places the thought. You will accept what is worthwhile and throw away the unneeded."[26]

Chertkov answered that he read Tolstoy's letter with joy and completely agrees with his corrections.

Soon after that - on 7 May 1903 - Tolstoy sent Chertkov his article, entitled "Afterward to Appeal To the Working Class" and on his behalf, asked:

"Write what you notice."

Chertkov wrote Tolstoy that he totally agreed with the contents of this article, but disapproved of the title:

"The title is very uninteresting and somehow awkward. Couldn't you just leave "Afterward to Appeal To the Working Class" as a subtitle and invent a title, expressing the common thought of the article? When I reread it, I will try, taking from your text, to come up with an appropriate title."[27]

Tolstoy answered that Chertkov's observation seems to him honest and offered:

"Why not give it the title: "Toward Political Leaders" and nothing more?"[28]

Under the title, The Free Word published the article during that year.

Corresponding with Chertkov concerning his articles, Tolstoy reports at the same time about himself and his general state of health to him.

Having begun the letter of 11 June, 1903 with work-related announcements that he corrected the proofs of one of the volumes released by Chertkov – *The Complete Collection of Tolstoy's Works, Banned in Russia*, tells him then about his mood and work:

"I am living very well. I am writing something in *Hadji Murat* about Nikolai Pavlovich, an individual chapter, which, although will be disproportionate to the whole, extremely fascinates me. Still, despite the apparent proximity to the end, I planned three things that I really want to start. Today I walked with the small children, eight and nine years old, (one – the daughter of the lackey, the other – son of Denisenko's niece), strolled in the forest, in the very overgrown part. We got lost, tired and returned happy and satisfied."

In other letters of Tolstoy's to Chertkov, written in the summer of 1903 the same cheerful tone is heard. In the beginning of August, explaining to V.G. and A.K. Chertkov why he hadn't answered their letters in a long time, wrote:

"This came about because I am too healthy. In the mornings I work – write, then go horseback riding twenty versts or more, lay down to rest before lunch, eat lunch, then fatigue, read letters, guests. And everyday say: today I will write letters – and I keep putting it off. The main reason is the morning mental work. I wrote during this time three tales that I gave to the Jewish collection as a donation to the victims of the Kishniev pogrom and pages I will send you. The tales are poor[29]. But it was necessary to free myself of them. And a story totally by accident – "Daughter and Father"[30], which I didn't set anywhere, is not bad. Already read a lot, thought and wrote two chapters of *Hadji Murat* about Nikolai Pavlovich. This is not finished, but what I planned and how it was planned seems to me good and important."[31]

At the end of August, Tolstoy got sick, having gotten bruises on his legs while riding horseback. The bruises got better, but Tolstoy continued to get sick. Nonetheless, he continues to work: writes an article "About Shakespeare and About Drama" and the preface to the publication by Chertkov in English of the biography of Garrison – a preacher who taught not to resist evil by force.

Chertkov was busy at this time with the preparation for publication of the string of volumes of *The Complete Collection of Tolstoy's Works, Banned in Russia*. He carried out this work with pedantic accuracy, often asking Tolstoy concerning individual parts or single words, calling one or another into doubt and sending Tolstoy galley proofs for corrections.

For example, in January 1904, Chertkov writes Tolstoy:

"We are now publishing that volume of *"The Complete Works"* which will be *"Short Retelling of the Gospel"*. But it seems that I have two variations of the preface for it: one already published by us in our individual publication of the *Short Gospel* with commentary from the detailed research... the other version was in manuscript form, in which I gave the enclosed galley proofs to be typeset. I think, almost even certain, that this version contains your *final* corrections. But since it is very important for *The Complete Collection*, that there not be the slightest doubt, I am sending you both versions, asking you to glance at them and tell me as urgently as possible which of them is final and complete."

Further, directing Tolstoy's attention to the fact that he used the words "church" and "sect" as synonyms, Chertkov writes that usually in the conception of the reader these words have different meanings. Therefore, to avoid misunderstanding, he offers to change both words in places where Tolstoy had in mind "church" and "sect", using only one of these terms. Underlining in the galley proofs these places in red pencil, Chertkov explains:

"In the first place, I don't dare to take upon myself such arbitrariness, and in the second place, you, perhaps, prefer to correct matters somehow differently, or leave them as they were initially."[32]

Tolstoy responded to this letter:

"I am hurrying as soon as possible to send these corrections. I understood everything and finally changed it differently. I hope that you will approve. Everything is wonderful. Probably this is the final version. I think about you with love and gratitude."[33]

War, breaking out in the Far East between Russia and Japan, moved aside the routine work in which Tolstoy was occupied. He wrote about this himself to Chertkov:

"The necessity to write about the war interrupted my artistic and philosophical work. I hope I will finish soon. The editor of "Woche" in Berlin wrote me, asking for an article about the war. I answered him that he appeal to you, since I send, it is understood, to you, and you spread it, as you find fitting."[34]

Tolstoy intensely works on an article about the war: "Bethink Yourselves" which, as it almost always was with his articles, did not come to him immediately, but the more he worked on it, the more he was excited by the process of work. In the beginning of April Tolstoy sends Chertkov the first ten chapters and continues to work on the rest of the article, making at the same time corrections on those chapters which he already sent to England.

And only at the end of April he finishes this article and makes an entry in his diary:

"At this time I already wrote the appendix to the article about war. Today I finished and am happy with it."[35]

Chertkov, having received the manuscript, writes that he is very glad to read it and finds it to be to a high degree necessary. Then he expresses his views concerning specific parts of the article.

Tolstoy prefaced every chapter with a long epigraph, containing thoughts about the intolerability of war, taken from various authors.

Chertkov writes concerning this:

"The epigraphs in and of themselves are excellent and evoke a strong impression. But placed between the chapters of your own article, they cut the thread of your argument too short and break that sincere mental merging of the reader with the author, which is necessary for the appropriate perception of his ideas. Generally speaking, the article consists of two parts – 1) your account; and 2) a wonderful collection of specific thoughts concerning the subject of your article. And it should be published in the form of these two individual parts... This would be the most beneficial and, I repeat, for your article and your epigraphs themselves, since, when they are placed between chapters of your article, then the reader either skips over them or reads them inattentively, in order not to loose the thread of your discussion."[36]

Tolstoy did not agree with this advice and answered Chertkov:

"The epigraphs, I think, are better left as they are. I, when I read the articles with the long epigraphs, can pass them up and then read them."[37]

Chertkov objected, joking that this vocation of Tolstoy appears just as the argument supporting the idea of placing epigraphs separately but Tolstoy remained with his opinion, and stipulating that during publication of the article in magazines, if the editors are not in agreement to publish excerpts from other authors, it is possible to make concessions, wrote Chertkov:

"On the placement of epigraphs alone, I don't agree. It seems to me that this will totally deprive the epigraphs of their meaning. I am sorry I don't agree with you, but add, that if you do this, however, the way you want, then I wouldn't be very distressed."[38]

Chertkov, already in his last letter, convincing Tolstoy to isolate the epigraphs from the text of the article, made a proviso, that, it is understood; fulfilled his desire with pedantic accuracy. He did not object concerning this, and the epigraphs remained in those places where Tolstoy put them.

Chertkov himself translated *"Bethink Yourselves"* into English and organized simultaneous appearance of this article in magazines in England, France and Germany and, following that, appeared in numerous individual publications in Europe and America.

The article hurt the feelings of people with a patriotic mood and Tolstoy wrote about this to Chertkov:

"I receive bitter letters for the article now: and it hurts me because I feel guilty. It is not allowed to devote oneself to indignation, it shouldn't be, and it should contain meek reasoning, persuasiveness. And I don't have this. And I feel guilty."[39]

Chertkov answered Tolstoy on this, that completely different comments on this article reach him – it made a big impression on a lot of people – and that no other of Tolstoy's writings during this time had such an impact. At the same time Chertkov did not agree with those reproaches, which Tolstoy made to himself about the tone of the article "Bethink Yourselves" and wrote him concerning this:

"There are cases, like in a fire, when it is necessary to shout in full voice, and this, your appeal was such a cry. And I, glancing from here, on the side, see how much it woke up the whole world and how thankful to you are those, whose voices are not sufficiently loud that they would not carry widely. If one could exude passions on the good side and ability to excite and become indignant (not against people, but against evil) from life, then life, in all relations, would lose in many senses. This does not interfere with that which has its own place and purpose in addition, and expression of ideas more peaceful, contemplative and common, in other words, that are not called forth by the impression of individual cases of horrible human disaster. These more peaceful expressions of thought, could, indeed, demand a more highly spiritual development and more balanced equilibrium between thought and feeling. Therefore they are used more rarely."[40]

Tolstoy at this time thought a lot about such work, which would give him the possibility to concentrate on those "peaceful, contemplative and common thoughts" which Chertkov wrote about.

Already in the first days of January 1904 he begins to work on the fulfillment of his old project – create the *Cycle of Reading*, in which ideas about questions of religion and ethics were gathered, taken from various sources and beside that, would be given suitable material for reading in the form of small artistic tales.

The Russo-Japanese war and the writing of the article "Bethink Yourselves" pushed this work aside. But having finished this article, Tolstoy returns to the *Cycle of Reading*, and makes an entry in his diary:

"The war worries me, but less because steam went to work."[41]

In the fall of 1904 Tolstoy works intensely on the *Cycle of Reading* and writes to Chertkov:

"I was very intensely busy with the *Cycle of Reading*, and now, it seems, that everything came out and what was left in my head is trash and I can't write anything and am glad because I am not distressed by this."[42]

In this letter he asks Chertkov to send him material for the *Cycle of Reading*, from the "Index" on which Chertkov worked together with his wife and coworkers over the period of many years, copying out thoughts of Tolstoy from all of his writings and assembling them in systematic order:

"I will send you everything when it is ready and will still ask you to edit, change, exclude", adds Tolstoy.

For Chertkov, this work of Tolstoy could be especially interesting, since he himself, despite the fact that the string of publishing matters take a lot of his time, continues to think intensely about those themes which interest Tolstoy.

Sometimes in one and the same letter Chertkov writes about this or that matter and about those common questions that occupy him at this time. So, for example, in the letter of 2 June, 1904 Chertkov writes about the fact that he is putting the epigraphs for the article "*Bethink Yourselves*" just as Tolstoy wants and at this time tells him about his arguments with the Englishman Briggs about freedom of will: Briggs' thoughts are completely negative toward free will, and Chertkov conceived them as incorrect, since, if one carries them to the end, they can lead to denial of the responsibility to fulfill goals in one's life and direct life's path in the determined direction.

After a short time, Chertkov again returns to this question and in two long letters from the 1st and 22nd November, tells how he gradually formed views on freedom of will.

In the first of these letters, Chertkov wrote:

"As I already somehow wrote you, I remember, that many years ago, during one of your conversations with a few of our fellow-thinkers, in which free will was accepted as an undoubted fact, I, partly because I put much thought into this question earlier, partly because the general unquestioning agreement with you and your co-conversationalists annoyed me – I noticed before leaving you that "generally speaking, free will doesn't exist at all." You looked at me attentively, were quiet and during my departure you told me softly and very seriously that "no, we are free and that you yourself recognize this", or something like that. I remember my mixed-up feeling after this, on one side, that you could never prove our free will if I began to object to you, but on the other side, that you, in essence, were right, for I indeed in my soul believed in the possibility of free will and I could not live without this recognition."

Further, taking and comparing Tolstoy's thoughts on this theme, expressed in the *Kingdom of God* and in his diaries, Chertkov expressed his conviction that without the recognition of free will the spiritual life of a person would come to random and irresponsible actions.

Tolstoy, busy at this time with work on the *Cycle of Reading*, briefly responds to Chertkov's letter, expressing agreement with his views:

"Concerning free will, I think your thoughts are justified but their expression is too complicated. They should be presented in a more simple form, like they do in algebra with equations, but the equation itself I think is correct."[43]

And further, telling about his work on the *Cycle of Reading*, Tolstoy lists those sections on which he would like to receive material for this book from the "Index" which Chertkov compiled.

Work on the *Cycle of Reading*, to which Tolstoy devoted time pleased him. He reluctantly tore himself away from it when life urgently demanded a response to current themes. Among them, in the beginning of 1905, Tolstoy began to be questioned from various sides about how he related to current events.

In January 1905 Tolstoy expressed his opinion in a small article "About the Social Movement in Russia" and, sending the manuscript to Chertkov wrote:

"It was unpleasant for me to write, because in it is much unsaid, such that I am placing in a long article about this subject. And now, sending it out, it seems to me that it is weak and better not to publish it. If you agree with this, then don't do it. If you will publish it, then type it as is. Don't send it back to me. There is not enough time and I would like to say more, it seems to me, more important. Time is very exciting and more than ever it is necessary not to give into hypnosis of the masses, and only with great energy, not distracting, do that which you did, if you consider, that which you did must be done."[44]

And in one of the following letters Tolstoy writes that he finished the above-mentioned "big article" – "*The Only Thing Is Needful*". At the same time he outlined an extensive plan of the works that he wanted to devote his strength:

"I buried myself in begun projects. To finish them is apparently impossible and there is only one exit from these beginnings – to die. But it is understood, as peasants say about good workers to die with a hammer in hand. Started projects: *Cycle of Reading*, stories for it – wrote one and didn't finish. By the way, I wrote the preface to Lamen, Pascal, Chelcicky and the "Teachings of the 12 Apostles". I chose from Chelcicky eight parts for the week's reading. All this, probably will not go in Russia but may be published abroad.

"The other work – this is an account of faith – simple, clear, popular, childlike. I work on this and it is very pleasant and useful for me, but as of yet, no results. I think sometimes that I don't have the strength for this. I will try, but if I fail someone else will do that. But it is necessary, necessary, necessary.

"The third work – my recollections, which I just begun. The fourth work – the *Cycle of Reading*, simple and understandable for children and people. The fourth work, continually occupying my thoughts – this is the account of my philosophical world-outlook. This I write excerpts of in my diary. Fifth – the main work – this is the improvement (of myself), my filth, weakness. This is all the work, necessarily which I recognize, important work, but there is still work and plans for work superficial for my satisfaction – these are old plans for artistic things, which again to write, and which to correct, and beside that articles on the topic of the day, like now begun with me about defenders of the people, and about the lie of property ownership and Henry George. Here I am boasting. Excuse me. This is your improper esteem of my activities carried to this deception. In healthy moments I remember that the time of departure, time to pack the suitcases, and the thing is only that the remaining days to live as God wants."[45]

230

Chertkov received this letter at the time when he faced a new prospective: the possibility arose to come to Russia and to see Tolstoy. Not long before, taking into consideration that the conditions in Russia changed somewhat, Chertkov decided to make an attempt to receive permission to go to Russia for three weeks for a meeting with his mother and with Tolstoy.

E.I. Chertkova decided to appeal to the tsar with a letter, asking permission for her son to come to Russia for three weeks. Chertkov, striving to get permission to go to Russia, nonetheless, considered it necessary to underline that he does not find it possible to ask for this permission, as mercy from the court, and doesn't take upon himself any kind of obligation concerning his conduct in the future.

He wrote about this to his mother:

"I thank you very, very much for your participation. Concerning your letter about me I totally understand, that you, with your point of view, used the word "mercy", but it could be unpleasant for me if the person to whom the letter was written, thinks, that I also look at this as "mercy". I don't consider this charity, but a temporary break from the cruel and morally illegal violence. It is exactly the same concerning my conduct, I can only say, that the *goal* of my request is not the desire to propagandize, but only to have rendezvous, but I can't give any promises, leaving myself full freedom to act, not binding decidedly to any restrictions. Therefore, I doubt success. But, if there will be success, then I hope very much, that it comes not on the basis of this misunderstanding."[46]

Despite Chertkov's expectation of permission for his travel to Russia to be given, there were a few provisos.

Chertkov wrote about this to Tolstoy:

"Dear friend, Lev Nikolaevich, I am writing only a few words to you, to announce that I received "permission" to visit Russia for three weeks, so as to see you at Yasnaya Polyana and mother in Petersburg. There is no necessity to express to you in words what joy it will be for me to have a personal meeting with you, if God allows, it will consist, especially to judge how this permission was given, discovering that I hardly will receive permission overall to return to Russia to live during my current activities: firstly, the period for arrival in Russia begins *not earlier* than the 1st of June, in view of anticipated disorderliness; secondly, I am allowed to stay *only* at your house and in Petersburg, thirdly, categorically insist that my stay in Russia not exceed three weeks. All this of course, is very flattering, although, unfortunately, totally not deserved, but at the same time discloses that it is not worth thinking about the complete return to Russia for the meantime. And therefore I am all the more happy about the opportunity to see you one more time face to face in this life. And so, I hope to visit you in June."[47]

Tolstoy, immediately after receiving this letter, answered him with a few lines:

"I, as if I had a premonition, having heard nothing about your actions for the trip to Russia, that I will see you. Now maybe we will meet. This will be a great joy for me."[48]

In the second half of May, Chertkov arrived in Russia and having been a few days in Petersburg, arrived at Yasnaya Polyana. He stayed there over a week and after his departure, Tolstoy wrote in his diary:

"On the third, Chertkov left. My relations with him were beyond expectation."[49]

The joyful mood that Tolstoy experienced during Chertkov's stay at Yasnaya Polyana was all the more strong in that Sofia Andreyevna met Chertkov politely and hospitably.

For the last few years before Chertkov's arrival, Tolstoy wrote and published almost exclusively those works which could not appear in Russia and by his wife, and the obligation that he send his manuscripts to Chertkov for publication abroad, could not but cause some kind of loss to her publishing. At the same time, for the past seven years of Chertkov's exile from Russia, naturally, to a considerable degree smoothed over that friction that was earlier felt between them. And in response to the letter in which Chertkov thanked her for the hospitality, Sofia Andreyevna wrote him:

"Your arrival in Russia and your stay with us was a real sincere holiday, unfortunately too short. It was joyful for me to see the happy face of Lev Nikolaevich when he looked at you and talked to you. And all of us, all throughout your stay in our house were unusually pleasant and joyful."[50]

232

Chertkov, on his behalf, described the same experience at the time of the meeting with Tolstoy in one of his letters to him after his return to England:

"How good and dear are those spiritual relations which unite us: in the air of such relations everything earthly, everything that is able to be expressed in words and that it is possible not to exceed to express, - all this – is secondary, but the main thing that unites us into one is our true lives, it does not need negotiations and discussions, but *there is* something in both of us, not needing to be expressed. And the last, especially clear thing revealed to me during our last meeting, when after so many years of separation, it seemed, it was a lot, about which to negotiate and came to an agreement, and meanwhile our relations continued, as if we only yesterday saw each other and will see each other again tomorrow."[51]

And in the first letter after his departure from Yasnaya Polyana, Chertkov also writes about the string of matters tied to publishing Tolstoy's works, as he had written before his trip to Russia. He announces that being in Moscow, en route to Petersburg, tried to provide for the publication of Tolstoy's new article "Great Sin" in *Russian Thought* without editorial permit, having negotiated this with N.V. Davydov, in the absence of the magazine's editor V.A. Goltsev.

"I went to Davydov's yesterday on the way to the train station. Goltsev, it turned out, is not in Moscow now. But I explained to Davydov how important it is not to make such cuts in the Russian edition which could add a denunciatory side to the one-sided character and strengthen the impression, that you began to relate to the government less negatively, than to the liberal's evil. He completely agreed with me and I decided to grant him control of Goltsev's handling of your article, who, as publisher, easily can make too many compromises for the sake of the possibility to put your article is his magazine."[52]

Having returned to England, Chertkov immediately takes on editing work, gives the article "Great Sin" for typesetting of individual publication in Russian and already on 8 July of the new style, sends proofs for correction to Tolstoy indicating a few ideas in need of clearer formulation in order to avoid misunderstanding. At the same time he edits the translation of this article in English, in order to put it into the newspaper *Times*, and, having finished this work, begins to edit the English translation of Tolstoy's article "The One Thing Is Needful".

Tolstoy, having returned the corrected proofs of the article "Great Sin", writes Chertkov about the translation and publication of others of his past works and tells about his writings:

"I received a letter from Crosby with the request to write the preface of his article about Shakespeare and decided to publish my article. Let it be in the form of a preface. At the same time – translate and publish "Divinity and Humanity". I hope this won't be bad. I send you the preface to the "Great Sin". At the same time, the work goes poorly, it seems, there is a lot I can and want to do and nothing comes of it. But events compel, demand an answer to them. Perhaps, I am mistaken, but it seems such."[53]

Chertkov, in his turn, tells about his activities. In a long letter begun on the 12th and finished on the 28th of August, Chertkov reports to Tolstoy:

"All this past time I was primarily busy with the translation and correction of your articles – the work is very enjoyable, although rather intense. I am very glad that these articles are all without exception, accepted in the *Times* and that they, following this, receive immediate worldwide dissemination. Yesterday I was completely surprised, having received an answer from the editor of the *Times* that he accepts "The One Thing Is Needful", which appears simultaneously in different countries on 29 and 31 August of the new style."

Continuing this letter after a break, Chertkov wrote:

"Today is the 28th. It means that I am writing this letter for more than two weeks. Various current troubles distracted me, by the way, the arrival of 180 Dukhobors from Yakutsk, for whom we had to prepare everything. I went to meet them in London and tomorrow I will go with Dimochka to take them to Liverpool. Several of them were our guests here. Now Olhovic, with his family and relatives are with them, having arrived from Russia on their own. In addition to them, individual Dukhobors from the Caucuses joined this party and a Dukhobor woman with a child stranded with us following an eye sickness. Needless to say, we have noticeably formed a real resettlement point, and this demands extensive and attentive correspondence and effort which swallows up much time."

Answering this letter, Tolstoy wrote Chertkov:

"I often think about that special fortune which befell my fate to have a friend and comrade such as you. One of the last times, how you worked for our (I want to think that its not our, but God's) case: my two articles, 180 Dukhobors, your future work. But yes, these accounts will be settled without us. I only want to say that I am glad and how glad I am that you are."[54]

Having received a letter from Tolstoy that he finds it possible to publish his article *"About Shakespeare and About Drama"* and his story "Divinity and Humanity", Chertkov begins to translate the article about Shakespeare and hands over the story "Divinity and Humanity" for typesetting. At the same time a few places in the story prompts Chertkov's critical observations, and, as always, he shares them with Tolstoy. Sending proofs of this story to Tolstoy, Chertkov writes:

"I am sending you the corrections of "Divinity and Humanity". Although I am not sure if this will please you, you will find my notes in the margins in pencil, expressing a few of our doubts, demanding your decision. If you want to make big changes in the account, then for God's sake, don't be shy, fearing to cause us extra work. Our publishing house exists mainly for the publication of your writings and it would be simply vexing if you were shyer with us, than your whole life with the commercial publishing houses. We will be glad, if it is necessary, to compile everything anew, although this thing seems to us superb just as it is."[55]

Tolstoy, as always, having read his story in proofs began again to work on it and wrote about this to Chertkov:

"I received your letter, dear friend, and the corrections of "Divinity and Humanity". I am afraid that I will make this a big bother for you, but have begun to read it, was horrified that the main part – Svetlogub's last hours – are disgustingly stupid. Thank you for sending this. To publish this would not only have been shameful, but also a pity to lose a chance to express much that is necessary. I am trying and intend to do this. I haven't done this yet because I have been busy."[56]

After two and a half weeks Tolstoy writes that he has added his corrections to the story, gave it out to be rewritten and thinks to quickly send out the manuscript. But then he again and again sets to work. Only after two months does he return the story and writes Chertkov:

"I changed and corrected so much of "Divinity and Humanity" that I cannot and will not any more. It is being rewritten and tomorrow sent to you."[57]

In the fall of 1905 Chertkov undertakes a few new steps toward systematic publication of Tolstoy's works in foreign languages. Organized by him a few years before, the publishing house *"Free Age Press"*, with the goal of publication of Tolstoy's writings as cheaply priced as possible had made good progress. The printing house even released, considerable for it's size – "What Do I Believe", "What To Do?", "About Life", "The Kingdom of God Is Within You", pricing them at 6 pence; or nearly 25 kopeks per copy. These publications were sold rather quickly, but their extremely low price resulted in almost total exhaustion of financial means of the firm.

In order to save the publishing house from liquidation, Chertkov intended to use the 1st editions of Tolstoy's new works for providing support to *"Free Age Press"* and planned a few measures toward this goal.

Chertkov, in a letter of 12 October 1905 wrote Tolstoy in detail about his plans. Tolstoy hurried to answer him in full agreement:

"The only thing that bothers me is that you wrote so much about the project and little or almost nothing about yourself. For me there is not and cannot be doubt that what you do, - is good, and in all these matters I am only ashamed that I unintentionally am the cause of worry and am afraid that I am often difficult for you. And many times, recollecting about this only more lively feel my gratitude to you."[58]

Following this Chertkovs begins a few measures so that Tolstoy's works, previously published abroad, could be published in Russia as possible more accurately and truthfully.

An abrupt weakening of the censure as a result of the 1905 Revolution allowed various publishing houses to begin reprinting Tolstoy's works in Russia, earlier banned and published abroad, moreover, they sometimes used those not published by Chertkov, but others, less accurate, for example, the Geneva book publisher's M.K. Elpidin. The additions that could have been restored from Tolstoy's manuscripts had not been taken into consideration and also certain parts of Tolstoy's text were often cut out for one reason or another.

In relation to this Chertkov decided to offer all Russian publishers to appeal to him for the approved text of Tolstoy's works, which they intended to republish and wrote Tolstoy concerning this:

"I, it is understood, would take the responsibility upon myself to provide every Russian publisher appealing to me with accurate copies of your writings, published already, and at the same time, would use all my influence so that the reading public not be misled concerning the common spirit and overall character of your writings when some part of a text is removed for censorship's sake without mentioning it."[59]

The concessions that the government was forced to make after the general strikes of October 1905 opened the possibility for Chertkov to transfer his activities to Russia. Tolstoy stated his point of view on current events in the article "End of the Century", sends the manuscript to Chertkov and at that time asks about his future plans:

"Today I again reviewed the article, made changes in it and additions and send it to you simultaneously with this letter, or the day after. This article, as you will see, has, besides internal meaning, already is timely and it is desirous to release it as soon as possible. I won't be disappointed by the results that it may have, but, however, think that at least a few people, reading it, will start to think about what they are doing and what is necessary to do. Now it is possible to publish in Russia and I am asked for text, but I hurried to send it to you and would like you to handle it, just as with all the others before. If I decide to publish here, then I will tell you beforehand.

The change in censure and freedom from censure will affect your life and activities. What do you think and what are you starting?"[60]

Chertkov takes measures for simultaneous publication of the article "End of the Century" in various countries, continues to carry on current work and at the same time thinks about his return to Russia. In answer to Tolstoy's question, Chertkov announces that he and Anna Konstantinovna consider it necessary to return to Russia in order to continue their work in publishing and disseminating Tolstoy's works. They planned, if events didn't interfere, to return to Russia in the spring and then settle in Finland because there, it will be, probably, more peaceful to live and work and they even plan to transfer there their printing house in time, since censorship conditions probably will be more favorable than in Russia.

At the same time, the Chertkovs hoped that, settling in Finland, they would be able to spend the summer in the surroundings of Yasnaya Polyana and be, in that case, in direct contact with Tolstoy.

In March 1906 Chertkov received notification that "by virtue of the order from 21 October 1905", he can return to Russia.

Chertkov planned, as he already wrote about this, to come to Russia with his family that summer, and, after living in Petersburg and close to Yasnaya Polyana, to settle for the winter in Finland. But the unhealthy condition of his wife did not allow Chertkov to fulfill this plan, and, finally, he decided to go to Russia alone at first, in order to return there with his family the following year.

In expectation of a personal meeting between Tolstoy and Chertkov in the first half of 1906, they wrote each other comparatively little, limiting for the most part letters about the string of publishing matters.

Tolstoy himself mentioned this in one of his letters:

"Its such a pity to me that we correspond only about matters, that is to say, about triviality."[61]

Chertkov writes him in response:

"I also feel that it is a pity that we only correspond "about business", and I hope that I just manage a little bit more to write to you "from the soul"... Now about matters: By the way, about the fact that you call them "triviality" I completely understand that *you* look at the whole insignificant external mechanism of publishing and disseminating your writings this way. For you, the serious, important side of the work – is to express your thoughts in the best way possible. And when they are formed on paper, the rest of it, how they are spread among people, – is not important and the details of it – trivialities. But for *me*, everything that is concerned with the publication of your writings, cannot be triviality, because this is one of the most important matters in my life, one of the services befallen on me to God and people. Therefore, though I am sorry that "business" correspondence with you, so often obstructs the road for more sincere exchange of thought, nonetheless, I consider my obligation to devote to these business matters as much attention and time as necessary so that the business goes successfully and correctly."[62]

In June Chertkov announced to Tolstoy that he plans to come to Yasnaya Polyana in the coming month.

Answering this letter Tolstoy wrote:

"Now I am very, very glad for your arrival and will count the days. Sofia Andreyevna is also waiting for you with sincerity and assigned a room for you in the wing. Everything will be comfortable."[63]

Chertkov arrived at Yasnaya Polyana on 27 July and left in the first days of August. Tolstoy noted his arrival in an entry in his diary:

"Chertkov is here and everything is pleasant for me."[64]

Maria Lvovna, visiting Yasnaya Polyana in the first days after Chertkov's arrival, wrote to Tatiana Lvovna:

"I am very sorry that you weren't with me at Yasnaya. It was very pleasant there. Papasha is healthy and cheerful, Chertkov is very nice, Sasha is very active and happy, mama, although she constantly has chest pain, runs all day for mushrooms in glasses and dirty aprons and everyone in good relations."[65]

Tolstoy, together with Chertkov, having visited Maria Lvovna in Pirogovo, where she lived at this time with her husband, wrote in his diary:

"At this time Chertkov arrived. I went with him to Masha's. I found Chertkov very pleasant, but I am afraid he has too high an opinion of me."[66]

Chertkov, on his side, wrote his mother that everyone met him very hospitably and amicably and that he feels himself pleasant at Yasnaya Polyana.

Chertkov found Tolstoy at that time, that he worked a lot, in particular finished his article "About the Meaning of the Russian Revolution", with a draft manuscript that Chertkov became acquainted with at Yasnaya Polyana. In one of his letters, written soon after Chertkov's return to England, Tolstoy summed up his work and wrote about thoughts which occupied him:

"As you probably know, I wrote a lot at this time: I finished the article "About the Revolution"[67], wrote about Henry George, preface to "Social Problems"[68], and the letter to a Chinaman[69], with which I am troubling you. If it isn't worth it and there is no one to translate it, then I will send it through the consul in Russian. And, as always happens with me, during the end of a work which has taken a long time, am undecided what to take on: I begin a new artistic work and drop it, I want to write "Recollections" and a new "Cycle of Reading", and mainly want to understand, in the simplest possible terms, what life is: what it is and how it should be lived. I only think about this in the last few days."[70]

This work on his writings and in his thoughts about life-understanding, which Tolstoy continually writes about in his diary, is not interrupted in him at this time, even in the most difficult moments.

In September 1906, Sofia Andreyevna endures a serious illness and professor Snegirev, summoned to Yasnaya Polyana, performed an operation on her, while Tolstoy hopes for a favorable outcome of the illness. He thinks with worry about the outcome of the operation, and, leaving at this time from home for the neighboring forest, intensely waits there for news that his daughter must bring him.

And all that day, not only does he put down his thoughts in his diary, but also makes notes about his preface to the book about Henry George,

In November Tolstoy had to experience a difficult ordeal: after a few days of illness with pneumonia, his daughter Maria Lvovna died. As he did during the days of Sofia Andreyevna's illness, he continued to work – thinking about life and death and writing his thoughts in his diary.

The day before Maria Lvovna's death, Tolstoy wrote Chertkov:

"She has lobar pneumonia, today is the 8th day and she is very, very bad. Her death, selfish for me, although she is my best friend of all those close to me, is not horrible and pitiful – it is not long before I have to live without her, but simply, not rationally, I feel sorry for her. She should be, for her years wanting to live, – and sorry simply for her suffering, – hers and those close. It is a pity and unpleasant these futile efforts of treatment to prolong life. But death is all the more and more, as in the past, become close to me, not terrifying, natural, necessary and so not opposing life, but bound with it as if in continuance, that to struggle with it is natural only in animal instinct and not reason. And therefore various reasonable, unreasonable and clever struggles with it, like medicine, unpleasant, not good.

There is much I want to write and will write certainly after, but now will only answer to the points in your letter:

"About Shakespeare" that Sytin[71] has, I remember, understand and approve. I am sorry that I forgot about "Divinity and Humanity" and put in "Cycle of Reading". "About Shakespeare" I received two sympathetic letters from England from Englishmen already, which were pleasing to me, and nasty swearwords from Russian readers, which also for me, were not without pleasantness. Did you write the article about Nietzsche? This is always useful and you can do this well, since you begin on that point of view with which an error is obviously seen. The only thing necessary – to forgive, not be angry, not reproach, but have pity, as we have pity on a sick person, comparing him with healthy ones. Pity for the person deprived of good in spiritual life, pity is more characteristic. It is strange for you to hear such words from me, when I many times, almost always, backed down from this rule in the sharpest way. Yes, but the person grows and the older the quicker. You don't believe how much has been opened for me of my badness in the past. Often I have to give and send my last writings, requested, and I almost always hesitate to send a lot, almost all, recollecting those unpleasant feelings, cruel condemnations which were expressed there. Only a very few are free from them. I would like to put an end to everything in the past and in the short time that remains, start again, less unpleasantly."

A postscript was added at the end of the letter:

"I wrote this letter this morning, and now is 1 am, Masha passed away. I still cannot appreciate the whole loss."[72]

A week after her death, Sofia Andreyevna, in a letter to her sister, T.A. Kuzminskaya, having described in detail the last days of Maria Lvovna's life, wrote about Tolstoy:

"I do not know what Lyovochka is experiencing. On the exterior he is peaceful, busy as before with his writings, walks, goes horseback riding, and even plays vint these days. Of all the children, Masha loved *him* the most and in her we lose that sincere support in which she was always prepared to help, sympathize with anything more than anything else that concerned her father."[73]

But her death did not pass without a trace for Tolstoy. He experienced that feeling of closeness of the end of his life and this mood found reflection in his letter to Chertkov, written a month after Maria Lvovna's death. Tolstoy, himself enduring a small bout of influenza, wrote Chertkov in response to his sympathetic letter concerning Maria Lvovna's death:

"Thank you, dear friend, for your letter. I did not answer for a long time because I was sick and now am still weak. But in spirit I am so serious, so good, like it never was before. It is strange to feel, that only on the day before death, you begin to live freely, freely for yourself, for God, but not for people."[74]

And even more precisely this mood was expressed in entries, made by Tolstoy, in his diary three days before Maria Lvovna's death:

"Masha seriously worries me. I love her very, very much. Yes I would like to put a dividing line under all my past life and begin a new short, but purer epilogue."[75]

IX
The Last Years

The last years of Tolstoy's life at Yasnaya Polyana, with the exception of a few months before his departure from home, externally differed little from the past. As then, every day after breakfast he takes a small solitary stroll, puts his thoughts in his diary, works on his manuscripts, and the second part of the day converses with those arriving to see him, reads and answers letters.

But at the same time these years of Tolstoy's life have their own peculiarities: much, having been noted already earlier, are revealed with great poignancy, approaching death, which he feels, is seen in entries in his diaries, his letters and in some actions.

Despite the fact that Tolstoy, as before, was stronger and firmer than the majority of people his age, he continues to experience a gradual decrease in strength. This sensation produces in him the same mood of special concentration on his internal life that was reflected in his diary during the time of Maria Lvovna's illness and in the letter to Chertkov after her death.

In August 1907 Tolstoy writes in his diary:

"I feel sizeable weakness of everything, especially memory, but in spirit am very, very good."[1]

In the final years Tolstoy experiences almost total memory loss a few times, and although usually these lapses subside in a few hours, they regardless call in him every time thoughts about the nearness of the end. He writes new articles, from time to time considers projects for artistic works, which he partially accomplishes, but many times notes in his diary and in his letters to Chertkov, that he does not feel himself lacking in strength necessary for artistic creation. And remembering an overheard conversation of two peasants, when the young peasant called the old man to bathe, and received the answer – "I already swam off" – Tolstoy loves to say about himself:

"I already swam off".

He continues to write his articles, but devotes especially a lot of time to work demanding less intense creative strength and at the same time widely reflecting on his life-understanding: the gathering and distribution of material for a new publication of the "Cycle of Reading", for the book of thoughts "For Everyday" and for the 31st release of the series "Life's Path" on which he worked a lot in 1910.

In the last years of Tolstoy's life the flow of letters increased at Yasnaya Polyana, and Tolstoy continuously answers the most varied questions.

People wrote him, it would seem, having little in common between themselves – from the barely literate peasant who tells him about his search for faith, or students asking him "how to live" or "what to read" and finishing with such leaders and writers as Gandhi or Bernard Shaw. They ask his advice on family matters, they want to find out his opinion on the upbringing of children, they send him their works for his judgment, finally, appealing to him with the request for material help, despite the fact that he gave up his own property a long time ago. In 1910, Tolstoy receives more than 30 letters a day and often answers 10-12 letters, either leaving the small inscription on the envelope of the received letter which is put as the basis of the answer, written under his instruction, or personally answering letters, which sometimes turned into a small article. This relation with people leaves Tolstoy often unpleasant episodes – often receives empty letters, not deserving of time lost on their reading, but there are many which are received which he reads with interest and joy.

Despite the fact that Tolstoy's external life, it would seem, goes well in these years, in reality, as his diaries show, much depresses him. These difficult emotions that he had to experience earlier not only did not diminish in the course of time but also are made sharper and sharper until, finally, in 1910 his life at Yasnaya Polyana becomes to a high degree burdensome.

Tolstoy earlier experienced the contradiction between his convictions and all the conditions of the Yasnaya Polyana estate with difficulty.

After the Revolution of 1905-1906 the relations between the peasants and landowners became strained, even there, where there were no agrarian revolts and this was noted at Yasnaya Polyana. In his diary Tolstoy noted the change that happened at the time: "The Revolution made the Russian people see suddenly the unfairness of their condition. The tale of the tsar in new dress – the child who told it like it is, that the tsar is nude, was the revolution."[2] And first of all it became clear in relations of the peasants toward the landowner's property.

Sofia Andreyevna, all the time lived in fear for her property and ready to protect it by any measure, asks that two police constables be sent to Yasnaya Polyana, one of them who lives on the estate until 1909, when other estates of the Tula region no longer kept constables in government service.

In November 1907 Sofia Andreyevna writes about the constables to T.A. Kuzminskaya:

"We now have two constables continually living with us – armed – one sleeps in the house. They go around the forest and the whole estate, asking those walking around for their documents and searching if they are armed."[3]

In another letter – 27 July 1908 – tells about her landowner's economy and again writes about the constables:

"It is fortunate, that you even have leisure time to write. And I am like boiling in tar. I changed the constables; I suffered with collecting money for mowing, every kopek I received myself and for mowing brought me 1400 rubles this year, and for the garden, 1200, so that I can maintain Yasnaya Polyana this year without additional payments, or I would have to add. For the rent of the land I also receive 1400 rubles."

But despite the presence of the constables on the landlord's estate, it was not without danger, and the same letter reports to Tatiana Andreyevna:

"These days they already robbed the wing: mattresses, lamps, curtains and the like, and still cut out honey from the beehive. To live in the countryside in Russia became intolerable. And the constables do not help at all."

When the constables finally leave, Sofia Andreyevna hires a mounted Circassian, who, guarding the forest, often beat the peasants coming onto the landlord's land, and Tolstoy had to listen to complaints of the victims who could not understand his words that he is not the lord of Yasnaya Polyana since he gave up all his property a long time ago, having given it to his family.

Animosity grows among the peasants and they don't always consider it necessary to hide it. In the summer of 1909, Tolstoy tells A.B. Goldenweiser that he heard how an old woman from whom a Yasnaya Polyana manager demanded payment of money or working off the damage, walks by the estate and, seeing the Tolstoy family eating breakfast, screamed:

"Eh, devils guzzle here!"[4]

Tolstoy makes an entry in his diary for June 10, 1907:

"I suffer more and more, almost physically, from inequality – of wealth and of the extravagances of our life amidst this poverty; and I can't reduce this disparity. Therein lies the secret tragedy of my life."

In one of his letters to Chertkov, Tolstoy, as if summing up his experiences, writes:

"Two things from different sides all the more and more have influence on me. On the side joy – this is all the more telling in letters and personal meetings – people coming together with us toward one goal, toward the approach to love, to God. The joy is not only that I, although a little, took part in this (this is foolish joy), but that we are not alone, and, going toward love, love each other. (This is something I write nonsense but with you it is possible to write stupid, you understand it as though it was not stupidity). The unpleasant side, all the more and more, to my embarrassment, tortures me, this is that environment – those conditions in which I live, especially land, this enslavement of people by means of landed property, in which, although indirectly and against will, suffering, but participate. Never did I feel about the sin of peasant's serfdom in 1/100 as sick, as I feel this sin."[5]

From time to time Tolstoy attempts to talk to Sofia Andreyevna concerning one or another of her measures for guarding the estate, but these conversations leave only a difficult and bad taste and didn't bring any kind of results. Sofia Andreyevna's character in former times unrestrained and capable of sharp and nasty outbursts, often setting up difficult scenes, when the matter concerned the defense of the interests of her family, as she understood them, – didn't soften with years.

Formerly, Sofia Andreyevna was surrounded by a large family and after every outburst of irritation sooner went into the usual circle of routine chores and worry about the children, demanding her direct participation. Now the children were grown and much changed in the Tolstoy home.

Tolstoy's son, Ilya Lvovich, wrote about this soon after his father's death:

"The children, all grown and living independently with families, moved aside on the second plan, the family factually fell apart."[6]

Sofia Andreyevna, instead of taking care of small children who sometimes fatigued but at the same time gave her joy, now was left with excessive persistent striving to preserve and widen her position, in order to leave as big an inheritance as possible for her sons and their families. This not only demanded guarding her estate rights but also making sure that the rights of ownership of Tolstoy's compositions would remain in the family.

Already in December 1897, Maria Lvovna told Tatiana Lvovna in a letter about how roughly Sofia Andreyevna demanded of Tolstoy the right to publish his new works in first edition in her publishing house, and asked in perplexity: "When will this be over, when mama calms down and begins to live?"[7]

At times, it seemed, that Sofia Andreyevna began to "calm down", but this impression turned out to be deceitful, and existence in the final year of Tolstoy's life at Yasnaya Polyana was made more distressing for him than at any time before.

The correspondence between Tolstoy and Chertkov during the last year of Tolstoy's life, with the exception of that period when Chertkov, living near Yasnaya Polyana, saw Tolstoy almost daily, continues its former intensity.

It was the same as in Tolstoy and Chertkov's initial acquaintance, their correspondence enveloped the whole circle of questions, which were close to them, beginning with thoughts about their life-understanding and ending with practical matters.

Letters about questions of faith as before occupy a rather sizeable place in their correspondence and in this sphere between Tolstoy and Chertkov exist complete agreement of opinion. In order to give some idea about letters of this order, one can take as examples small excerpts from the correspondence of Tolstoy and Chertkov on these themes.

In January 1907 Chertkov writes Tolstoy a letter in which he tells him about his relation toward prayers, and about how, in his opinion, that it is necessary to understand and explain to others the word "God":

"What joy this is, this ability of a person to find in himself God, splitting and contrasting this true eternal *I* to another one: small, insignificant, who has become conceited and grabs everything in his hands. I don't know how it is with you but my prayers usually start with such division of myself, and only after clearly recognizing and positioning these two "persons" inside myself, I can address one from the point of view of another and sustain a meaningful conversation in which my eternal I indicates my mistakes to me what I should do and, mainly, distract me from my base I into the heavenly area of light, reason, peace and joy... I think it would be a mistake to start with declaring God as something existing by Himself and demanding an absolute recognition; it is better to start with one's own "I" and to approach God common to everyone by the thread, which starts in myself, discovering not just a tie to but a *participation* in God. Speaking about the word "God" I would like to make *one more* addition to my book on revolution explaining why we keep using and can't stop using these words: "God," "religion." Because I know that for many these words are the obstacles – I am talking about those who would wish to understand but still unable, not about those who doesn't want to – those will not be satisfied by any explanations."

Having received this letter and the addition, made by Chertkov, for the article "About Revolution", written in 1904 and again reviewed for the second edition, Tolstoy wrote Chertkov:

"Nice, dear friend. I just received and read your letter and addition to the article "About Revolution". The feeling aroused in me, often excited in other instances (yesterday evening I read about Crosby and his relations toward me – not towards me, Lev Nikolaevich, but towards me, what's true within me), this feeling, especially strong when it was produced by your letter: why was this joy given to me? How did it happen that people love the same things as I do, and more than myself, and serve the same something which I feel to feeble to serve now? I couldn't make and corrections and observations for you to your addition. The only thing I would desire, that is have the possibility for greater dissemination, - but true dissemination in the souls of people – not in our power."[8]

In future letters Chertkov continues to share with Tolstoy his thoughts about God, finally sending him his notes about the word "God", which grew into a small article and should have been placed in the book "About Revolution", in the form of a special supplement.

Tolstoy, agreeing with Chertkov's thoughts, however, marked off places in the manuscript, which in his opinion were excessive, and notes these clauses, which, it seems to him, were not formulated accurately or well enough.

He writes about this to Chertkov:

"I received and read your letter about God, making notes. During the meeting, if there is one, I will tell you, but if not, than I will write if I will be alive.

The introduction and the thought itself are very good, but I don't like the form of expression, it doesn't correspond with the meaning of the subject. I always equally praised your writing, that I am glad for the chance to censure, to show in this my sincerity."[9]

In other letters, Tolstoy tells about himself and his projects. In the beginning of 1907 Tolstoy carries on at home studies with peasant children from Yasnaya Polyana with great interest while trying to state his life-understanding in suitable form for children.

He writes about this to Chertkov:

"I did not write for a long time and did not respond to your last letter because everything is swallowed up by study with the boys. I cannot boast. But I feel that, if God orders me to live still, then it might produce something useful. Everything is still in a chaotic condition, but the benefits in many aspects, which I feel from these relations, cannot be appreciated enough. It is clear to me that they are much smarter and better than I thought, and I am more stupid than I imagined. "Still wont be like children". In them a person is still seen, as someone who made him intended. He is already dirtied, but nevertheless sometimes you see in him all the beauty."[10]

249

In expectation of Chertkov's arrival, Tolstoy finds a home for them in the spring of 1907 close to Yasnaya Polyana, near the village of Yasenka, and, as in the summer of 1894, when Chertkov planned for the first time to spend the summer near Yasnaya Polyana, writes in detail about how he found them a place, expresses his views about the possible price of furnishing and remodeling. At the same time he writes that Sofia Andreyevna joyfully accepted the news of the Chertkov's arrival. But the thought of a prolonged stay of the Chertkovs near Yasnaya Polyana alarmed Sofia Andreyevna and she wrote her sister: "The Chertkovs are arriving soon to live at Yasenka. But little joy is expected from this."[11]

Having received the news that the Chertkovs arrived in Russia, Tolstoy telegraphed them in Moscow: "Inexpressibly glad. Give instructions. We are at your service."[12]

In his diary of July 20 Tolstoy makes an entry about the Chertkovs:

"The main thing – the Chertkovs. Joyful relations with them."

The Chertkovs lived in Yasenka until the middle of September. Tolstoy found himself at this time in such continual contact with them, as in those years when they spent the summer in Dyomenka before Chertkov's exile.

After Chertkov's departure, Tolstoy writes him in Moscow, where he had to stay with his family on the way to England:

"Strange and sad that you are not here …….. These points stand for everything that I think and feel about you, but I don't want to spoil it with words."[13]

In the first letter to Chertkov, addressed to England, Tolstoy writes to the whole family:

"Now I wrote a mountain of letters, dear, dear friends, Galya, Dima and Dimochka, and to you I write last. I write you last because it is necessary to think what to write, in order not to say something false, but to you I can write whatever comes out, you understand everything, whatever there is to understand, and excuse everything if there is nothing to understand or what's bad. Thank you for your letter from Moscow. It was very joyful for me... You are probably already home. Write. I have been very diligently working on a new "Cycle of Reading" and am roughly finished. Here Repin is painting

Sofia Andreyevna's and my portraits. This matter is empty, but I submit so as not to offend."

And at the end of the letter, Tolstoy, returning thoughtfully to the past summer, added:

"This summer was very, very good to us. Thank you for this, but I don't think about the future."[14]

In his letters to Chertkov after his return to England in 1907, Tolstoy, as always, keeps him in the loop of his work, announces about his work on the book "For Every Day", which he calls in his letters the new "Cycle of Reading" and writes about his health in general.

In the beginning of November Tolstoy writes Chertkov:

"I have only been busy all this time with the new "Cycle of Reading". I correct it, change it, and still am not finished. Today again I wrote chapters. As it always is, when I am busy with something, it seems, that it is the most important project."[15]

In the next letter Tolstoy writes Chertkov about himself:

"The older I get, the more physically weak, but I feel better and better. How I wish everyone such a blessing and how I am firmly convinced that everyone will receive it. So many people love me and how it has become easier for me to love people."[16]

In October 1907, Tolstoy's secretary N.N. Gusev was arrested. This arrest was especially unpleasant for Tolstoy because the charge against Gusev should more correctly have been brought against Tolstoy himself. During a search of Gusev's, a brochure was found, published in Russia, of Tolstoy's "The Only Thing Needful", where some excerpts, removed from the Russian edition by the censors and copied out by Gusev from the edition of "*Free Word*" done in England. Tolstoy gave sharp characteristics to Russian autocrats, beginning with Ivan the Terrible and ending with the "Dumb Hussar's Officer", Nicholas II.

The local authorities were at first prone to consider Gusev as the author of these excerpts. It demanded Tolstoy's interference, attesting to his authorship, and after prolonged efforts, Gusev was finally freed. Tolstoy resorted to the assistance of his acquaintance, Count D.A. Olsufyev, member of the government council, during this incident. In a letter to him Tolstoy mentioned, by the way, that he was sorry about the sharpness of the expressions that characterized the Russian Tsars.

Sometime before this Chertkov indicated to Tolstoy the sharpness of a few of these opinions: initially Tolstoy used words in this article not only abusive but unpublishable. Tolstoy agreed with Chertkov, and those expressions did not appear in print even in publications abroad, but the common thought of his opinion about the tsars remained unchanged. Now, having received from Tolstoy a copy of his letter to Count Olsufyev, Chertkov expressed apprehension that the regret of Tolstoy concerning the sharpness of his opinions about the tsars could leave the impression as though he retracted a few of his assertions under the influence of persecution of his fellow-thinkers. Chertkov wrote about this to Tolstoy:

"Allow me to candidly list for you these questions which confuse me: 1) Why the repentance for your harsh expressions about government representatives appeared only when one of your fellow-thinkers underwent persecution, that is, when happened that which you so desired and that should happen to each of us, your friends, if only we will fulfill our duty? 2) Why don't you express repentance for opinions, much more harsh, about other people, for example revolutionaries and liberals, who don't persecute your friends? 3) If revolutionaries could cause some kind of suffering for any of your fellow-thinkers for the spread of your writings in which you harshly and candidly express your opinion about them – revolutionaries –, then would this call on your side a declaration to revolutionaries that you repent from your harsh opinion of them? 4) It is a proper time to repent in front of people in your denunciatory opinions of them, when these people cause people close to us that same evil for which you denounce them?"[17]

Tolstoy, answering Chertkov, did not agree with his doubts:

"To all your questions," – wrote Tolstoy, – "I answer (please don't insist, don't argue) yes, yes, yes, repent, regret because then there was no reason to say that, which is offensive to a person, although he would be super-tsar. The same as I would repent if someone suffered because of my offensive words to them from revolutionaries I would repent even if they did not suffer. It is simply hurtful to me about Gusev and embarrassed with myself for unkind words. You know better than me, how everything is able to be said kindly and how this is more sincere; how it is not necessary and therefore ashamed..."

Further, having told Chertkov about the letter from Ikonnikov, locked up in jail for refusal of military service, Tolstoy wrote:

"What joy to live with your soul in people who lift you to the summit, on which they themselves are lifted. How much joy I have and everyday more and more. Yesterday was the barber from the small town of Sevsk in the Orlov Region. He was inflamed by that perceived truth and desire to go to preach it. Among these joys, you know my great and longstanding – I wont tell you the joy of my friendship, but my spiritual unity with you. And you want to argue with me, but for arguments it is necessary to have two, and I cannot argue with you because I know that we agree."[18]

In the following letters Tolstoy and Chertkov do not return to this theme. Both are busy with their next projects and from time to time report to one another about them.

In the winter of 1907-1908 the Chertkovs prepare for their final transfer to Russia, planned for the summer of 1908, finish their business in England and intensely push forward the compilation of "Index of Tolstoy's Thoughts", the outline of which they wanted to finish before their return to Russia. F.A. Strahov helped them in this work, having arrived in Russia with this goal, along with a few other people recopying sayings inserted into the "Index".

Tolstoy continues his work on the "Cycle of Reading" and the book "For Everyday". In February 1908, having received a letter from Chertkov with his observations concerning the work, Tolstoy writes him:

"I accept your observations on the "Cycle of Reading" as true and ask that you make them more. I cannot tell you how much joy it gives me this work on the "Cycle of Reading". I finished the corrections on the old "Cycle", I hope that it will be considerably better than the first. I did not receive anything from Sytin[19]. I also finished in rough form the new "Cycle of Reading", but am not touching it. I want to write about the situation of the Christian world – I even began. Only work is necessary, only it satisfies – this work is internal and that is farther and more. Many visit me, I write a lot, and try not to sin with these visitors and correspondents, but it works. But I don't despair."[20]

In the beginning of 1908 Chertkov came to Russia for a short time in order to prepare for his family's arrival and spent mid-January and the first days of March at Yasnaya Polyana. Tolstoy, as he did after Chertkov's previous, notes in his diary and in letters to Chertkov that relations with him were joyful.

After Chertkov's return to England in March 1908, Tolstoy, instead of writing him a letter, speaks to him in front of a phonograph, gifted not long before by Edison. Chertkov then could, having received this roll, hear Tolstoy's live speech:

"I want, although through the phonograph, to tell you a few words, my dear friend. Your visits always were for me joyful, but this one was especially dear to me as personal contact with you. My health is very good – physically and especially spiritually. Only now realize that which before seemed strange: that it is possible in old age to feel one longstanding gratitude for intense, increasing internal good."[21]

Despite the fact that Tolstoy's health continues to weaken and that in the spring of 1908 he twice, on March 2 and April 12, experiences a sharp loss of memory for several hours – he continues to work a lot and begins to write a new article – "The Law of Force and The Law of Love". In a letter, the beginning of which Tolstoy dictated into the phonograph, but the end wrote himself, he tells Chertkov about this article:

"My article, to my surprise, I like it and it progresses."

And in the postscript to this letter, Tolstoy adds:

"I want to add still that I am healthy, work and think. My anniversary, to my great relief was skipped. Very much work, both old and new "Cycle of Reading" (today I sent February and they have January), and on articles, and preparation of lessons for the children, and on letters, of which there are many."[22]

Having roughly finished his article, Tolstoy turns to different work, totally enveloping him. Daily newspapers at this time carry news about tens of death sentences which court-martials imposed. Tolstoy suffered deeply from these announcements and in May 1908 begins to write an article "I Cannot Be Quiet".

On June 1 Tolstoy dictates a letter to Chertkov:

"I am sending you, dear friend, a few pages, written by me about the current death penalties we have. This so tortures me that I cannot be calm, until I express all my feelings that are generated in me. I hope that you will help me put this, if it is possible, in Russian newspapers, or, in any case, abroad. I don't write you by hand, because today I feel very weak, and don't want to postpone the topic I am writing about. I am waiting for you with great impatience and love. I leave for you to decide about the double Chapter 5: discard or leave it in and then the next chapters – from 5 make 6 and so on."

The next day, sending this letter to Chertkov, Tolstoy writes that he asks him, if it will be necessary to include this or that correction into the manuscript and one more time underlines that he considers it necessary to publish the article as soon as possible:

"Please, if you can, publish it quickly. It is necessary for me, for my conscience."[23]

Chertkov, having received "I Cannot Be Quiet", quickly wrote Tolstoy, having made his usual few observations concerning specific parts of the article.

Tolstoy answered in a telegram:

"I totally approve the changes. Publish it soon. Tolstoy."[24]

The next day, having received his manuscript with Chertkov's corrections, Tolstoy wrote:

"I telegraphed you, dear friend, already knowing, that everything that you do, will be wonderful. Now I received the article and everything is not so, but better than I expected... If there were no Chertkov then it would be necessary to invent him. For me, in any case, for my pleasure – little, for that which I found out, greater good in total unity. If you find it necessary and safe, put in the small additions and corrections which Gusev sent you."[25]

In his diary Tolstoy made an entry about this article:

"Chertkov corrected it wonderfully."[26]

Chertkov takes measures so that the article "I Cannot Be Quiet" was published as soon as possible in Russia and abroad. On the 3rd of July 1908 the article appeared simultaneously in Russian and foreign languages, while in one, Germany, it was published in two hundred periodic publications.

During the second half of June, the Chertkovs, having returned to Russia, settled close to Yasnaya Polyana, acquiring an estate in Telyatinki. From this time until March 1909, when Chertkov was exiled from the Tula region, correspondence between Tolstoy and Chertkov was replaced by personal contact: for this period Tolstoy wrote Chertkov only a few small notes, with the exception of one letter, representing the certification of Chertkov's right to publish letters to Tolstoy from various people.

Living in Telyatinki does not directly contribute to publishing activities, but as before, persistently watched that Tolstoy's writings be published on those foundations which Tolstoy earlier established and would not be turned over as the publisher's property. At the same time he, just as earlier, prepared so that in time to guarantee as complete as possible a publication of Tolstoy's writings, gathering his draft manuscripts and letters.

With this goal, Chertkov asks Tolstoy to guarantee in writing permission, already given earlier, to publish letters that Tolstoy wrote to various people. To avoid misunderstanding, Tolstoy writes Chertkov a special letter:

"Vladimir Grigorievich! In view of the fact that you are preparing all my writings for publication and would desire for this to have the right to freely use my personal letters to various people – I certify, in this case, that you or those whom you in your presence of after you instruct to continue this project, would find it desirous to include in publication my writings, some or others of my personal letters to whomever, copies of which you have or will receive from me or from other means, then I grant you and those continuing your work, full rights to do this, agreeing to your or their consideration.

I am giving you this permission because, proposing, that a few of my letters might have a general interest, I am sure, that, as you, and those to whom you grant to continue your work, can more or less find an expedient way to use them; and still because, in general, not recognizing literary ownership, I would not desire, that my letters remained personal property of those people to whom they were addressed. Lev Tolstoy."[27]

Having settled near Yasnaya Polyana, Chertkov continually sees Tolstoy, just as in previous years, helps him in a few matters:

translates his letters into English, compiles draft manuscripts which Tolstoy, as before, gave to him for preservation, talks with visitors whom Tolstoy sends to him.

Chertkov gives Tolstoy assistance by various means. Already in 1907, having recommended the qualities of the secretary N.N. Gusev to Tolstoy, Chertkov takes it upon himself his compensation, and, after Gusev's exile, finds Tolstoy another secretary, V.F. Bulgakov, who lives at Telyatinki, in order not to be completely dependant materially on Sofia Andreyevna.

The Chertkov home at Telyatinki becomes in some sense the center to where people were drawn, having sympathetic views with Tolstoy – here they feel themselves more at ease than at Yasnaya Polyana, where they are bound by alien conditions of the landlord's home.

The Chertkov's son, the 19-year-old youth, closely befriends the peasant youth of neighboring villages and his comrades from this environment continually are at Chertkov's home.

The Chertkov home soon attracts the attention of the local administration: often suspicious people stay there, from the point of view of the authorities, who don't rush and send their passports for registration. Chertkov gladly enters into conversation with local peasants and with the peasant youth who are at Telyatinki, not hiding his views of the church or government. The local priest, local police and a few landowners consider him politically unreliable and start sending reports about this.

Already in October 1908 the Governor of Tula urgently orders the police chief to establish secret observation of Chertkov, since "it has come to note" that he is spreading "anti-government views" among the peasant youth. The police chief quickly begins to send reports not only about activities but also Chertkov's plans. So, announcing that Chertkov is giving peasants a "Calendar for Each", published by Mediator, and the article "I Cannot Be Quiet", the police chief adds:

"About what I report to Your Nobility and add that Chertkov publishes in his own publishing house a calendar directed against the government under the title "Around Reading", and such will be published in short time. Measures against the spread of this brochure are taken."[28]

In February 1909 the Governor of Tula reports to the Minister of Internal Affairs that Chertkov is occupied with "agitation and propaganda", as a result of this, the "mood of local peasants happens highly noticeably changed for the worse" and asks permission to use his right in accordance with the Law of Increased Security to banish unreliable people. Having mentioned the closeness of Chertkov to Tolstoy, the Governor writes:

"To fear that the latter will respond to measures taken against Chertkov and stir up in the community greater interest toward the activities of Chertkov, in my opinion, there is no basis, in accordance with the receipt of my completely confidential, private information from Tolstoy's family, mainly from his sons, Andrei and Michael, Lev Nikolaevich himself is oppressed by Chertkov's influence, but cannot, due to the lack in strength of character, escape from this influence, while many basic views of Chertkov, which are too extreme, are not shared by Count Tolstoy, in his world-outlook, lately, apparently begins a turning point to the side of softening of the extreme of his teaching which his followers preach, coming, to the words of Count Tolstoy himself, much farther, than he foresaw and desired."[29]

The Minister of Internal Affairs agreed to Chertkov's exile from the Tula region "without execution of a search of the indicated person", and on March 5, the temporary Governor of Tula, signed a decree concerning this exile, since his stay there appears "dangerous for the general peace and quiet". The decree about the exile found Chertkov sick and he was given a postponement until the end of the month.

Chertkov's exile from the Tula Region outraged not only Tolstoy but also Sofia Andreyevna. She quickly wrote a letter to the editor of the newspaper *Russian Gazette*, in which she expressed her indignation of the measure taken in relation to Chertkov. In two months, on May 9, 1909, she wrote her sister about those measures with the same indignation: "They say that the Tula nobility petitioned for Chertkov's exile. But in all of Russia there are not more mean, uneducated and bad nobles, as in the Tula Region. They found someone to listen. And what kind of despotism has begun in Russia; without a trial, without guilt, on the basis of almost old wife's gossip, punish a 50 year-old respected person so as to drive him out of his own home, away from his family, embitter the people and us and the Chertkov family."

Chertkov left for Petersburg, hoping to obtain a repeal there of the decree concerning his exile from the Tula Region.

In the first days of April, Tolstoy wrote him in Petersburg:

"I am starting your notebook with a letter to you, dear friend, Vladimir Grigorievich. You yourself know certainly how much I miss you, how you are the most important and necessary for *me*."

In the same letter Tolstoy announced to Chertkov about his work on the article "Inevitable Revolution":

"I am writing letters and dawdle over my article. I hope that I am not mistaken, working on what I am working on, because the only motive somehow not in vain to use the remaining strength. Please, don't write me, if you don't want to, but if you do want to, then write and I will be very glad in my heart to feel you, again the very real *you*. Yesterday and today I received very good letters. Such joys, that with so many, alien externally people you live in the same emotions so close."

On the 8th of April Chertkov, answering this letter, as if to sum up that which he had to experience lately, begins with a short illness which he endured at the beginning of March and ends with the forced departure from Telyatinki:

"All this time after the illness and experienced worry my consciousness is put in some kind of small, poor in content, not lively condition, more contemplative than active, as you certainly noticed during my latest visits to Yasnaya Polyana. This condition continues even now. The only good in it is that I don't accept this as real life, but hold in my heart of hearts the idea, recollection, an echo of true spiritual life, and therefore the possibility of a new blossoming. Thank you, dear friend, for your sincere letter, and in general for all your love, for everything that you gave me, if it is possible to thank you for that. You say you miss me? My situation is different. I am knocked off of a track on which I went and certainly, like passengers after a wreck, I cannot still regain consciousness, be oriented. In the past I left from one place, arrived in another, of my own initiative, knowing why I do this and what I plan to do further. When they exiled us from Russia, we went with the whole family from places where we only temporarily lived as guests. Now it is totally different: I am knocked out from one of those places, where I grew roots and left those who are closest to me, (with the exception of my mother) and place, conditions very dear to my heart. And I feel myself somehow confused. Don't think only, that I am complaining about my fate, or pitying myself and grieving. No, thank God, I am holding myself together and don't experience, even temporarily, attacks of real depression. I only wanted to tell you about the strange condition of some kind of emptiness in which I am in now."

Tolstoy answered Chertkov with a long letter in which he wrote:

"I want to write you, dear friend, about my internal spiritual life, which, thank God, does not leave me. I want to write that I experienced in the last days that, very certainly, which seems to many as completely insignificant, already well-known, old, but about you I know, that you will understand what I felt, if not how I felt it, however loving me like you do, will understand what gives me joy and worry. And this is the main thing. Four days ago, at night, when I think best, I began to think about something painful, and suddenly it became clear to me that that which is painful may be painful for Tolstoy, but for *me* it is not and cannot be anything painful, difficult for me, for my real *I*, everything is easy, everything is good. And when I understood, clearly understood this, I began to sort out everything which bothers, tortures me and clearly acknowledged that this solves everything: wants Tolstoy to think badly about a person, condemn someone for thoughts, doesn't want Tolstoy, having been torn away from work, to converse with a person who he considers simple, ask *him*, only, *me*. *He* finally decides, and his decision is always such, that from their fulfillment is always good, joyful. This joyful condition of a clear division in two beings: one pitiful, vile, and base and the other omnipotent, clean, holy, done with me lately and I want to share this joy with you. If something appears difficult, confusing (such as in your situation), it is worth only to clearly split these two living as one, beings and everything now will become easy and simple.

Chertkov wants to return to Telyatinki, wants to continue to direct his son, and doesn't want to be separated from his wife – to continue many years of work. All this can be good, but maybe not completely, it is necessary to ask him, that him who was not born and will not die and who wants only good and not only for Chertkov but for the whole world and inseparably fuses with Chertkov. It is necessary to ask him and he decides and his decision will be good for everyone.

I am writing you this because this is clear division of me into Tolstoy and *I* suddenly made in me especially sharp and gave me new strength and joy. Perhaps this will not be with you, but I wanted to share with you my joy."[30]

Chertkov himself already shared with Tolstoy similar reflections often and having received this letter, answered, that at times experiences the same feelings and considers these times the most joyful in his life.

In Petersburg, Chertkov energetically pleads for his return to the Tula Region, but all his efforts seem without results.

Tolstoy writes him, that he waits with worry for a decision in his case. At the same time, Tolstoy reminds him that the absence of personal meetings cannot cause a dent in their friendship:

"I haven't written you in a long time, Vladimir Grigorievich, I am not writing an appeal, our relationship is above this. I think about you too much – too, because I want to be ready for the external separation on earth. As you, as I in our good moments, we know that our bond cannot be broken, not by Stolypin and not even death. Such a bond, like I have with you, like we have, allows me to think – about many, many people whom we did not see and of whose existence we do not know, and with such living as well as dead. I feel this, in good moments, and then personal contact, joyful and painful, fall back to the second, hundredth plan. I wanted to say "enough" – let's talk about me, about you, about those close to us, about matters, but the surprising thing is I cannot be interested in these things. And it is necessary."

261

And further, Tolstoy tells Chertkov about his family, remaining in Telyatinki and about his work, mentioning that he wants to fulfill Chertkov's desire, which he continually advised Tolstoy to write in artistic form:

"I see Galya almost every other day and find her always peaceful, reasonable, kind. I don't see Dimochka that much, and would like to talk with him about soul searching in his young soul. Horrible years of youth with its rapidity and ignorance. Everything at home is, as before, OK. Thank God, there is a lot of work, which seems to be necessary. I want to fulfill your desire, and not only for you, but for me, so clearly, that it is necessary and willing to start, but my hands don't get started and are mainly weak. 2-3 hours a day I feel in myself the strength to write, but am too weak."[31]

Chertkov, carrying out efforts for his return, at that time continues to take care of the publication of Tolstoy's compositions and prepares the basis for publishing the new "Cycle of Reading", received finally the title "For Everyday". He writes Tolstoy about those difficulties which he met bringing this publication to fruition:

"Sytin was here, and I, with him, at last finally made arrangements concerning the publication of the new "Cycle of Reading". It seems that the censure conditions are getting worse day by day, that to publish anything at all written by you has become very risky. Sytin and I, however, made arrangements thus: we will start the monthly release of the new "Cycle of Reading", beginning with June (in order that the first release immediately went up for sale). Publication will be here in Petersburg, without the logo of Sytin's firm, although this publication will be his. Hiryakov is crossing out everything that could displease the censors. To start, ten copies will be published which will be sent to the censors. If the publication is not stopped, then we will start the real publication."[32]

In another letter Chertkov announces that he carried on negotiations with Sytin about the reprint of the old "Cycle of Reading" and explained the impossibility of publishing it in full due to censure obstacles. Therefore Chertkov made arrangements with Sytin such that Hiryakov crossed out the risky text so that the publication could take place.

At the end of May 1909, Tolstoy sent Chertkov in Petersburg excerpts from his latest diaries:

"I am sending you some of my latest diaries," – wrote Tolstoy. "I know that this is interesting for you, – that which I have in my soul does to you what you have in your soul does to me. I am not sending the entire diaries because I decided to write them for myself. And if one knows that they will be read, then I, at least, cannot be completely simple and sincere with myself."

Further, having announced that "at this time I spent time" on the article "Inevitable Revolution", which he considers finished, and that he "rummaged" around the article "The Single Commandment", which he also finished, Tolstoy answers Chertkov's letter about the reprints of the "Cycle of Reading":

"Please encourage Sytin to publish the second publication of the "Cycle of Reading". This booklet is very, very necessary, and I, as always, want to give it to the people, and I have no more. Let Hiryakov cross out everything dangerous. I am very thankful to him for his very boring work, and let him ruthlessly cross out. Even if a lot was crossed out, however, there remains a lot of good. And I already thought about publishing it myself. I hope that when it is released, he will send me many copies, so I can pass them out."[33]

Chertkov answered that he totally understands the feeling preventing Tolstoy from giving his diary to read in its entirety. At the time Chertkov expressed fear for the fate of Tolstoy's diaries, if they remained not copied:

"It would be a great pity to me if your diaries remained decidedly not copied by anyone, even Alexandra Lvovna, since this is dangerous, as if in the case of fire, as in your death: those for whom it's contents are important and necessary could be deprived of it."[34]

At the same time, Chertkov wrote Tolstoy that he is sending him the final corrections of the June release of "For Everyday" and that this booklet will soon come to light if it wont be confiscated by the censors.

Already at the end of May Tolstoy wrote Chertkov that he plans to visit his daughter Tatiana Lvovna at her husband, M.S. Suhotin's family estate, Kochety, positioned near the boarder of the Tula and

Orlov Regions, and invited Chertkov to use this opportunity in order to see each other.

On June 8th, Tolstoy left for Kochety and returned from there in the beginning of July. In Kochety, he worked a lot on an article, "The Single Commandment", although he announced to Chertkov not long before this that the article was finished.

Tolstoy wrote about this work to Chertkov:

"I am at Tanya's, and it is very good for me here. I am writing "The Single Commandment". It seems to me that this is necessary, and I am now in these good conditions, that any month, week, day, must, in probability, consider the last. And therefore, I cannot choose that which I consider more necessary from the impending work... You write about what is the most important to help the people, or, more specifically, somehow to repay them. And it is understood, you are right, but I feel my feebleness, my weakness. This article began for the simple reader, but finished, the article is almost incomprehensible to the simple reader. But I don't despair, I will try."[35]

In the next letter Tolstoy continued to develop those same ideas:

"Yesterday I read for ours (five people) my article "Single Commandment", which, as it seems to me, can stimulate in people good thoughts and feelings. But reading it yesterday to people of our class - disfigured, pitiful people - I was convinced (it is good to be convinced of this at age 81), that everything that I write is stupid, because it doesn't appeal to that public for which it is necessary, – to the millions of workers, illiterate and semiliterate, but to those not perverted, reasonable people. And for the first time, not only with the mind, but also with the whole being, understood the complete stupidity, such that I did, and measured those months, days, hours which I have left, to turn to writing for them, transmit to them that which I, it seems to me, know, and they, it seems to me, don't know: write for them in both reasonable and artistic form."[36]

In Kochety, Tolstoy receives news that Chertkov was finally refused permission to return to the Tula Region.

In a letter to Chertkov, after the receipt of this news, Tolstoy wrote:

"I will try to see you, wherever you are. Although it is unpleasant to say this, and foolish, and often unfair, it seems to me, that I will soon leave and I don't suppress this idea – it is useful and pleasant, and therefore I would like to see you before the departure."[37]

Tatiana Lvovna thought up a way in which Chertkov could see Tolstoy at Kochety, not breaking his order prohibiting residence in the Tula Region. She offered to rent Chertkov a place in the village of Suvorovo, situated four versts from Kochety, but located within the territory of the Orlov Region, and Chertkov having settled there, could visit Kochety, returning for lodging for the night to the izba rented for him.

Chertkov arrived in Suvorovo at the end of June and spent a few days there.

In this arrival, just as in others, Chertkov could be acquainted with a string of Tolstoy's works. Sending him his article "Single Commandment", Tolstoy wrote:

"I am sending you, dear friend, "Single Commandment". If you find time, read it with a pencil in hand. Your observations are very important to me. I hope to be at your place at 5pm."[38]

Having been convinced that it is not worth it to return to Telyatinki in the near future, Chertkov decided not to remain in Petersburg.

Just as some twenty years ago, Chertkov settles together with Anna Konstantinovna on the estate of his relatives, the Pashkovs, in Krekshino, in the Moscow region. Here in the summer of 1909, he finishes his popular account, begun already a long time ago, of Tolstoy's article "About Life". At the same time Chertkov writes reminiscences of one of the episodes of his youth, having an influence on his future development – "Duty in Military Hospitals"[39]

Sending this manuscript to Tolstoy, Chertkov wrote:

"Attached are my recollections, you can see, more or less, as in the letter to you, since I indeed wrote a few parts, instead of letters to you. Please read consistently from the beginning and, if it is not too difficult for you, with a pencil in hand."[40]

Tolstoy was very pleased with these reminiscences. He read them aloud at Yasnaya Polyana and after the reading told A.B. Goldenweiser:

"What a surprising person Chertkov is. And how he is completely, especially unlike others."[41]

In the summer of 1909 Tolstoy had to experience many painful experiences. Soon after his return from Kochety, a sharp clash between Sofia Andreyevna and Alexandra Lvovna took place over a peasant, whom the police constable held for fishing in the Yasnaya Polyana pond and planned to beat.

Tolstoy wrote several times in his diary that he felt ill after conversations with Sofia Andreyevna and that he had thoughts of leaving Yasnaya Polyana.

Having received an invitation to participate in the World Congress that would take place in August 1909 in Stockholm, Tolstoy planned to go to Sweden. Sofia Andreyevna declared that she did not permit this trip. And when Tolstoy does not agree with her arguments, she uses her other resources.

Tolstoy writes in his diary:

"After dinner I began to talk about the trip to Sweden, and there was a terrible hysterical outburst of anger. She wanted to poison herself with morphine. I ripped it out of her hands and threw it downstairs. When I went to bed and thought about it calmly, I decided to give up the trip. I went and told her. She is pitiful, and I'm truly sorry for her. But how edifying. I didn't undertake anything, except internal work on myself. And just as I got myself in hand, everything was settled."[42]

Despite the fact that the trip to Sweden did not take place, Sofia Andreyevna's mood does not change for the better, and as before, it was difficult at Yasnaya Polyana.

As always, Tolstoy tries to escape into his work and writes rather a lot during this time. Having finished, at last, the article "Single Commandment", he starts an article about science.

Tolstoy often writes to Chertkov at this time, and as always, sends him manuscripts, asking to give his opinions, shares his thoughts and especially warmly writes about the closeness, which he feels, thinking about him:

"It seems to me, – writes Tolstoy, – that I in weakness, not stopping, write a lot of emptiness and, mainly, repetition. You, as a real friend, tell me, don't be afraid to distress me. Now beside "Inevitable Revolution", is "Single Commandment", and still about science. There is no basis for this flow to stop. Please tell me. To come to your place – is a joyful dream. I hope to fulfill it. I am writing almost nothing more beside that you are close to me, close, and I am joyful not only to be with you but to think about you."[43]

In another letter Tolstoy tells Chertkov about his mood and reflections concerning those difficult episodes that he had to experience at this time:

"I lived badly at this time, it was not kind. And as soon as there is no love – there is no joy, no life, no God. One hole in the bucket – and all the water pours out... Yes, God – love, this is for me such clear, undoubted truth, but lately it is clearer not what I see but feel with all my being, that to reveal love in life, to us, worthless people, especially those with a base, sinful past, is not easy, and here at every step dilemmas and in the name of love, fulfilling one demand of love destroys another. One solution is to live only in the present, carry a cross every day, hour, minute. But I am so sick, and all the more and more want to die. Before I wanted to in the evening, but now in the morning too. And this is not pleasant for me. Don't think I am complaining to you. I don't have the right or desire and for most times only thankful, especially when I am alone."[44]

Chertkov, in his turn, writes Tolstoy about those thoughts which were born in him by Tolstoy's letters, reports, about his measures for publication of Tolstoy's new works, in particular informs him that the article "Inevitable Revolution" has already been sent to England for translation into English. He sends a copy and translation of his letters to the Englishman Wright, who, having placed the article about Tolstoy in the Encyclopedia Britannica, sent the account of Tolstoy's religious views to Chertkov for his opinion. Chertkov found that Wright did not completely accurately transmit Tolstoy's ideas about immortality and hurried to explain Tolstoy's point of view to him.

Tolstoy approved Chertkov's letter to Wright and answered:

"I received your letter, – dear friend – and was very glad about the spiritual unity which I recognize in you."[45]

Settling in Krekshino, the Chertkovs invite Tolstoy to visit a few times, together with Sofia Andreyevna, Alexandra Lvovna, the doctor D.P. Makovitzky, and the old servant of the Tolstoy's I.V. Sidorkov.

Tolstoy decided to go to Chertkov's and wrote him several days before the departure:

"I very much want to and every day wait for the possibility to go to you. This should not be later than the 2nd. I try not to be oppressed by what ties me. I shame myself for this, comparing my situation with the condition of others, a thousand times worse... These days, five days, I intently don't work. Many various plans – I want to say a lot, but already my strength is poor, and sometimes it is good to keep quiet. Sasha helps me greatly with correspondence, etc. How often do I envy those old men – especially the Buddhists – who leave in late years into the desert."

At the same time Tolstoy wrote about his string of works:

"I, beside Mohammed[46], compiled a booklet of sayings of Lao-Tse with a small preface.[47] Ivan Ivanovich and I want to collect and publish booklets, costing a kopek, of all religious sages. This I think is necessary. In addition to "For Everyday", in June he publishes simple booklets for a kopek, not entitled "For Everyday" but "For the Soul"[48]. Just like he wants to publish everything. What's with Sytin?"[49]

And in the end of the letter, Tolstoy again writes about his mood:

"I don't tell others this, but I will tell you, that lately I am melancholy, sick. It is understood because I myself am bad. But I am not depressed, I am trying to be better."[50]

On the 3rd of September, Tolstoy, together with his wife and daughter, Makovitzky and Sidorkov left for Krekshino and on the way stopped in Moscow. Tolstoy was not in Moscow for a few years and his unexpected arrival caused a sensation. Newspapers were full of correspondent's articles, and on the return trip to Yasnaya Polyana toward the time of departure of Tolstoy's train, a huge crowd gathered, organizing an ovation for him.

In Krekshino, the Chertkovs tried to do everything necessary so that Tolstoy could live with them there, not disrupting his habits and preserving all his usual daily routines. And, as in Yasnaya Polyana, he strolled on foot or on horseback every day, wrote during the day in his room, and in the evening talked with guests or listened to music.

Tolstoy stayed in Krekshino from the 4th to the 18th of September and before his departure decided to make a will, which had to have judicial validity, since his desires, expressed earlier in his diaries and letters to Chertkov, formally, were not binding for heirs and it was possible to fear that his will would remain unfulfilled.

Tolstoy often declared his refusal of literary property on everything that he wrote after 1881, but Sofia Andreyevna continually said she did not agree with his will.

As long as Tolstoy was alive it was impossible to interfere with free printing and reprinting of his new works. But Sofia Andreyevna did not hide her aspiration to firm up Tolstoy's literary legacy for her and her family.

Tolstoy often had to carry on painful conversations with his wife on this theme.

In the beginning of May 1908, already before Chertkov's return to Russia, Tolstoy, having written in his diary about receiving a few letters which upset him, then made an entry about this conversation with Sofia Andreyevna:

"Today no letters, but a conversation about the right to my compositions after my death. It was difficult to carry on."[51]

In the beginning of December 1908, Sofia Andreyevna asked Chertkov what he intended to do with the drafts and pages of Tolstoy's unpublished works in his possession. Chertkov answered that he will take care of their publication, and then will transfer those manuscripts there where they will preserve them.

Responding to this, Sofia Andreyevna stated that Tolstoy gave up only those of his works, written after 1881 for general use, which already appeared in print, but those of his works, which were still not published, belong to the family. And although Tolstoy was present during this conversation, and very decidedly objected against such an interpretation, she insisted on her own way and finally said that he still "can surrender".

In July 1909, experiencing difficult days at Yasnaya Polyana, Tolstoy made an entry in his diary:

"I think all the more about leaving and to give instructions about the estate."[52]

In Krekshino, on 18 September 1909 Tolstoy fulfilled his intention to "give instructions" about his inheritance.

In the will, which Tolstoy made at this time, his works, written before 1881, remained in lifelong use of Sofia Andreyevna. All the rest of the works, written before 1881 but not published, and all written after 1881 were left to Chertkov in order that he provided for their free publication. After Chertkov's death, his right would be transferred to whomever he entrusts this matter.

This will was written with witnesses, but to avoid complications, Sofia Andreyevna was not informed.

The Tolstoys, en route from Krekshino to Yasnaya Polyana remained in Moscow for one day and Alexandra Lvovna used this opportunity in order to show the text of the will to the lawyer N.K. Muravyov and to explain how much it was formally correct.

It turned out that this will had no legal force – it was necessary to indicate a single person or institution to whom to will the possession of Tolstoy's works, so that already in the future the heir would execute the will after his death.

Chertkov refused to be the legal heir of Tolstoy's literary property. Therefore Tolstoy decided to write a will in the name of his daughter, Alexandra Lvovna, having expressed in an explanatory letter attached to the will his desire that factually his works not constitute anyone's personal property and that all of his manuscripts would be given to Chertkov who was occupied with their revision and publication on those bases as he carried out this matter during Tolstoy's life.

At the end of October, F.A. Strahov brought the text of the will, worked out with Muravyov's close participation, to Yasnaya Polyana.

In a few days Strahov, having returned to Moscow, announced that Tolstoy decided to make an important change in the initial text of the will – to leave all his writings, including those that were published before 1881 for common use. In accordance with this desire, Muravyov put the changes in the text of the will. Tolstoy signed this will on November 1, 1909, while it was, just as the first time, decided to avoid oppressive family complications, not to relate this information to Sofia Andreyevna.[53]

After his return from Krekshino Tolstoy, as before, often writes Chertkov, and often remind him of diary entries by their tone. In one of these letters Tolstoy writes Chertkov:

"My physical condition is good. Not as good as it can be, when you are glad for everything, and not emotional but good because, despite the physical indisposition – the liver – must be, and from that melancholy I hold on and work in that sphere, which is omnipotent. It is funny to say, but the older I get, the more I feel myself the student, transferred from the higher classes to the lower, study the ABCs, then, as I imagined, I knew *all*. The ABCs that I study and cannot learn are that during various such meetings, relations, first of all, pray, in addition, first of all, pray before you, and begin to write, think, and even do also. And I cannot do all this: I say stupid, foolish, evil and only then (I remember), that it is necessary first of all to pray. Rarely, very rarely, succeed, but am not depressed, although a little moved. It is comforting that during this, that, which is important is not that which I will reach, but that which I am not stopping to attain. And it can be good. I don't know if this is good or foolish, but lately I very, very much want to die, mainly from that horrible difference, contradiction, which I recognize between my understanding of life – not mentally, but by my whole being – and completely and hopelessly not agreeable, contradiction – people of the world. It has to be like it is necessary, but as if you feel that you cannot do anything and it's not necessary. But this is personal triviality."[54]

Chertkov writes Tolstoy in response:

"I want to tell you, dear, kind friend, and mainly, brother in spiritual life, that I am very glad and grateful to you that you inform me about your internal emotional condition: this is especially necessary for me and dear, since I am separated from you. And it is dear to me to know all joyful and sad, what is happening to you."[55]

And further Chertkov writes that the desire for death resulting from the contradiction between convictions and daily life is sinful temptation, because everyone is obliged to fulfill his duty, not thinking about the consequences. At the same time, no one should earlier mentally limit those possibilities which are hidden in him: not only at 30 years, but at 80 and 95 people must make a step which lifts them to a higher level and gives an exit from that impasse where it seemed, went his life.

Tolstoy responded to Chertkov's letter:

"I am glad now, that I wrote you in my moment of weakness. This produced your good, cheerful letter."[56]

In other letters Tolstoy writes Chertkov about the string of projects – expresses his desire to accelerate the publication "For Everyday", complaining about Sytin, very slowly publishing the string of releases, telling about visitors, staying at Yasnaya Polyana and announcing about his works. He is writing at this time "The Passerby and the Peasant" and, as always, often reworks this article.

Chertkov, having received the manuscript of "The Passerby and the Peasant", uses the opportunity to write Tolstoy again about the fact that the artistic form of the account is especially convincing since it doesn't evoke the desire to argue.

Having reminded that this thing should carry a bigger impression, than those articles, in which there is no dialogue, Chertkov writes Tolstoy:

"My personal egotistical element which always interferes with perception of the good is removed when I read artistic work. I am present only as a spectator observing other people, transferring into *their* souls, forgetting myself. And to forget oneself is the best precondition to feel and to appreciate what is good, and to take the side of what is really fair and just. Logic could be convincing, even irresistible when it is presenting something absolutely true, but under one condition only: a listener has to be impartial; but the *majority* of people have no deep faith and they can be impartial *only* when they forget themselves. The same is about feelings: appeal to a stranger to become more kind – most likely he will become more malicious. But use the artistic images to make him be carried into the situations and souls of the others in order for him to forget himself and yourself, to feel good and evil *in them;* and if you, the artist, yourself are sincerely joyful about good and saddened by evil, then you will *for sure* pass this feeling to all your listeners and spectators in accordance with their keenness. That is why the episodes like yours "The Talks of the Passerby with the Peasant," or "The Talk with the Passers-by," or "Child's Wisdom," despite their basic reasoning tone, impress the heart and mind of the reader with its touch of feeling (exactly like your purely artistic works) much more than if the same was expressed in the form of discourse."[57]

Having finished "The Passerby and the Peasant", Tolstoy starts other projects.

In November, Tolstoy writes Chertkov:

"I never forgot and will not forget what you did and what you are doing for the spread of my writing, and I never am in charge and will never be in charge of them like you. I also know that all my latest writings are just boring repetitions, and am not depressed. There are more important and spiritual projects. I know also, that I "swam off", that is, expressed in literary form what I had to say, and that everything I write now, is very weak, but it will be habitually approved. I don't have any illusions on this score. But I am very well, especially having such friends as you."[58]

And at that time he persistently works on new writings, in which observations of peasant life, redone in artistic form, joins with discussion – "Three Days in the Countryside". In the beginning of January1910, these works were finished, although Tolstoy continues still, as usual, for a long time making corrections and changes to the manuscript.

Tolstoy writes about this to Chertkov:

"This work, it seems, is not worthy, I finished – I am glad that I am through with them. You are to blame that they are more or less in artistic form. All of this together must make one whole. And as bad as this is, each individual part, together this might be useful. Together this is the way: "First Day in the Village – Wandering People. The Second Day in the Village – Livers and Dyers... Third Day in the Village – Taxes, and the Fourth – Dream. Two of these are rewritten, two will be rewritten in the next few days and sent to you. I would very much like to see you. Its strange, but you are so close to me that to write you is somehow uncomfortable. I want to say too much, but I can't say it all – I would not succeed – so there."[59]

Chertkov, having received the manuscripts of "Wandering People" and "Dream", writes Tolstoy:

"Wandering People" is magnificent, new, very touching, forceful and convincing."

Further, Chertkov passes on to Tolstoy observations that Anna Konstantinovna made: in the conclusion where it says that the wanderers must entice "feelings of compassion" – it would be better to say "feelings of embarrassment and compassion".

Concerning the manuscript "Dream" Chertkov makes, on his side, observations, close to those, which he in his time expressed, concerning juxtaposition of artistic scenes and Poznyshev's reasoning in "Kreutzer's Sonata":

"Dream", it is understood is a thing very rich in content, but the artistic persuasiveness in the description of the dream is destroyed because you put long discussions there, wonderful in and of themselves, but such that by their thought and even in form account belonging and can belong only for you yourself. And therefore I think, that this thing to a degree would win in artistic integrity, and therefore in convincing impressions if your own argument was totally picked out of the description of the dream, in which ought to leave only that by it's tone indeed corresponds to that "combined" friend of yours, who you heard in the dream. In the enclosed copy I tried to make this change, and, it seems to me, that the article wins a lot from this, both that artistic requirements are observed and not one of your own thoughts were lost."

And, having offered still a few more small changes, Chertkov wrote at the end of the letter:

"I will not apologize for my audacity that I offer you these changes, since by experience know that, whether you agree or not with my opinion, you won't be angry with me for expressing what I think without embarrassment."[60]

Having received this letter, Tolstoy made an entry in his diary:

"Yesterday, it seems, was Chertkov's letter with corrections of "The Dream". How terrific."[61]

Answering Chertkov, Tolstoy wrote:

"I just received, dear friend, your letter with the corrected article. I cannot express to you the entire degree of my approval of your corrections of "The Dream". Please, release it in its corrected form. I will shamelessly use your labor, passing it off as mine. This is not a joke, but sincere truth. In addition the word "embarrassment" also should be used. I am sending you back the article with the small changes in the transition from dream to debate. If I didn't like you, as a brother in faith, a friend in unity of views, I would not be able not to like you for the gratitude of your invaluable assistance from all sides toward the goal we are both trying to serve our lives." [62]

Studying Chertkov's letters to Tolstoy in the last year of his life, it is clearly seen that Tolstoy's expression about how Chertkov assists "from all sides", does not appear exaggerated. With his usual persistence and straightforwardness, not trying to avoid conflicts with other people, Chertkov continues to fulfill obligations, taken upon himself, of Tolstoy's only representative in all matters concerning his literary works.

When P.A. Sergeyenko begins to prepare for publishing a collection of Tolstoy's letters, Chertkov insists on putting on the book the words "reprinting is allowed", in order that the publishers could not consider Tolstoy's published letters as somebody's property. When Sergeyenko avoids giving agreement to this request, Chertkov sends him a formal letter, and Tolstoy makes a postscript of his agreement with Chertkov's letter.

At the same time Chertkov publishes the letter in newspapers, in which in "the capacity of Tolstoy's authorized representative concerning seeing through to publication of his writings which first appeared", announces that Tolstoy, not being against publication of his letters, entrusted him to declare that he asks those people, publishing these letters, observe two conditions:

"First, not desiring that any of his writings would become anyone's property, but desiring that after their first appearance in print, they remain accessible to all for republication free of charge, as he stated already in print in the 80s, Lev Nikolaevich asks publishers to make and appropriate statement prefacing his letters that they don't have any rights to literary property. Second, desiring

275

to thoroughly avoid anything inappropriate contained in his letters that went into print, from Lev Nikolaevich's point of view, or of those receiving his letters, or references to third-parties in the letters, and at the same time, not having time for this goal himself to examine and edit his letters, Tolstoy asks publishers to deliver these letters before-hand to me for examination and editing."[63]

When the editors of "Russian Gazette" published Tolstoy's article "About Pseudo-Science", cut out those thoughts, which the newspaper especially did not agree[64] without his permission, Chertkov writes an article "Two Censorships for Tolstoy", which restored all the omitted parts and decidedly protests against the actions of the editors of the newspaper.[65]

At the same time Chertkov takes various measures in order to facilitate the process of work for Tolstoy, beginning with the invitation of a secretary, and then copier, who live at Telyatinki, daily being at Yasnaya Polyana and ending with the acquisition of fountain pens for him from the best English firms.

Tolstoy in the beginning of 1910, as in 1909, often makes entries in his diary about how upsetting for him that condition in which he must live at Yasnaya Polyana, and writes that he has not the former persistence in work. Nevertheless, he continues to work a lot, reworking "For Every Day" in small booklets on various themes, putting together a series "The Path of Life", and answering letters received from the most varied people. Sofia Andreyevna wrote her sister on the 13th of March about his general health and ability to work:

"He himself, however, is weakening, sometimes doesn't eat the whole day, sometimes lethargic. And then again, as if nothing, goes horseback riding and works a lot in the morning. This custom is so high that he cannot live without it."

In March 1910, Tolstoy, thanks to Chertkov that he afforded him the opportunity to use the help of his secretary – V.F. Bulgakov – and the copier S.M. Belinky, writes about his work:

"It seems to me, yes, I am completely sure, that I don't need anything, but it turns out that two such workers, not stopping, working but cannot finish everything. But all this resulted from the exaggerated significance seen in me and I in my weakness give in to this temptation."[66]

Tolstoy often at this time sends Chertkov his responses to letters from abroad, asking to translate them into English, and sometimes offers Chertkov himself to answer one or another letter in English.

Having received a letter from Gandhi, Tolstoy writes Chertkov:

"Now and yesterday evening read the book sent to me along with the letter (one previously, one after) from Gandhi, one of the Indian thinkers and fighter against English domination, opposing it by means of passive resistance. He is a very close person to us. He read my writings, translated my letter to Indians into Indian[67], his book *"Indian Home Rule"*[68] in Indian was banned by the British government. He asks my opinion of his book. I would like to write him a detailed letter.[69] Would you translate such a letter for me?"[70]

In other letters Tolstoy writes Chertkov about his health. In time, despite the upsetting atmosphere around him, he feels good. At the end of March, he writes Chertkov:

"I should refrain from boasting, but I would like to very much in front of you: in my soul everything is better and better. God grant that you had, probably and also have now the same. Plants grow quickly in the beginning, and then slowly, but spiritual life goes in reverse."[71]

But then the continual contradiction between Tolstoy and his surrounding environment distresses him. In the middle of April he writes in his diary:

"I woke up at 5, and all the time thought, how to get out, what to do. And I don't know. To write I thought. And to write is nasty, remaining in this life. Talk with her? Leave? Change a bit? It seems the last thing I will and can do. But difficult nevertheless."[72]

Soon after this Tolstoy writes Chertkov:

"I, dear friend, am in the same depressed condition: I cannot write, and it is necessary to make a continual effort not to succumb to unkind emotions."

In the same letter Tolstoy tells about his work on the comedy "She Is A Cause of All Qualities", which he wrote for a home performance organized at Telyatinki by Chertkov's son and his friends:

"I decided not to give them the play, since it is poor. And they wait for something from me, at least, not totally stupid. But, in my present condition, I cannot write."[73]

Tolstoy's daughter, Tatiana Suhotina, invites him to visit her at the Kochety estate. Tolstoy gladly accepts this invitation and in the beginning of May leaves Yasnaya Polyana. At the same time, he uses this opportunity in order to meet with Chertkov. Already in the beginning of April Tolstoy writes Chertkov:

"I miss you very much, and I always dream that somehow this stupidity will be solved. Miss you, especially because there are things that I cannot tell anyone, except you, and which no one will tell me, except you."[74]

Not long before his departure for the Suhotin's, Tolstoy asks Chertkov if he would be going to Kochety.

Chertkov decides to go to Kochety and, by invitation of the Suhotins, staying this time, not in the neighboring village of the Orlov Region, but with them on the estate.

Tolstoy writes in his diary:

"Great joy: Chertkov arrived."[75]

The first day after Chertkov' arrival, Tolstoy gave him his diary for recopying, having said that he at first felt some embarrassment at the thought of his diary would be read, but then decided to write as if no one would ever read what he writes.

Tolstoy felt well in Kochety and wrote considerably a lot, reworked and corrected the preface to "*The Path of Life*", worked on the comedy "She Is A Cause of All Qualities" and an article about suicide. At the same time he strolled for a long time in the park and around the estate, continually starting conversations with peasants, being glad that here they don't know him and accept him only as a simple old man, and read a lot, rereading the French thinkers Montaigne, La Boetie, La Rochefoucauld, books which he found in the Suhotin's old library.

Chertkov stayed at Kochety almost two weeks from the 7th to the 19th of May. He rewrote the preface to "*The Path of Life*" for Tolstoy at this time, looked at, as a favor to Tolstoy, the beginning of the article about suicide and talked with him a lot on varied subjects.[76]

Tolstoy returned to Yasnaya Polyana on May 20th, and on the following day he was forced to have an unpleasant conversation with Sofia Andreyevna – the village old women complained to Tolstoy that they were not allowed to walk across the estate to the state forest, where they could get grass to feed their livestock. Sofia Andreyevna, finally, agreed to change her instruction, but the situation did not improve. In a week a still more difficult conversation took place with her. When Tolstoy, in response to Sofia Andreyevna's words that she was tired of managing household affairs, advised to her to give it up and leave, she began to scream that she was being pushed out of her home and went into a fit of hysterics. Finally she calmed down, but Tolstoy, during the course of that whole day had an intermittent heart beat.[77]

Soon after this, Tolstoy wrote in his diary:

"I have a very pleasant, good feeling toward Sonya – a good, spiritual, loving one. I feel well at heart despite my inactivity."[78]

But already in three days, Tolstoy, returning from his walk, found the Circassian mounted patrol, catching an old peasant in the landlord's woods of Yasnaya Polyana and bringing him to the estate.

Tolstoy writes in his diary that it is very difficult for him and again thoughts come up about leaving. The next day, walking in the woods, meets a young peasant and after the conversation with him, makes an entry in his diary:

"I met a young one, he asks if he can walk there or will the Circassian beat him. And I felt so terribly."[79]

Tolstoy felt so burdensome at being at Yasnaya Polyana that he was glad at the possibility, although not for long, to leave there. Already before the trip to Kochety, Chertkov wrote Tolstoy in one of his letters, that he rented a summer cottage in the village of Meshchersky in the Podolsky Region of the Moscow Province, a three-hour train ride from Yasnaya Polyana and invited him to visit.

Soon after Tolstoy's return from Kochety, he wrote Chertkov:

"I am expecting a joyful trip to you and remember the joy from our meeting at the Suhotins. I am occupied these last days with the most disagreeable two projects: the play: i.e.) nonsense, and the reworking of the preface to the booklet *For Every Day*", which I consider – true or not – important. Hello to Galya. I will see her, not at Telyatinki, but at your place, if I will live."[80]

Tolstoy went with Alexandra Lvovna and Dr. Makovitsky on the June 12 and returned on the 23rd. And as in the trip to the Chertkovs in Krekshino, he continued his work at their house – he finished the preface to the series *"The Path of Life"* and wrote "Response To the Invitation To the Slavonic Conference in Sofia".[81]

At the same time he walked in the neighborhood, talked with the local peasants, visited the hospital for mentally ill for the Troitsky and Meshchersky villages with great interest, and was at the textile factory, where he questioned about salary and working conditions.

At that time when Tolstoy was at the Chertkovs, they received news that Chertkov will be permitted to be at Telyatinki while his mother is living there. The Chertkovs decided to return in a few days.

Tolstoy was at the Chertkovs until June 23rd.

That morning he made an entry in his diary:

"Yesterday I had just gone to bed, still had not fallen asleep, when a telegram arrived: "I beg you, come on the 23rd. I will go and am glad for the chance to do my duty. God help me."

The evening of that day, having returned to Yasnaya Polyana, Tolstoy wrote in his diary:

"Found things worse than expected: hysterics and bad temper. It's not possible to describe. I didn't behave badly, but not very well either, not gently enough."[82]

After Tolstoy's return from the Chertkovs, the most painful period of his life at Yasnaya Polyana began. Much has been written about the last months of Tolstoy's life at Yasnaya Polyana, and there is no necessity in detail to concentrate on them again. For this would require setting forth and analyzing a considerable amount of material, and such a task might become the subject of special work. Therefore here it is necessary to limit oneself to listing the basic facts that are not doubted and only in this way will it be necessary in order that the history of the relationship of Tolstoy and Chertkov not remain incomplete.

Returning from the Chertkovs, Tolstoy found Sofia Andreyevna in a condition of extreme irritation, and immediately scenes of severe hysteria begin. This atmosphere was getting more and more tense until the very departure of Tolstoy from the home.

Already in 1898, in one of the letters to Tatiana Andreyevna, Sofia Andreyevna wrote about having bouts of irritability, and she herself called them "my alarms and madness"

Now these "alarms and madness", agonizing for Tolstoy, and for her too, begin to repeat themselves day to day. Entries in Tolstoy's diaries show how painfully he was affected at this time by the mood and behavior of Sofia Andreyevna.

Tolstoy's friendship with Chertkov, who, over the period of many years, managed all projects concerned with publishing Tolstoy's works, had at his disposal drafts of a large part of Tolstoy's manuscripts for the last twenty-five years and enjoyed his unlimited trust, served, in Sofia Andreyevna's opinion, as the most important obstacle for fulfilling her desire, in order that Tolstoy's literary works passed down to her family. At the same time, she created the notion, as if Chertkov decided to cause a rift between her and her husband. And she begins to feel sharp hatred toward Chertkov, accepting the form of some kind of obsession, to a considerable degree penetrating all her behavior in the last months of Tolstoy's life.

She desires by any means to stop Tolstoy's meetings with Chertkov and to receive entrusted manuscripts, given to Chertkov by Tolstoy.

Already in 1909 she was indignant at Chertkov's expulsion from the Tula Region, and in a letter to her sister called him an honorable man. Now she despairs at the thought of his return, tells everyone that Chertkov continually takes Tolstoy's manuscripts away from him and took the goal upon himself of completely estrange him from his wife.

A.B. Goldenweiser, spending the summer of 1910 near Yasnaya Polyana, and continually being there, wrote in his diary:

"Before the very arrival of Lev Nikolaevich, in the evening, she said that she was sick, departed, lay in bed and began to cry. She did not give Lev Nikolaevich the possibility to sleep the whole night; immediately showed him all the entries where she wrote that he and Chertkov want to lock her up in insane asylum, that he is in love with Chertkov, that he always had the propensity to love men, etc. Sofia Andreyevna said of Chertkov: I will drive him out of here. I will drive Lev Nikolaevich from Chertkov. Wherever he goes, I will go too."[83]

Chertkov returned to Telyatinki on June 27.

Sofia Andreyevna, desiring to disrupt his meeting with Tolstoy, insisted that Tolstoy go together with her to visit their son Sergei Lvovich at his estate. But they weren't at Sergei Lvovich's long, having left on the 28th and they returned to Yasnaya Polyana on the 29th of June. The next day Chertkov arrived at Yasnaya Polyana.

From June 30th to July 24th Tolstoy and Chertkov saw each other no less than in previous years, when Chertkov lived near Yasnaya Polyana. But Sofia Andreyevna does everything to disrupt their meetings, beginning with eavesdropping at the door when they spoke to one another, and ending with painful hysterical scenes, which she continually makes for Tolstoy.

Having found out that Tolstoy's diaries for the past ten years were preserved at Chertkov's, she demanded that they be taken from him and given to her. Tolstoy declines this demand, but Sofia Andreyevna resumes conversations on this topic daily, turning to hysterics, threatens suicide. Finally Tolstoy decides to take his diaries back, but not to give them to Sofia Andreyevna, but that they be preserved in a neutral place – a safe deposit box of a bank.

On July 14, Tolstoy wrote Sofia Andreyevna a letter, subsequently often appearing in print, in which he announced to her about his decision. In this same letter he wrote that since his meetings with Chertkov are so distressing to her, he is ready to break them off, but warned her that if life does not become "nice and peaceful" that he would leave Yasnaya Polyana.

That day Tolstoy wrote in his diary:

"A very depressing night. Began writing her a letter in the morning and finished it. Went to her room. She demanded the very things that I promised and granted. I don't know whether I did right, whether I wasn't too weak or submissive. But I couldn't do otherwise. They've gone to get the diaries. She is still in the same petulant condition, not eating or drinking…Sasha brought the diaries. She went twice. And Sonya has calmed down and thanked me. I think it is all right. I received a touching letter from Batey[85]*. I am going to bed. Am not completely healthy and weak. Spiritually OK."

Sending for the diaries, Tolstoy wrote Chertkov:

"You understand, dear friend, how distressing for me to sacrifice our contacts, I hope this is a temporary deprivation, contact with you, but I know that you love not me, Lev Tolstoy, but my soul. And my soul – your soul, and its demands are the same. Sasha will tell you everything. I'm OK, really OK. And I will be already completely fine, and still better when I get from you what I am waiting for – your unity with me in the name of what we both live for. Everything will be OK if we don't weaken. God help us. L.T. Write."

Worrying, Tolstoy forgot to write that he asks to give his diaries to Alexandra Lvovna.

He wrote Chertkov a second letter the very same day:

"I was so worried this morning, that, having written you, thought, that I had written the main thing: that you immediately give Sasha back the diaries. Now I ask you about this. Sasha will immediately bring them to the bank. It is very painful, but will be better. Be strong in kindness and you, dear friend."

After Tolstoy took his diaries, Sofia Andreyevna declared that she would not be against Chertkov being at Yasnaya Polyana, and this was how the break in personal contact between Tolstoy and Chertkov was postponed.

In his letter to Sofia Andreyevna, Tolstoy made an effort to soften her mood, but the situation did not change from this. Tolstoy still did not intend to change his mind concerning his works, stated in his will.

In July 1910 he rewrote his will twice, having decided to make a codicil, that in the event of Alexandra Lvovna's death, her rights and obligations would go to Tatiana Lvovna. On the 22nd Tolstoy and witnesses signed the will, in its final form, and then, as before, Sofia Andreyevna was not informed about it.

Painful scenes in the Yasnaya Polyana home did not stop. Sofia Andreyevna asks that Tolstoy give her the key to the safety deposit box in the bank, where the diaries are kept and, having been denied, runs to her room and, having grabbed a bottle with opium, screams that she drank the whole thing and poisoned herself. But when Tolstoy runs at her screams, she declares that she said this "on purpose".

On his daughter's advice, Tolstoy decides to talk to doctors about Sofia Andreyevna's physical condition.

Dr. G.I. Rossolimo, a neuropathologist, was invited to Yasnaya Polyana, to make a diagnosis:

"Degenerative double constitution, paranoid and hysterical with predominance of the first, at any moment episodic exacerbation".

Dr. Rossolimo arrived with Dr. D.V. Nikitin, who often took care of Tolstoy and his family. After listing the usual measures, recommended for nervous-patients, – baths, walks, etc., – they expressed their opinion that it would be desirous if Lev Nikolaevich and Sofia Andreyevna lived apart from one another for some time.

Sofia Andreyevna's sharp hostility toward Chertkov did not decrease, even after the diaries were taken from him.

Tolstoy writes in his diary on July 18th:

"Uncontrollable hatred of Chertkov."

On July 24th, Sofia Andreyevna writes her sister a letter, filled with harsh opinions about Chertkov. She maintains that she cannot feel calm about the fate of Tolstoy's diaries:

"The diaries were taken from Chertkov, but Lyovochka put them in a state bank in Tula under his name and in a short time again surreptitiously can give them to Chertkov, to whom he is subordinate and with whom is simply in love."

The thought that Chertkov remains to live close to Yasnaya Polyana horrifies her:

"I cannot think without horror, – continues Sofia Andreyevna, – that the government left Chertkov in our neighborhood. The village constable said that the people became completely different without Chertkov, much better and quieter. Chertkov incites Lev Nikolaevich with his influence to write evilly and revolutionary."

Tolstoy and Chertkov decide for a time to stop meeting each other.

Tolstoy writes Chertkov concerning this decision:

"I think it isn't necessary for me to tell you how painful for you and for me is the break in our personal contact, but it is necessary. I think also it is not necessary to tell you that the demand for this of me is for, in the name of what we both live. I comfort myself and think that this cessation is only temporary, that the painful condition will pass. We will correspond."[86]

A continual exchange of letters begin between Tolstoy and Chertkov. Chertkov decidedly expresses his conviction that Sofia Andreyevna should not be given any further concessions, since each new concession calls for further demands and only stimulate that unrestrainability, which, all the more and more reveals Sofia Andreyevna. Tolstoy, agreeing a lot with Chertkov, writes that he feels pity toward her.

In other letters he tells about his own health, shares his thoughts with Chertkov, writes about the translation into English of his responses to English letters, about the necessity of speeding up publication which Sytin releases and about other strings of projects.

The atmosphere at Yasnaya Polyana remains as before burdensome. Tolstoy often makes diary entries about this. At the same time, knowing, that his diaries could be read by others and, in particular, Sofia Andreyevna, who tries to read what he writes, although surreptitiously, picking up the keys to the drawer of his writing desk, he carries another diary, which is called "for myself alone" and carefully hides it, often changing it's place.

Tolstoy writes in the first entries in this diary, concerning his will, that even if the smallest possibility exists, that what he wrote is helpful to people, it would be wrong to deprive them "of this spiritual food" for the benefit of a few of his sons. But the following day, after conversations with Biryukov, negatively relating to the composition of the will, he writes in his diary:

"Chertkov has involved me in a struggle, and this struggle is both very depressing and very repugnant to me. I'll try to conduct it with love (its strange to say how far away I am from it.)[87]

In a letter of 2 August Tolstoy, reporting to Chertkov about his conversation with Biryukov, having told him that it was not necessary to draw up the will secretly from the family, wrote, that he agreed with Biryukov. At the same time Tolstoy wrote that they should not use the judicial form of the will, instituted by the government, which he disclaims, and it would be better not to undertake anything.

Chertkov responded with a long letter, which thoroughly reminded him of the motives which supported the preparation of the will, and argued that this was the only way to guarantee the desire which Tolstoy already often expressed over the last several years.

Tolstoy wrote in response to this:

"I am writing on sheets of paper because I am in the woods, on a stroll. And from yesterday evening to this morning I am thinking about your last letter. Two main feelings were born in me from it: disgust toward the display of flagrant greed and insensitivity, which I either did not see or saw and forgot; and grief and repentance in that I gave you pain in my letter, in which I expressed regret about what was done. The conclusion that I made from the letter is that Pavel Ivanovich was not right and I was not right either, agreeing with him, and that I fully approve of your activities, but I am not happy with my activities, I feel that I could have behaved better, although I don't know how. Now I don't regret what I did, that is, that I wrote the will they way it was written, and can only be thankful to you for your participation which you had in this matter."[88]

In another letter Tolstoy wrote Chertkov that he would like to see him, but cannot do this, since Sofia Andreyevna is still in her previous condition and instills in him a feeling of pity.

"I am sitting in the garden", – wrote Tolstoy, – "I cannot work today, I think about you and here I am writing you. There is nothing for me to say to you that you don't know. I will say one thing, that in the recent past I have been somehow ashamed, funny, and at the same time it is unpleasant to avoid you, but I can't, can't do anything else. I feel sorry for her, and she, undoubtedly, deserves pity more than I do, therefore I would be foolish, pitying her to increase her suffering. I, although I am tired, in essence am well, so well, that in the recent past, external success of my activities, previously occupying me very much, does not interest me at all. Everything closer and closer approaches exposure, probably good, foreseeable mystery and this approaching can only attract, please me."[89]

From time to time, Tolstoy writes about his projects. He thinks about new works, but at this time cannot work on anything except responses to letters and corrections of *"The Path of Life"*:

"I am not doing anything, except for letters," – writes Tolstoy, – "but would very much like to write, specifically artistically. And when I think about it, I want to still more because I know, that this will give you pleasure. Perhaps it will produce a real egg, but if its nonsense, then there is nothing to do."[90]

Already at the end of July Tolstoy received a letter from Tatiana Lvovna, inviting him to visit Kochety. He began to think about this trip, hoping to rest a bit from those conditions in which he had to live at Yasnaya Polyana. Sofia Andreyevna expressed the desire to go with him, and Tolstoy questioned her if it was worth her doing this:

"Whatever you want. If you want to, lets go."

Tolstoy stayed at Kochety for more than a month – from August 15 to September 22 – and, as always, often wrote Chertkov at this time. It is not necessary to stop here and have a detailed discussion of their correspondence during this period, more so, that Tolstoy's letters to Chertkov, written in Kochety, are published in A.B. Goldenweiser's book, *"Close to Tolstoy"*.

Tolstoy felt considerably better at Kochety than at Yasnaya Polyana, although a lot was burdensome here too. Contradictions between Tolstoy's views and the conditions, in which he had to live, existed at Kochety and even could be said to a higher degree.

Tolstoy himself wrote about this to Chertkov:

"It burdens me, as always, and especially here, life's luxuries amid the poverty of the people. Here peasants say: "God's kingdom is in heaven, but here is the landlord's heaven." And here luxury is especially great, and this word stuck in my head and heightens the consciousness of embarrassment of my life."[91]

Sofia Andreyevna, especially in the beginning of her stay at Kochety, was much more reserved than at Yasnaya Polyana. True, during this period, she talks about the very same topics which worried her at Yasnaya Polyana with irritation almost every week, and Tolstoy often writes in his diary that she is "pitiful and painful" for him. However, she was a guest there, and this influenced her behavior to a certain degree.

On the 30th of August, Sofia Andreyevna returned to Yasnaya Polyana for five days, and then returned again for a week at Kochety. At Yasnaya Polyana she took down Chertkov's portrait that hung in Tolstoy's study, invited a priest to her home, who performed a te deum service, and was, as before irritated and excited.

Returning to Kochety and having stayed from the 5th to the 12th of September, she, after a short time again resumed her usual conversations of ownership of Tolstoy's literary works and about Chertkov, and how it is evident by Tolstoy's diaries, again begin hysterical scenes, burdensome to the highest degree.

Chertkov makes efforts at this time to have a talk with Sofia Andreyevna and writes her a long letter, trying to explain his behavior, but receives a response from her, which, as before, blames him for "taking away" Tolstoy's diaries and manuscripts, and instigated Tolstoy's hostile feelings toward his wife."[92]

Four days after Sofia Andreyevna left Kochety, Tolstoy writes Chertkov a letter in which he tells about his stay there:

"I am writing you, dear friend, in order to tell you that I, as before, am in average condition both physically and emotionally. I try to look at my painful, moreover difficult relations with Sofia Andreyevna, as an ordeal, necessary for me, and which I could turn into good for myself but rarely succeed in it. I will say one thing, that in the recent past "not by brains, but by sides", as the peasants say, went so far that I clearly understood the border between resistance – when you pay evil for evil, and resistance – hot giving up in the activity which you consider your duty to God and people. I rested these four days and thought about my line of action before returning, which I already don't want and can no longer put off. I have to return around the 20th, more so after than before.

I did nothing important here. Yesterday and today was occupied with a letter to Grot, brother of the philosopher, for the placement into his collection about Nikolai Grot. The letter is not important, about the difference of religious and so-called scientific philosophical understanding of life. Nikolai Grot did not have this religious understanding. I already wrote you everything that I wanted to write, and I didn't write anything, so it's better not to write this and be reconciled with this inaction. But I can't, however want.

"I would also very much like to see you, and I, although don't know how, but think that I can arrange this, when I arrive. And, it is understood, to whom, after informing about this, it will be unpleasant."[93]

Tolstoy left Kochety for Yasnaya Polyana on September 22. He made a diary entry on that day:

"I am going to Yasnaya Polyana and horror overtakes me at the thought of what awaits me there. I will do only what needs to be done.[94] And only keep quiet and remember that in her soul– is God."

Sofia Andreyevna met Tolstoy with reproaches that he did not return to Yasnaya Polyana for a long time and the next day resumed hysterical scenes that were repeated daily.

Tolstoy writes in his diary that he feels the demand for artistic work, but cannot realize it in such painful emotional conditions that he experiences. He continues to occupy himself mainly with responses to correspondence and corrections to the booklet *"The Path of Life"*.

Refraining from meetings with Chertkov, Tolstoy continues to maintain contact with him by way of correspondence. He sends Chertkov his long letter to Grot about philosophy and religion and to Czech students about socialism, which turned into an article, remaining unfinished. Chertkov in his turn, sends Tolstoy a manuscript of the first four chapters of his long article *"About Proper Thinking"*, on which he began working while he still lived in Rzhevsk, and his diary from July 14 to October 1, 1910.

Tolstoy read Chertkov's diary and made an inscription on it:

"Thank you that you sent them, gave me the opportunity, as much as possible to see into your soul."

Tolstoy wrote about Chertkov's manuscript:

"The first three chapters of your article were very good, the 4th, "Complex Thinking", it seems to me was too complex and unclear."[95]

Chertkov, having received Tolstoy's letter to Grot, returned it, having made little work on the copy of the letter: he removed text that concerned Grot himself. The result was a note about philosophy and religion.

Tolstoy wrote Chertkov concerning this:

"I can't thank you enough, dear friend, for all that you do for me, not only pleasing but good."

And having mentioned about M.A. Schmidt's portrait, sent by Chertkov, and brochure, published in the journal "World News", Tolstoy continued:

"...3) and main thing about Grot. I still was not able to read, only glanced and see and know, that the article won from your friendly and unselfish work useful for our project. Today I received a letter from Grot. You read it and decide how you consider better. 4) About the article on socialism. Also only skimmed and also believe that it will be useful."[96]

Chertkov answered this letter:

"You touch me with your gratitude for the small work on your writings, which I from time to time fulfill as carefully as I can and fulfillment which gives me only pleasure. Lacking is only one of the greatest joys – personal contact with you – I ask you, dear friend, more often turn to me for that small assistance, which I can provide you now and then."[97]

On the 3rd of October Tolstoy experienced to a serious degree one of those painful bouts, which he had in the final years, – fainting with convulsions, sharp weakening of memory and general weakness, lasting two days. Under the influence of Tolstoy's illness, Sofia Andreyevna was more restrained for the period of several days.

At the same time Tatiana Lvovna and Sergei Lvovich, arriving at Yasnaya Polyana, tried to influence Sofia Andreyevna and soften her mood. Tolstoy, recovering from his illness, wrote Chertkov:

"She is sick and everything else, but it is impossible not to pity her and not be tolerant of her. And in this I ask, in the name of our friendship, which nothing can change, because you did too much and do for the sake of what is dear to both of us and I can't not remember this. External conditions can separate us, but that which we – allow me to say for you – friend to friend, nothing and no one can weaken. I only, as practical advice in this instance, say: be tolerant. With her it is impossible to take her seriously or to reason logically. I say all this because, if this comes about, something I believe is possible, in former natural relations, then don't put obstacles before something I want very much."[98]

The day after this letter, Sofia Andreyevna agreed to instruct Tatiana Lvovna to invite Chertkov to Yasnaya Polyana. On his side, Tolstoy asked Alexandra Lvovna to give Chertkov the invitation to come to Yasnaya Polyana.

Chertkov arrived at Tolstoy's on the evening of 7 October, but he did not resume his visits because Sofia Andreyevna's hostile relations toward him remained unchanged.

After Chertkov's departure, Tolstoy made an entry in his diary:

"Chertkov was here. Very simple and clear. We talked about everything except our strained relations. It is better. He left after 9. Sonya again had an hysterical fit, it was painful."[99]

On Sofia Andreyevna's side continued reproaches, causing painful hysterical scenes.

Chertkov writes Tolstoy:

"Alexandra Lvovna told me all about what's happening to you, and I want to tell you one thing: leave in the name of God, leave as soon as possible to Kochety while the Suhotins are still there. If you don't do this for yourself, then do it for Sofia Andreyevna. She is apparently completely taken down the track of emotional excitement and endless demands which she herself has no strength to leave. And therefore on you lies the moral obligation to put all obstacles you can think of in her path, which as painful to her as to others, and not allow it to go with growing speed which certainly will happen if you stay in the same atmosphere and under the same conditions. And the method, in order to help her, you have only one – that well-tried method that already several times helped, as much as it is possible to help, namely to change the environment, leave for Kochety. And it is worth doing immediately."[100]

At this time Chertkov writes a long letter to Hristo Dosev, a Bulgarian, sharing Tolstoy's views. Dosev's letter to Anna Chertkov expresses bewilderment concerning the fact that Tolstoy remains living at Yasnaya Polyana, and expresses fear that his external life will compromise in people's eyes all meaning and significance of his words and thoughts.

Responding to this letter, Chertkov writes Dosev that Tolstoy remains at Yasnaya Polyana not because it is pleasant – living in his home for him was for a long time already painful, – but because he wouldn't like to act egotistically by avoiding to carry a cross, which was destined for him". Also Chertkov expressed his conviction that Tolstoy still could realize the desire often appearing in him to leave home, if he feels that he has to leave.[101]

At the same time Chertkov accomplishes another small project. Hearing the rumor that Sofia Andreyevna thought to sell the rights of publication of Tolstoy's works, written before 1881 and meant for her use, to the printing house "Enlightenment" for a million rubles, Chertkov drew up a draft for Tolstoy, which had to be published in the form of letters to the editorship of newspapers. In this statement, Tolstoy warned that the intention of one or another publisher about the purchase of his works cannot be realized, since the publication of his works, written before 1881, belong to Sofia Andreyevna, without the right of transfer, but the works, appearing in print after this year could all be reproduced free of charge.

Tolstoy, having received copies of Chertkov's letters to Dosev and the draft statement, responded at first with a short note:

"I am not responding to your letters which are all joy for me. After. I signed the declaration, but it's still not necessary to send it. When I find that it is necessary, I will let you know. I don't thank you, but am glad for that soulful unity, which I acknowledge and especially lively experience."[102]

That very day Tolstoy wrote Chertkov:

"I read your letter and other papers. That I can say anything else, dear friend, except that I always feel for you... I don't want to say. Our relations are such that words, excess words are not necessary and one is scared to say them."

Life at Yasnaya Polyana remained painful: agonizing scenes came one after another, and in almost every entry in Tolstoy's intimate diary repeats the word – "painful".

And all the more often Tolstoy has the thought that it is necessary to put an end to this and leave home.

Earlier, when Tolstoy had the idea to leave home, in order to eliminate the contradiction between his convictions and those of the lordly environment surrounding him, he, remaining at home, often wrote in his diary that he did not do this, not wanting to sharply disturb the peace in the family and cause pain to those close to him. Now his presence at home only increased Sofia Andreyevna's irritability, giving her the opportunity to again and again lay one and the same claim and make one and the same reproaches.

Further presence at Yasnaya Polyana made no sense.

Nonetheless, it was not easy for Tolstoy to make the final decision.

For two days before his departure from home he writes in his diary:

"All the same trying feelings, suspicion, spying, and sinful desire, such that she gave me reason to leave. I'm so bad. I think of leaving and about her situation – and pity and I can't do it."[103]

Tolstoy shares his thoughts about leaving home with Alexandra Lvovna and Chertkov, but he still cannot decide to make the last step. On 26 October Tolstoy writes Chertkov a letter – the last one written to him from Yasnaya Polyana:

"Today I felt for the first time with especial clarity – even with sadness – how much I miss you. There is a whole sphere of thoughts and feelings, which I cannot share with anyone as naturally – knowing that I am totally understood – as with you. Today was a few of those feelings-thoughts. One of these is about (I experienced in a dream today a heart tremor, which woke me, and falling asleep, remembered a long dream, as I walked downhill, held on to branches but nevertheless slipped and fell, i.e.) woke up. All this dream-seeing, which seemed about the past appeared in a flash), such that one thought – that at the moment of death will be this similar heart tremor in a dream state, timeless moment, and all my life will be this retrospective dream. Now we are at the very height of this retrospective dream. Sometimes it seems to me to be true and sometimes it seems like nonsense.

The second thought-feeling is again such, today a vision of me, already the third in the last two months, a wonderful artistic dream. I will try to write it and previous one down, although it would be in the form of a synopsis.

The third, this is not as much of a thought as a feeling, and a bad feeling – the desire of changes in my situation. I feel something unnecessary, embarrassing in my situation, and sometimes I look at it – as it is – as on a blessing, but sometimes, I oppose it, am indignant.

Sasha told you about my plan, which I think about sometimes in moments of weakness. Do it, so that Sasha's words about this and mine now about their mention, would not be said.

I miss you very much. One can't say everything on paper. But something perhaps. I write you about me. You write about yourself as it comes out. How you understand me from a simple hint so I will understand you. Well goodbye. If I undertake anything, then, it is understood, I will inform you. Maybe even use your help."[104]

Chertkov in his response letter also does not organize any concrete plans, concerning the possibility of Tolstoy's departure. He writes Tolstoy that he understands his thoughts about life, as about a dream:

"I remember how once you pictured the interpretation of our life as a dream and I was enchanted with it. Since then, in the best moments of my spiritual life, especially when I am tired by daily commotion or sad about someone dear who already left us – this idea about life as a dream, from which we are going to wake up appears in me joyfully and vividly."[105]

The next day, 27 October – the day before Tolstoy's departure – Chertkov writes him a long letter. He convinces Tolstoy to try to work on his manuscripts just as he did earlier, after his morning stroll, and not take on letters that Tolstoy recently began to answer in the morning, almost totally having stopped working on his articles and artistic works.

"With the approach of your period of old age, – writes Chertkov, – it is very probable that this intense energy of thoughts don't perceptibly manifest itself in you in the morning; but there can't be any doubt that the morning hours, after night dreams – are the most dear and fruitful for mental work. And beside that, as I well know, you receive mail at this time, and before, like with a clear head concentrated on independent work, you look through all the letters you receive that day. It seems to me that in purely practical relations – this is a big mistake. That could be compared with a situation when you before withdrawing into your soul in order to work in all its depth, the need for whatever mental work it presents, you would let a crowd of people into your room, one of whom would persistently ask you for material help, others – spiritual, others would expose and abuse you, others would express their sympathy for you, still others would bring you into their internal life, etc., etc."

Tolstoy spent the day as usual, – read and wrote letters, rode his horse and went to sleep at 11:30pm. Nothing indicated that this would be the last day he would spend at Yasnaya Polyana. But this morning Tolstoy roughly outlined the letter, which he intended to leave Sofia Andreyevna, if he finally decided to leave home. That night, having heard a rustle, having seen the light on in his study, and having understood that Sofia Andreyevna is searching for and, perhaps reading his diary, he decided to immediately leave.

A little later, having gotten up from bed, he corrected and rewrote his farewell letter to Sofia Andreyevna, began packing his things, woke Alexandra Lvovna and D.P. Makovitzky, and announced his intentions to them.

He left the house still in darkness, having at first decided to go to Optina Cloister, not far from Shamardin, where his sister the nun Maria Nikolaevna Tolstaya lived. He went to rent a hut in Shamardin, thinking to settle in the village. But, fearing that Sofia Andreyevna would come there, he decided to go further. Together with Alexandra Lvovna and Dr. Makovitzky, Tolstoy traveled south, having gotten tickets in the direction of Rostov-on-Don.

Alexandra Lvovna made arrangements with Chertkov that Tolstoy would let him know how he is, writing telegrams with the code name Nikolaev, and Alexandra Lvovna chose the name Frolova.

Leaving Shamardin on October 31, Tolstoy wrote a letter to Chertkov, asking him to tell him about everything happening at

Yasnaya Polyana and giving instructions to receive and resend his letters. In the postscript of this letter Tolstoy wrote:

"We were scared that Sofia Andreyevna would come to the monastery and decided to leave immediately. We are going south, probably to the Caucuses. Since it doesn't matter to me where to go, I decided to choose the south, especially because Sasha is coughing. It is understood that we will inform you where we will be. If you want to send a telegram, then send them to Rostov in the name of Frolova. I would like to know very much what is happening there. If everything is the same, then write only two words. I am healthy and glad to be with Sasha."

The next day, November 1, Chertkov received two telegrams almost at the same time:

"Yesterday I got sick. I am afraid of the publicity. Today is better. We are going further. Take measures. Inform us. Nikolaev".

And after that a telegram arrived from Alexandra Lvovna:

"Yesterday we got off at Astapovo. High fever, semi-conscious. In the morning the temperature was normal, now again is shivering. There is not point to go. He expressed his desire to see you. Frolova."

Chertkov left on the very first train and arrived at Astapovo on the second of November.

Chertkov spent the last days of Tolstoy's life near him, helping in looking after the patient and carefully recording his last words.[106]

Tolstoy's death did not interrupt the job of publishing his works, which served as Chertkov's main work during his life.

A new phase began in Chertkov's activities, finishing editing the anniversary publication of the complete works of Tolstoy, the basic texts of which to a considerable degree were found in manuscripts, letters and materials which Chertkov saved and gathered over the period of many years with exceptional persistence.

ENDNOTES

Chapter I (15-27)

1. Diaries of S.A. Tolstoy, Part II, publishers M. and C. Sabashnikov. Moscow 1929, p. 105.
2. L.N. Tolstoy, Confession. Complete Collection of Compositions under the editing of P.I. Biryukov, T. XV, publisher I.D. Sytin, p. 12.
3. Letter of L.N. Tolstoy to Countess A.A. Tolstoy, February 1880. Correspondence of L.N. Tolstoy with Countess A.A. Tolstoy, publisher Tolstoy Museum, St. Petersburg 1911, p. 328.
4. Letter of L.N. Tolstoy to N.N. Strahov from 11 October 1882. Correspondence of L.N. Tolstoy with N.N. Strahov. Publisher Tolstoy Museum, St. Petersburg 1914, p. 299.
5. Letter of S.A. Tolstoy to T.A. Kuzminskaya, November 1879. State Tolstoy Museum.
6. Brief autobiography of Countess S.A. Tolstoy, "The Beginning", 1921, № 1, p. 153.
7. Tolstoy's diary. Entry of 15 March 1884.
8. Letter of Count L.N. Tolstoy to His Wife, 2nd edition, Moscow 1915, p. 335
9. "L. Tolstoy and V.V. Stasov" Correspondence 1878-1906. Publisher "Surf", Leningrad 1929, p. 54, 56.
10. Letter of L.N. Tolstoy to N.N. Strahov from 11 October 1872. "Letters of L.N. Tolstoy 1848-1910" under the editing of P.A. Sergeyenko, publisher "Book" Moscow 1910, p. 94.
11. Letter of N.N. Strahov to L.N. Tolstoy from 25 April 1878. Correspondence of L.N Tolstoy and N.N. Strahov. Petersburg. 1914, p. 166.
12. Letter of N.N. Strahov to L.N. Tolstoy from 29 November 1881. Correspondence of L.N Tolstoy and N.N. Strahov. Petersburg. 1914, p. 289.
13. Ibid. p. 288.
14. V.I. Alekseyev. Reminiscence of L.N. Tolstoy. Manuscript of the State Tolstoy Museum.
15. Letter of L.N. Tolstoy to V.I. Alekseyev from 5 October 1881. State Tolstoy Museum.
16. V.I. Alekseyev. Reminiscence of L.N. Tolstoy. Manuscript of the State Tolstoy Museum.
17. Letter of L.N. Tolstoy to V.I. Alekseyev, December 1884. State Tolstoy Museum.
18. T.L Suhotina-Tolstaya. Friend and Guest at Yasnaya Polyana. Moscow 1923, p. 36.
19. K.S. Shohor-Troitsky. Syutyayev and Bondarev. "Tolstoy's Annual for 1913" Department: Articles and Materials. St. Petersburg, 1913, p. 5.
20. Letter of L.N. Tolstoy to M.A. Engelhardt, December 1882-January 1883. Copy in Chertkov's archives.

Chapter II (28-52)

1. Diary of V.G. Chertkov. Entry of 18 March 1893. Chertkov's archives.
2. Letter of Count A.A. Bobrinskoy to V.G. Chertkov. Letters to V.G. Chertkov for 1872. Chertkov's archives.
3. Letter of N. Maltsev to V.G. Chertkov of 1 October 1873. Chertkov's archives.
4. V.G. Chertkov. Duty in Military Hospitals. Page from reminiscences, publishers "Unity" and "Soldier-Citizen". Moscow 1918, p. 3
5. Letter of V.G. Chertkov to E.I. Chertkova from 22 December 1872. Chertkov's archives.
6. V.G. Chertkov. Duty in Military Hospitals. Page from reminiscences, publishers "Unity" and "Soldier-Citizen". Moscow 1918, p. 5
7. Diary of V.G. Chertkov. Entry of 8 January 1884. Chertkov's archives.
8. Letter of R.A. Pisarev to V.G. Chertkov from 10 October 1879. Chertkov's archives.
9. Letter of Baron Fredericks to G.A. Chertkov from 29 July 1879. Chertkov's archives.
10. Letter of V.G. Chertkov to E.I. Chertkova from 26 December 1879. Chertkov's archives.
11. Undated letter from Prince S. Vasilchikov to V.G. Chertkov in 1880. Chertkov's archives.
12. Letter of R.A. Pisarev to V.G. Chertkov from 9 April 1880. Chertkov's archives.
13. Letter of V.S. Shramm to V.G. Chertkov from 6 August 1872. Chertkov's archives.
14. Letter of V.S. Shramm to V.G. Chertkov from 6 November 1872. Chertkov's archives.
15. Letter of R.A. Pisarev to V.G. Chertkov from 14 April 1881. Chertkov's archives.
16. Undated letter from Prince V.P Golitzyne to V.G. Chertkov. Letters to V.G. Chertkov for 1881. Chertkov's archives.
17. Letter from Prince V.P Golitzyne to V.G. Chertkov of 12 November 1881. Chertkov's archives.
18. Letter from D.F. Trepov to V.G. Chertkov of 24 October 1881. Chertkov's archives.
19. Chertkov's diary of 1905. Chertkov's archives.
20. Chertkov's diary. Entry of 8 January 1884. Chertkov's archives.
21. Letter of R.A. Pisarev to V.G. Chertkov from 12 September 1881. Chertkov's archives.
22. Undated letter of R.A. Pisarev to V.G. Chertkov. Letters to Chertkov for 1882. Chertkov's archives.
23. Letter of V.S. Shramm to V.G. Chertkov from 17 December 1881. Chertkov's archives.

24.   Letter from E.I. Chertkov to V.G. Chertkov of 25 November 1882. Chertkov's archives.
25.   Letter from E.I. Chertkov to V.G. Chertkov of 17 March 1883. Chertkov's archives.
26.   Undated letter from E.I. Chertkova to V.G. Chertkov. Letters to Chertkov for 1883. Chertkov's archives.
27.   Letter from V.G. Chertkov to E.I. Chertkova. Winter of 1883. Chertkov's archives.
28.   Letter from V.G. Chertkov to E.I. Chertkova of 9 February 1884. Chertkov's archives.
29.   Chertkov's observation about N.V. Davydov's book "From The Past". Chertkov's archives.
30.   G.A. Rusanov. Reminiscences. "Tolstoy's Annual For 1912". Moscow 1913.
31.   N.V. Davydov's telegram to V.G. Chertkov on October 23 1883. Chertkov's archives.

Chapter III (53-74)

1.   V.G. Chertkov. Observation about the acquaintance with Tolstoy, prepared for P.I. Biryukov. "Lev Nikolaevich Tolstoy. Biography", volume II , 2nd edition, Moscow, 1913, p. 470
2.   Letter from V.G. Chertkov to E.I. Chertkova of 9 December 1883. Chertkov's archives.
3.   Letter from Chertkov to Tolstoy of 14 November 1883. Chertkov's archives.
4.   Letter from V.G. Chertkov to E.I. Chertkova of 24 November 1883. Chertkov's archives.
5.   V.G. Chertkov diary entry of 10 December 1883. Chertkov's archives.
6.   Letter from Tolstoy to Chertkov of 5 December 1883.
7.   Letter from Chertkov to Tolstoy of 7 December 1883.
8.   Letter from S.A. Tolstoy to T.A. Kuzminskaya. January 1884. State Tolstoy Museum.
9.   Tolstoy's diary from 1884. Entries of 16 and 9 March.
10. Letter from Tolstoy to A.S. Buturlin of 19 February 1884. Copy in Chertkov's archives.
11. Letter from S.A. Tolstoy to T.A. Kuzminskaya of 28 February 1884. State Tolstoy Museum.
12. Tolstoy's diary from 1884. Entries of 18 March, 23 and 19 April.
13. Tolstoy's diary from 1884. Entries of 6 April.
14. Letter from Chertkov to Tolstoy from the end of January 1884.
15. Letter from Chertkov to Tolstoy of 13 March 1884.
16. Letter from Tolstoy to Chertkov of the beginning of March 1884.
17. Letter from Chertkov to Tolstoy of 8-9 March 1884.
18. Letter from Tolstoy to Chertkov of 18 March 1884.

19. Letter from Tolstoy to Chertkov of March 1884.
20. Letter from Tolstoy to Chertkov of 28 March 1884.
21. Letter from Chertkov to Tolstoy of 25 March 1884.
22. Letter from Chertkov to Tolstoy of 8 April 1884.
23. Letter from Chertkov to Tolstoy of 31 May 1884.
24. Letter from Tolstoy to Chertkov of 9 June 1884.
25. Letter from Chertkov to Tolstoy of 4 July 1884.
26. Letter from Tolstoy to Chertkov of 18 April 1884.
27. Tolstoy's diary. Entry of 25 June 1884.
28. Letter from Chertkov to Tolstoy of 4 July 1884.
29. Letter from Chertkov to Tolstoy of 15 July 1884.
30. Tolstoy's diary. Entry of 7 May 1884.
31. Tolstoy's diary. Entry of 3 July 1884.
32. Letter from Tolstoy to Chertkov of 24 July 1884.
33. Tolstoy's diary. Entry of 15 August 1884.
34. Letter from Chertkov to Tolstoy of 15 September 1884.
35. Letter from Chertkov to Tolstoy of 26 September 1884.
36. Letter from Chertkov to Tolstoy of 15 September 1884.
37. Letter from Tolstoy to Chertkov of 28-29 August 1884.
38. Letter from Tolstoy to Chertkov of 5-7 September 1884.
39. Letter from Tolstoy to Chertkov of 7 November 1884.
40. Letter from Tolstoy to Chertkov of 1 October 1884.
41. Letter from Tolstoy to Chertkov of 10 October 1884.

Chapter IV (75-99)

1. Letter from Chertkov to Tolstoy of 24 October 15 1884.
2. I. D. Sytin. "From My Past." In the collection "Half a Century for a Book" marking the 50th anniversary of Sytin's publishing activity. Moscow, 1916, p. 21.
3. Letter from Chertkov to Tolstoy of 27-28 November 1884.
4. Letter from I.N. Kramskoy to V.G. Chertkov of 27 October 1884. Chertkov's archives.
5. Letter from Chertkov to Tolstoy of 1 December 1884.
6. Letter from Tolstoy to Chertkov of 2 December 1884.
7. Letter from Chertkov to Tolstoy of 28 September 1884.
8. Letter from Chertkov to Tolstoy of 8 December 1884.
9. Letter from Tolstoy to Chertkov of 17 December 1884.
10. Letter from Tolstoy to Chertkov of 5-6 February 1885.
11. Letter from Tolstoy to Chertkov of 2-3 January 1885.
12. Letter from Chertkov to Tolstoy of 12 January 1885.
13. Letter from Chertkov to Tolstoy of 24 February 1885.
14. Letter from Tolstoy to Chertkov of 1-2 June 1885.
15. Letter from Chertkov to Tolstoy of 1 May 1885.
16. Letter from Chertkov to Tolstoy of 5-6 May 1885.

17. Letter from Tolstoy to Chertkov of 9 December 1884.
18. Letter from Tolstoy to S.A. Tolstaya of 14 March 1885. Letters of Count Tolstoy to His Wife. 2nd edition, M. 1915, p. 262
19. Letter from Tolstoy to Prince L.D. Ourusoff of 12 April 1885. State Tolstoy Museum.
20. Letter from Tolstoy to Chertkov of 2 May 1885.
21. Letter from Tolstoy to Chertkov of 6-7 December 1885.
22. Letter from Chertkov to Tolstoy of 4 June 1885.
23. Letter from Tolstoy to Chertkov of 9-10 June 1885.
24. Letter from Tolstoy to Chertkov of 23-24 July 1885.
25. Letter from Tolstoy to Chertkov of 6-7 June 1885.
26. Letter from Chertkov to Tolstoy of 14 June 1885.
27. Letter from Tolstoy to Chertkov of 23-24 June 1885.
28. Letter from S.A. Tolstaya to T.A. Kuzminskaya of 9 January 1885. State Tolstoy Museum.
29. Letter from I.E. Repin to Chertkov of 29 August 1887.
30. Letter from Chertkov to Tolstoy of 17 September 1886.
31. V.G. Chertkov's diary. Entry of 9 November 1885. Chertkov's archives.
32. Letter from Tolstoy to Chertkov of 6-7 December 1885.
33. Letter from Tolstoy to Chertkov of 9-15 December 1885.
34. Letter from S.A. Tolstaya to T.A. Kuzminskaya, almost fully printed in V.A. Zhdanov's book "Love of Tolstoy's Life", 2nd volume, published by M. and S. Sabashnikov, Moscow 1928, pp. 58-59.
35. Letter from Chertkov to Tolstoy of 4-5 October 1885.
36. Letter from Chertkov to Tolstoy of 8 August 1886.
37. Letter from Tolstoy to Chertkov of 1 September 1886.
38. Letter from Tolstoy to V.G. and A.K Chertkov of 6 November 1886.

Chapter V (pp. 100-135)

1. Letter from Tolstoy to Chertkov of 19-21 January 1887.
2. Chertkov's diary. Entry of February 27 1887. Chertkov's archives.
3. Letter from Chertkov to Tolstoy of 9-10 February 1887.
4. Letter from Tolstoy to Chertkov of 13 February 1887.
5. Letter from Tolstoy to Chertkov of 14 September 1887.
6. Letter from Chertkov to Tolstoy of 2 January 1887.
7. Letter from Tolstoy to Chertkov of 6-7 February 1887.
8. Letter from Chertkov to Tolstoy of 9 February 1887.
9. Letter from Tolstoy to Chertkov of 13 February 1887.
10. Letter from Tolstoy to Chertkov of 2 April 1887.
11. Undated letter from V.G. Chertkov to E.I. Chertkova sent in 1884 or 1885. Chertkov's archives.
12. Letter from Chertkov to Tolstoy of 10 December 1886.
13. Letter from V.G. Chertkov to E.I. Chertkova of 1 December 1886. Chertkov's archives.

301

14. Letter from Tolstoy to Chertkov of 21 July 1887.
15. Letter from Tolstoy to Chertkov of 16 October 1887.
16. Letter from Tolstoy to Chertkov of 2 November 1887.
17. Letter from Chertkov to Tolstoy of 19 November 1887.
18. Letter from Tolstoy to Chertkov of 22 November 1887.
19. Letter from Tolstoy to Chertkov of 27 November–1 December 1887.
20. Letter from Tolstoy to Chertkov of 6 December 1887.
21. Letter from Chertkov to Tolstoy of 27 December 1887.
22. Letter from Chertkov to E.I Chertkova of 24 February 1888. Chertkov's archives.
23. Letter from Chertkov to Tolstoy of 1 May 1888.
24. Letter from Tolstoy to Chertkov of 20-28 September 1888.
25. Letter from Chertkov to Tolstoy of 7 June 1889
26. Letter from Tolstoy to Chertkov of 27 August 1889.
27. Letter from Tolstoy to Chertkov of 21 December 1888.
28. Letter from Tolstoy to Chertkov of 5 July 1888.
29. Letter from Tolstoy to Chertkov of 11 December 1892.
30. Letter from Chertkov to Tolstoy of 27 October 1889.
31. Tolstoy's diary. Entry of 31 October 1889.
32. Tolstoy's diary. Entry of 27 January 1890.
33. Undated letter from Tolstoy to Chertkov, sent, probably, toward the beginning of February 1890. Tolstoy's archives.
34. Letter from Tolstoy to Chertkov of 11 June 1890.
35. Letter from Chertkov to Tolstoy of 4 September 1890.
36. Letter from Tolstoy to Chertkov of 17 September 1890.
37. Letter from N.N. Strahov to Tolstoy of 29 October 1893. Correspondence of Tolstoy with Strahov, published by the Tolstoy Museum. Petersburg 1914, p. 453
38. Letter from Tolstoy to Chertkov of 11 December 1892.
39. Letter from Tolstoy to Chertkov of 3 February 1893.
40. Letter from Tolstoy to Chertkov of 14 December 1891.
41. Letter from Chertkov to Tolstoy of 28 April 1891
42. Letter from Tolstoy to Chertkov of 22 June 1892.
43. Letter from Chertkov to M.L.Tolstaya of 28 July 1890. Copy in Chertkov's archives.
44. Letter from Tolstoy to Chertkov of 8 April 1890.
45. Letter from Chertkov to Tolstoy of 16 August 1890.
46. Letter from Chertkov to Tolstoy of 8 August 1886.
47. Letter from Tolstoy to Chertkov of 24 April 1890.
48. Letter from M.L.Tolstaya to Chertkov. July 1890. Chertkov's archives.
49. Letter from M.L.Tolstaya to Chertkov of 22 February 1894. Chertkov's archives.
50. Tolstoy's diary. Entry of 2 May 1891.
51. Tolstoy's diary. Entry of 10 June 27 1891.
52. Letter from Tolstoy to Chertkov of 18-19 March 1891.

53. Tolstoy's diary. Entry of 1 October 1892.
54. Letter from Tolstoy to N.N. Ge of 28 November 1892. Correspondence of Tolstoy and Ge published by "Academia" Moskva–Leningrad. 1930, p. 129.
55. Letter from Tolstoy to Chertkov of 19 October 1892.
56. Letter from Tolstoy to Chertkov of 29 February 1888.
57. Tolstoy's diary. Entry of 14 July 1891.
58. Letter from Chertkov to P.I. Biryukov of 31 January 1889. Copy in Chertkov's archives.
59. Letter from Tolstoy to V.G. and A.K Chertkov of 18 May 1889.
60. Letter from Chertkov to Tolstoy of 22 July 1889.
61. Letter from A.G. Chertkova to V.G. Chertkov of 7 June 1888. Chertkov's archives.
62. Letter from Chertkov to Tolstoy of 12 June 1887.
63. Letter from Chertkov to Tolstoy of 8-9 April 1888.
64. Letter from Chertkov to Tolstoy of 18 March 1888.
65. Letter from Chertkov to Tolstoy of 18 March 1888.
66. Letter from Chertkov to Tolstoy of 15 November 1891.
67. Letter from Chertkov to Tolstoy of 22 December 1891.
68. Letter from Chertkov to A.I. Ertel of 25 December 1895. Letters of A.I. Ertel. Moscow 1909, p. 343.
69. Undated letter from Chertkov to N.D. Kivshenko, sent toward the end of the 1880s. Copy in Chertkov's archives.
70. Letter from Chertkov to Tolstoy of 12 November 1891.
71. Letter from A.I. Ertel to Chertkov of 30 March 1891. Letters of A.I. Ertel. Moscow 1909, p. 259
72. Letter from Chertkov to Tolstoy of 10 April 1893.
73. Letter from Tolstoy to Chertkov 3 April 1893.

Chapter VI (pp. 136-168)

1. Chertkov's diary. Entry of 18 March 1893. Chertkov's archives.
2. Letter from Chertkov to Tolstoy of 6 March 1893.
3. Letter from Chertkov to E.I Chertkova of 14 March 1893. Chertkov's archives.
4. Letter from Chertkov to E.I Chertkova of 9 April 1893. Chertkov's archives.
5. Letter from Tolstoy to Chertkov of 3 May 1893.
6. Letter from Chertkov to Tolstoy of 16 June 1893.
7. Letter from Chertkov to Tolstoy of 15 June 1893.
8. Letter from Tolstoy to Chertkov of 22 June 1893.
9. Letter from A.K. Chertkova to Tolstoy of 27 August 1893. Copy in Chertkov's archives.
10. Letter from Tolstoy to A.K. Chertkova of 4 September 1893.
11. Letter from P.I. Biryukov to Chertkov of 4 November 1893. Chertkov's archives.

12. Letter from Tolstoy to Chertkov of 21 July 1893.
13. E.I. Popov. Life and Death of E.N. Drozhin (1866-1894). With a preface by L.N. Tolstoy. Published by F. Gotgeimer. Berlin. 1895.
14. Letter from Tolstoy to Chertkov of 5 November 1893.
15. Letter from Chertkov to Tolstoy of 18 November 1893.
16. Letter from Tolstoy to Chertkov of 24 December 1893.
17. Letter from E.I Chertkova to Chertkov of 1 January 1894. Chertkov's archives.
18. Printed in the book "Lev Tolstoy and the Russian Tsars". Published by the book publishers "Freedom" and "Unity". Moscow 1919, pp.15-19
19. Letter from Tolstoy to Chertkov of 9 December 1893.
20. Letter from Tolstoy to Chertkov of 3 November 1893.
21. Letter from Tolstoy to Chertkov of 5 November 1893.
22. Letter from Chertkov to Tolstoy of 12 November 1893.
23. Letter from M.L. Tolstaya to V.G. Chertkov of 3 December 1894. Chertkov's archives.
24. Letter from Tolstoy to Chertkov of 18 March 1894.
25. Letter from Tolstoy to His Wife, 2nd edition. M. 1915, p. 469.
26. Letter from Tolstoy to V.G. and A.K. Chertkov of 7 April 1894.
27. Letter from Tolstoy to Chertkov of 30 April 1894.
28. Letter from S.A. Tolstaya to T.A. Kuzminskaya of 8 April 1894. State Tolstoy Museum.
29. Letter from Tolstoy to Chertkov of 12 May 1894.
30. Tolstoy's diary. Entry of 13 July 1894.
31. "Noble Son" – joking reference to the Chertkov's five year old son, Dima.
32. Letter from Tolstoy to V.G. and A.K. Chertkov of 18 August 1894.
33. Letter from Chertkov to Tolstoy of 14 October 1894.
34. Tolstoy's diary. Entry of 30 October 1894.
35. Letter from Chertkov to Tolstoy of 18 November 1894.
36. Letter from Tolstoy to Chertkov of 16 January 1895.
37. Letter from D.F. Trepov to Chertkov of 12 June 1895. Chertkov's archives.
38. Tolstoy's diary. Entry of 6 September 1894.
39. Letter from Chertkov to Tolstoy of 25 January 1895.
40. Letter from Tolstoy to Chertkov of 24 February 1895.
41. Letter from Chertkov to Tolstoy of 28 February 1895.
42. Letter from M.L. Tolstaya to Chertkov of 10 March 1895. Chertkov's archives.
43. Letter from Tolstoy to Chertkov of 26 April 1895.
44. "Tolstoy's Yearly" for 1912. Petersburg. 1913. p. 10.
45. Letter from Tolstoy to Chertkov of 26 November 1894.
46. Letter from Tolstoy to Chertkov of 8 June 1895.
47. Letter from Chertkov to Tolstoy of 5 October 1895.
48. Letter from Chertkov to Tolstoy of 19-24 September 1895.
49. Letter from Tolstoy to Chertkov of 7 October 1895.
50. Letter from Chertkov to Tolstoy of 13 October 1895.

51. Letter from S.A. Tolstaya to T.A. Kuzminskaya of 12 July 1896. State Tolstoy Museum.
52. Letter from Chertkov to Tolstoy of 8 May 1885.
53. Tolstoy's diary. Entry of 5 August 1895.
54. Letter from Tolstoy to Chertkov of 21 September 1895.
55. Letter from Tolstoy to Chertkov of 30 October – 6 November 1896.
56. Letter from Tolstoy to Chertkov of 2 December 1896.
57. Help! A Call to the Public About the Persecution of Dukhobors from Caucusus. Prepared by P. Biryukov, I. Tregubov and V. Chertkov. With a postscript by L.N. Tolstoy. Published by V. Chertkov, London, 1897.
58. Letter from Chertkov to Tolstoy of 11 January 1897.
59. Letter from Tolstoy to Chertkov of 25 January 1897.
60. Letter from Chertkov to Goremykin of 2 February 1897. Copy in Chertkov's archives.
61. Tolstoy's diary. Entry of 7 February 1897.
62. Letter from Tolstoy to D.A. Hilkov of 12 February 1897. Copy in Chertkov's archives.
63. Letter from S.A. Tolstaya to T.A. Kuzminskaya of 12 February 1897. State Tolstoy Museum.
64. Letter from Chertkov to E.I. Chertkova of 22 April 1897. Chertkov's archives.

Chapter VII (pp. 169-208)

1. Letter from Tolstoy to Chertkov of 8 March 1897.
2. Letter from M.L. Tolstaya to Chertkov of 27 March 1897. Chertkov's archives.
3. Letter from Tolstoy to Chertkov of 7 May 1897
4. Letter from Tolstoy to Chertkov of 26 May 1897
5. Letter from Tolstoy to M.L. Tolstaya of 12 January 1897. Copy in Chertkov's archives.
6. Letter from M.L. Tolstaya to Chertkov of 19 January 1896. Chertkov's archives.
7. Letter from M.L. Tolstaya to Chertkov of 24 March 1897. Chertkov's archives.
8. Letter from S.A. Tolstaya to T.A. Kuzminskaya of 14 September 1898. State Tolstoy   Museum.
9. Tolstoy's diary. Entry of June 25 1894.
10. Letter from S.A. Tolstaya to T.A. Kuzminskaya of 24 March 1897. State Tolstoy Museum.
11. Letter from M.L. Tolstaya to A.K. Chertkova of 8 July 1897. Chertkov's archives.
12. Letter from Tolstoy to S.A. Tolstaya of 8 July 1897. Letters of Count Tolstoy to his wife 1862-1910. Moscow 1915, p. 524.

13. Letter from Tolstoy to S.N. Tolstoy of 22 February 1897. State Tolstoy Museum.
14. Letter from Tolstoy to Chertkov of 11 March 1897.
15. Letter from Chertkov to Tolstoy of 31 March 1897.
16. Letter from P.A. Kropotkin to Chertkov from 10 June 1897. Chertkov's archives.
17. Letter from Chertkov to Tolstoy of 19 June 1897.
18. Letter from Tolstoy to Chertkov of 19 June 1897.
19. Catalog of publications of Vladimir Chertkov. Purleigh, Essex, England, 1898.
20. Letter from Chertkov to Tolstoy of 16 June 1897.
21. Letter from Tolstoy to Chertkov of 19 June 1897.
22. Letter from M.L. Tolstaya to Chertkov of 27 March 1897. Chertkov's archives.
23. Letter from Tolstoy to Chertkov of 30 April 1897.
24. Letter from Tolstoy to Chertkov of 7 May 1897.
25. Letter from Chertkov to Tolstoy of 28 July 1897.
26. Letter from Tolstoy to Chertkov of 8 August 1897.
27. Letter from N. Ya. Grot to Tolstoy of 26 November 1897. Tolstoy's archives.
28. Letter from Chertkov to Tolstoy of 21 December 1897.
29. Letter from Tolstoy to Chertkov of 13 December 1897.
30. Letter from Chertkov to Tolstoy of 31 December 1897.
31. Letter from Tolstoy to Chertkov of 14 February 1898.
32. Letter from Tolstoy to Chertkov of 16 July 1897.
33. V. Chertkov. "Where is Your Brother?" Purleigh, Essex. 1898.
34. Letter from Tolstoy to Chertkov of 4 May 1898.
35. Letter from Chertkov to Tolstoy of 15 September 1898.
36. Letter from Tolstoy to Chertkov of 17 March 1898.
37. Letter from Tolstoy to Chertkov of 9 October 1898.
38. Letter from Tolstoy to Chertkov of 12 August 1898.
39. Letter from Tolstoy to Chertkov of 15 October 1898.
40. Letter from Tolstoy to Chertkov of 16 October 1898.
41. Letter from Tolstoy to Chertkov of 31 October 1898.
42. Tolstoy's diary. Entry of 2 November 1898.
43. Letter from Chertkov to Tolstoy of 2 December 1898.
44. Letter from M.L. Tolstaya-Obolenskaya to Chertkov of 23 November 1898. Chertkov's archives.
45. Letter from Tolstoy to V.G. and A.K Chertkov of 15 March 1899.
46. Letter from Tolstoy to Chertkov of 4 April 1899.
47. Letter from Chertkov to Tolstoy of 21 November 1899.
48. Letter from Tolstoy to Chertkov of 5 December 1898.
49. "Pages of the Free Word". Periodical publication under the editorship of V. Chertkov. No. 1, November 1898.
50. "Pages of the Free Word", No. 8, 1899.

51. Account of the book publisher "Free Word" V. and A. Chertkov for the period of 1897-1900. A. Chertkov, Christchurch, 1901. Account of the book publisher "Free Word" V. and A. Chertkov for 1901. A. Chertkov, Christchurch 1902.
52. Student movement of 1899. Collection edited by A. and V. Chertkov. 1899. Persecutions in Finland. Collection edited by V. Chertkov. 1900.
53. Letter from P.A. Kropotkin to Chertkov of 30 June 1901. Chertkov's archives.
54. Letter from Tolstoy to Chertkov of 14 September 1901.
55. Letter from Tolstoy to Chertkov of 31 December 1899.
56. Letter from Tolstoy to Chertkov of 1 September 1900.
57. Letter from Chertkov to Tolstoy of 19 September 1900.
58. Letter from Chertkov to Tolstoy of 29 December 1900.
59. Letter from Chertkov to Tolstoy of 26 January 1901.
60. Letter from Tolstoy to Chertkov of 12 December 1900.
61. Letter from Tolstoy to Chertkov of 18 July 1901.
62. Letter from Tolstoy to Chertkov of 30 March 1901.
63. Letter from Chertkov to Nikolai II of 6 February 1901. Copy in Chertkov's archives.
64. Letter from Tolstoy to Chertkov of 12 August 1901.
65. Letter from M.L. Tolstaya-Obolenskaya to Chertkov of 15 September 1901. Chertkov's archives.
66. Letter from N.L. Obolensky to Chertkov of 28 September 1901. Chertkov's archives.
67. Letter from Tolstoy to Chertkov of 30 November 1901.
68. Letter from Chertkov to Tolstoy of 10 February 1902.
69. Letter from P.A. Bulange to Chertkov of 20 February 1902. Chertkov's archives.

Chapter VIII (209-242)

1. Tolstoy's diary. Entry of 20 September 1902.
2. Letter from S.A. Tolstaya to A.B. Goldenweiser of 13 March 1902. A.B. Goldenweiser. Close to Tolstoy, volume I, Moscow 1922, p. 83.
3. Letter from S.A. Tolstaya to T.A. Kuzminskaya of 22 October 1898. State Tolstoy Museum.
4. Letter from S.A. Tolstaya to T.A. Kuzminskaya of 2 July 1903. State Tolstoy Museum.
5. Letter from S.A. Tolstaya to T.A. Kuzminskaya of 17 November 1903. State Tolstoy Museum.
6. Letter from S.A. Tolstaya to T.A. Kuzminskaya of 3 April 1903. State Tolstoy Museum.
7. Letter from O.K. Tolstaya to A.K. Chertkova from 16 March 1904. Chertkov's archives.
8. Letter from Chertkov to Tolstoy of 27 May 1900.

9. Letter from Chertkov to Tolstoy of 19 June 1901.
10. Letter from M.L. Tolstaya-Obolenskaya to Chertkov of 16 January 1901. Chertkov's archives.
11. Letter from Tolstoy to Chertkov of 7 September 1902.
12. Letter from Tolstoy to Chertkov 19 April 1903.
13. S.A. Tolstaya's diary 1897-1909. Publisher "Sever" (North). Moscow 1932, p. 204.
14. Published in the diary entries of L.N. Tolstoy, under the editorship of V.G. Chertkov 1895-1899 Moscow 1916, pp. 257-258.
15. Letter from Tolstoy to Chertkov from the beginning of July 1902.
16. Letter from Tolstoy to Chertkov 22 July 1902.
17. Letter from Tolstoy to A.K. Chertkova of 17 August 1902.
18. Letter from Tolstoy to Chertkov of 2 September 1902.
19. Letter from Tolstoy to Chertkov of 11 October 1902.
20. Letter from Tolstoy to Chertkov of 11 January 1903.
21. "Reminiscences of Childhood", written for the biography, prepared by P.I. Biryukov.
22. Letter from Tolstoy to Chertkov of 11 January 1903.
23. Letter from Chertkov to Tolstoy of 23 March 1903.
24. Letter from Tolstoy to Chertkov of 22 March 1903.
25. First published in the magazine "Svobodnoe Slovo" (Free Word): 1903, Nos. 5, 6, 7, 8; 1904, Nos. 9, 10. Separate edition: V. Chertkov. About Revolution. Violent Revolution Or Christian Liberation. With a preface by L.N. Tolstoy. Published by Svobodnoe Slovo (Free Word), Christchurch, 1904. Second expanded edition published in Russia, Moscow, 1907.
26. Letter from Tolstoy to Chertkov of 29 March 1903.
27. Letter from Chertkov to Tolstoy of 27 May 1903.
28. Letter from Tolstoy to Chertkov of 22 May 1903.
29. Tales: "Assirian Tsar Assardakhon," "Three Questions" and "Labor, Death and Sickness." First planned for collection "Pomoshch" (Gilf–Help), published in Yiddish by "Folksbuilding", Warsaw, 1903, where first two tales were published. In Russian first two were published by Posrednik (Mediator), Moscow 1904, and the last one in supplement to magazine "Svobodnoe Slovo" (Free Word), 1904, No. 9.
30. The story "After the Ball", first published in "Posthumous Artistic Works of L.N. Tolstoy", published by A.L. Tolstaya, volume I, Moscow 1911.
31. Letter from Tolstoy to V.G and A.K. Chertkov of 9 August 1903.
32. Letter from Chertkov to Tolstoy of 22 January 1904.
33. Letter from Tolstoy to Chertkov of 19 January 1904.
34. Letter from Tolstoy to Chertkov of 19 February 1904.
35. Tolstoy's diary. Entry of 29 April 1904.
36. Letter from Chertkov to Tolstoy of 2 May 1904
37. Letter from Tolstoy to Chertkov of 27 April 1904.
38. Letter from Tolstoy to Chertkov of 13 May 1904.
39. Letter from Tolstoy to Chertkov of 1 July 1904.

40. Letter from Chertkov to Tolstoy of 27 July 1904.
41. Tolstoy' diary. Entry of 2 August 1904.
42. Letter from Tolstoy to Chertkov of 27 November 1904.
43. Letter from Tolstoy to Chertkov of 27 November 1904.
44. Letter from Tolstoy to Chertkov of 22 January 1905.
45. Letter from Tolstoy to Chertkov of 17 April 1905.
46. Letter from V.G. Chertkov to E.I. Chertkova of 13 April 1905. Chertkov's archives.
47. Letter from Chertkov to Tolstoy of 26 April 1905.
48. Letter from Tolstoy to Chertkov of 24 April 1905.
49. Tolstoy's diary. Entry of 6 June 1905.
50. Letter from S.A. Tolstaya to V.G. Chertkov of 6 July 1905. Chertkov's archives.
51. Letter from Chertkov to Tolstoy of 21 September 1905.
52. Letter from Chertkov to Tolstoy of 6 June 1905.
53. Letter from Tolstoy to Chertkov of 6 July 1905.
54. Letter from Tolstoy to Chertkov of 4 September 1905.
55. Letter from Chertkov to Tolstoy of 9 October 1905.
56. Letter from Tolstoy to Chertkov of 18 October 1905.
57. Letter from Tolstoy to Chertkov of 19 December 1905.
58. Letter from Tolstoy to Chertkov of 7 October 1905.
59. Letter from Chertkov to Tolstoy of 4 January 1906.
60. Letter from Tolstoy to Chertkov of 4 November 1905.
61. Letter from Tolstoy to Chertkov of 1 March 1906.
62. Letter from Chertkov to Tolstoy of 24 March н.с. 1906.
63. Letter from Tolstoy to Chertkov of 27 June 1906.
64. Tolstoy's diary. Entry of 30 July 1906.
65. Letter from M.L. Tolstaya-Obolenskaya to T.L Tolstaya-Suhotina of 3 August 1906. State Tolstoy Museum.
66. Tolstoy's diary. Entry of 24 August 1906.
67. L.N. Tolstoy. "About the Meaning of the Russian Revolution". Published by "Posrednik" (Mediator). [Moscow 1906].
68. Preface to G. Drozhin's book "Public Tasks", translated by S.D. Nikolaev, Published by "Posrednik" (Mediator), Moscow 1907.
69. Letter to Ku-Hung-Ming, October 1906, published under the title: L.N. Tolstoy. Letter to the Chinese Man. Published by "Posrednik" (Mediator), Moscow 1907.
70. Letter from Tolstoy to Chertkov of 3 October 1906.
71. Tolstoy's article "About Shakespeare and Drama" appeared in Russia for the first time in I.D. Sytin's publication "Russian Word" (No. 277, 278, 279, 280, 281, 282, 285 for 1906.). Tolstoy, during his meeting with Chertkov in 1905, permitted him to publish this article as well as the story "Heavenly and Human" in order that the royalty, which could be received from the first publication of these works, would be used to cover the cost of inexpensive

309

English publication of Tolstoy's works. Chertkov in his letter of 3 December 1906, to which Tolstoy answers, reminded him of this conversation.

72.   Letter from Tolstoy to Chertkov of 26 November 1906.

73.   Letter from S.A. Tolstaya to T.A. Kuzminskaya of 3 December 1906. State Tolstoy Museum.

74.   Letter from Tolstoy to Chertkov of 28 December 1906.

75.   Tolstoy's diary. Entry of 23 November 1906.

Chapter IX (243-296)

1.   Tolstoy's diary. Entry of 8 August 1907.

2.   Tolstoy's diary. Entry of 11 March 1910.

3.   Letter from S.A. Tolstaya to T.A. Kuzminskaya of 9 November 1907. State Tolstoy Museum.

4.   A.B. Goldenweiser. "Those Close to Tolstoy", volume I, Moscow 1922, p. 316.

5.   Letter from Tolstoy to Chertkov of 25 May 1909.

6.   I. Tolstoy "Who Is The Guilty One?" – "Russian Word" 1910. No. 209.

7.   Letter of M.L Tolstaya to T.L. Tolstaya of 13 December 1897. State Tolstoy Museum.

8.   Letter from Tolstoy to Chertkov of 21 January 1907.

9.   Letter from Tolstoy to Chertkov of 19 May 1907.

10.   Letter from Tolstoy to Chertkov of 6 April 1907.

11.   Letter from S.A. Tolstaya to T.A. Kuzminskaya of 13 June 1907. State Tolstoy Museum.

12.   Telegram from Tolstoy to Chertkov of 15 June 1907.

13.   Letter from Tolstoy to Chertkov of 16 September 1907.

14.   Letter from Tolstoy to Chertkov of 26 September 1907.

15.   Letter from Tolstoy to Chertkov of 2 November 1907.

16.   Letter from Tolstoy to Chertkov of 17 November 1907.

17.   Letter from Chertkov to Tolstoy of 10 December 1907.

18.   Letter from Tolstoy to Chertkov of 9 December 1907.

19.   I.D. Sytin released the second printing of the "Cycle of Reading" at that time.

20.   Letter from Tolstoy to Chertkov of 10 February 1908.

21.   Letter from Tolstoy to Chertkov of 11 March 1908.

22.   Letter from Tolstoy to Chertkov of 25 March 1908.

23.   Letter from Tolstoy to Chertkov of 2 June 1908.

24.   Telegram from Tolstoy to Chertkov of 8 June 1908.

25.   Letter from Tolstoy to Chertkov of 9 June 1910.

26.   Tolstoy's diary. Entry of 10 June 1908.

27.   Letter from Tolstoy to Chertkov of 30 January 1909.

28.   File "About subversive activity of V.G. Chertkov" from a Secret Department of Tula Governor's Office. Tolstoy Museum, p. 35.

29.   Ibid., p. 46.

30. Letter from Tolstoy to Chertkov of 11 January 1909.
31. Letter from Tolstoy to Chertkov of 12 May 1909.
32. Letter from Chertkov to Tolstoy of 23 April 1909.
33. Letter from Tolstoy to Chertkov of 25? May 1909.
34. Letter from Chertkov to Tolstoy of 25 May 1909.
35. Letter from Tolstoy to Chertkov of 18 June 1909.
36. Letter from Tolstoy to Chertkov of 23 June 1909.
37. Letter from Tolstoy to Chertkov of 24 June 1909.
38. Letter from Tolstoy to Chertkov of 1 July 1909.
39. V.G. Chertkov. "Page From Reminiscences. Duty in Military Hospitals" – "Bulletin of Europe", 1909, No. 11. Separate publication of Sytin, Moscow 1911 "Unity" and "Soldier-Citizen". Moscow 1918.
40. Letter from Chertkov to Tolstoy of 8 August 1909.
41. A.B. Goldenweiser. "Close to Tolstoy", volume I, Moscow 1922, p. 285.
42. Tolstoy's diary. Entry of 26 July 1909.
43. Letter from Tolstoy to Chertkov of 23 July 1909.
44. Letter from Tolstoy to Chertkov of 2 August 1909.
45. Letter from Tolstoy to Chertkov of 28 August 1909.
46. Sayings of Mohammad, not put in the Koran. Selected by L.N. Tolstoy. Translated into English by S.D. Nikolaev. Published by "Posrednik" (Mediator), Moscow 1910.
47. Sayings of the Chinese sage Lao-Tse, selected by L.N. Tolstoy. Published by "Posrednik" (Mediator), Moscow 1910.
48. Under this title appeared at least one booklet from the series "For the Soul" thought up by Tolstoy and I.I. Gorbunov-Posadov. The sayings of thinkers of different countries in different centuries, selected by L.N. Tolstoy. Published by "Posrednik" (Mediator), Moscow 1910.
49. Tolstoy had in mind the publication of I.D. Sytin "For Every Day", which came out in individual releases very slowly.
50. Letter from Tolstoy to Chertkov of 31 August 1909.
51. Tolstoy's diary. Entry of 5 May 1909.
52. Tolstoy's diary. Entry of 22 July 1909.
53. Text of the will reproduced as a photo in "Tolstoy Annual Collection" for 1913. Published in St.-Petersburg, 1914, pp. 25-30. The account of its preparation is given in a book "Tolstoy's Departure" by V. G. Chertkov, Moscow 1922.
54. Letter from Tolstoy to Chertkov of 12 October 1909.
55. Letter from Chertkov to Tolstoy of 20 October 1909.
56. Letter from Tolstoy to Chertkov of 22 October 1909.
57. Letter from Chertkov to Tolstoy of 25-26 December 1909.
58. Letter from Tolstoy to Chertkov of 19 November 1909.
59. Letter from Tolstoy to Chertkov of 14 January 1910.
60. Letter from Chertkov to Tolstoy of 24 January 1910.
61. Tolstoy's diary. Entry of 27-28 January 1910.
62. Letter from Tolstoy to Chertkov of 27 January 1910.

63. "New Russia" of 25 December 1909. No. 354.

64. "Russian News" of 10 November 1909.

65. V.G. Chertkov. "Two censures for Tolstoy"—"Life for Everyone", 1910, No. 2.

66. Letter from Tolstoy to Chertkov of 1 March 1910.

67. Letter from Tolstoy to T. Das, in Russian, first published in the Collected Works of Tolstoy, under the editorship of P.I. Biryukov, published by Sytin, volume XX p. 240.

68. M. Gandhi. Indian Home Rule, Natal 1910. [M. Gandhi. Indian self-government.]

69. Letter from Tolstoy to Gandhi of 25 April 1910. Copy in the Tolstoy State Museum.

70. Letter from Tolstoy to Chertkov of 22 April 1910.

71. Letter from Tolstoy to Chertkov of 24 March 1910.

72. Tolstoy's diary. Entry of 13 April 1910.

73. Letter from Tolstoy to Chertkov of 17 April 1910.

74. Letter from Tolstoy to Chertkov of 8 April 1910.

75. Tolstoy's diary. Entry of 7 May 1910.

76. Chertkov made entries in his diary at this time about conversations with Tolstoy and afterwards published them in an article "Meeting with L.N. Tolstoy in Kochety at M.S. and T.L. Suhotin's". Tolstoy's Annual for 1913. Saint Petersburg. 1914.

77. A.B. Goldenweiser. "Those Close to Tolstoy", volume II, Moscow 1922, pp. 34-35.

78. Tolstoy's diary. Entry of 2 June 1910.

79. Tolstoy's diary. Entry of 6 June 1910.

80. Letter from Tolstoy to Chertkov of 3 June 1910.

81. Collected Works of Tolstoy, under the editorship of P.I. Biryukov, published by Sytin, volume XX p. 475.

82. Tolstoy's diary. Entry of 23 June 1910.

83. A.B. Goldenweiser. "Those Close to Tolstoy", volume II, Moscow 1922, p. 69.

84. Letter from Tolstoy to His Wife. 2nd edition, M. 1915, pp. 588-589.

85. "Батей": Chertkov was called such in his family.

86. Letter from Tolstoy to Chertkov of 26 July 1910.

87. Tolstoy's intimate diary. Entry of 31 July 1910.

88. Letter from Tolstoy to Chertkov of 12 August 1910.

89. Letter from Tolstoy to Chertkov of 7 August 1910.

90. Letter from Tolstoy to Chertkov of 14 August 1910.

91. Letter from Tolstoy to Chertkov of 25 August 1910.

92. Letter from Chertkov to Sofia Andreevna and her answer published in Goldenweiser's book, "Those Close to Tolstoy", volume II, Moscow 1923.

93. Letter from Tolstoy to Chertkov of 16 September 1910.

94. Tolstoy's favorite French saying "Do what you must, and what will be will be". This saying is not finished, it is finished only in the last handwritten entry in Tolstoy's diary.
95. Letter from Tolstoy to Chertkov of 1 October 1910.
96. Letter from Tolstoy to Chertkov of 11 October 1910.
97. Letter from Chertkov to Tolstoy of 10 October 1910.
98. Letter from Tolstoy to Chertkov of 6 October 1910.
99. Tolstoy's intimate diary. Entry of 7 October 1910.
100. Letter from Chertkov to Tolstoy of 14 October 1910.
101. Letter from Chertkov to Dosev published in the books: V.G. Chertkov. "Departure of Tolstoy", Moscow 1922, pp. 16-24 and A.B. Goldenweiser's "Those Close to Tolstoy" volume II, Moscow 1923, pp. 324-333.
102. Letter from Tolstoy to Chertkov 22 October 1910.
103. Tolstoy's intimate diary. Entry of 26 October 1910.
104. Letter from Tolstoy to Chertkov of 26 October 1910.
105. Letter from Chertkov to Tolstoy of 26 October 1910.
106. These letters were used by Chertkov in his brochure "The Last Days of Lev Tolstoy", published by Sytin, Moscow 1911.

INDEX

Ageyev, Afanasii Nikolaevich 202
Alexander II 23, 28, 29
Alexander III 28, 29, 143-45, 152
Alexeyev, Pyotr Semyonovich 118
Alexeyev, Vasili Ivanovich 22-3
Alyehin, Mitrofan Vasilievich 128
Alyehin, Arkadii Vasilievich 128
Alyehin, Arkadii Yegorovich 128
Antonii, Mitropolitan of St. Petersburg 204
Antonin, Marcus Aurelius 18, 24
Archer, Herbert 192-3

Ballou, Adin 119
Bariatinskaya, Elena Mikhailovna, Princess, nee Countess Orlova- Denisova 46
Barikova, Anna Pavlovna, nee Kamenskaya 115
Battersby 89
Bedford, Duke 37
Belinky, Samuil Moiseyevich 276
Bestuzhev-Ryumin, Konstantin Nikolaevich 33
Biryukov, Pavel Ivanovich: a.k.a. Posha
  80, 87, 89, 92-3, 98, 140-41, 158, 162-63, 165-67, 188, 197, 221, 285-86
Bobrinsky, Alexei Aleksandrovich 32
Bondarev, Timofei Mikhailovich 152
Briggs, William 228
Buddha 115-6
Bulange, Pavel Aleksandrovich 207
Bulgakov, Valentin Fyodorovich 257, 276
Bulygin, Mikhail Vasilievich 217
Burnsby, G.S.W. 37
Buturlin, Aleksandr Sergeyevich 59

Catherine II 251
Cervantes, Miguel 100
Chelcicky, Pyotr 230
Cherevin, Pyotr Aleksandrovich 46
Chernyshev, Zahar Grigorievich 28
Chertkov, Grigorii Aleksandrovich 46
Chertkov, Grigorii Ivanovich 28, 65
Chertkov, Grigorii Grigorievich 29
Chertkov, Mikhail Grigorievich 29

314

Chertkov, Mikhail Ivanovich 28
Chertkov, Vladimir Vladimirovich: a.k.a. Dima 150, 152, 196, 250
Chertkova, Alexandra Grigorievna 131
Chertkova, Anna Konstantinovna, nee Dietrichs: a.k.a. Galya 95, 98, 107-8, 110, 122, 130, 132, 137, 140, 148-9, 152, 154, 169, 172-3, 192, 195, 197-9, 201, 206, 218, 223, 238, 250, 262, 280
Chertkova, Elizaveta Ivanovna, nee Chernysheva-Kruglikova 28, 34, 45-6, 65, 93, 105, 143, 145, 166, 199, 231
Chertkova, Olga Vladimirovna: a.k.a. Lusya 108
Crosby, Ernest 234, 248

Davydov, Nikolai Vasilievich 50-52
Degtyarova, Ekaterina Vasilievna 169
Denisenko, Elena Sergeyevna 223
Dosev, Hristo Fydosievich 291, 292
Drenteln, Elizaveta Sergeyevna, Doctor 110
Drozhin, Yevdokim Nikitich 141-3, 146, 158, 162,
Dumas, Alexander 152

Edison, Thomas Alva 254
Elpidin, Mikhail Konstantinovich 237
Engelhardt, Mikhail Aleksandrovich 26, 27
Epictetus 115
Ertel, Aleksandr Ivanovich 115, 133, 134

Fedorov, Nikolai Fyodorovich 26
Feoktistov, Yevgenii Mikhailovich 103
Fifield, Arthur Charles 202
Franklin, Benjamin 100
Fredericks, Vladimir Borisovich 37

Gagarin, Sergei Sergeyevich, Prince 46
Gandhi, 244, 277
Garrison William Lloyd 224
Garshin, Vsevolod Mikhailovich 77, 131
Ge, Nikolai Nikolaevich 24, 128
George, Henri 230, 240
Gertsen, Aleksandr Ivanovich 200
Geyden, Alexander Fyodorovich, Count 43, 80
Goldenweiser, Alexander Borisovich 209, 246, 266, 281, 287
Goldsmith, Oliver 100
Golenishchev-Kutuzov, Count A.V. 43
Golitzine, Pavel Pavlovich, Prince 100

315

Golitzine, Vasily Pavlovich, Prince 42, 43
Goltsev, Victor Aleksandrovich 223
Goncharov, Ivan Aleksandrovich 41
Gorbunov, Ivan Ivanovich (Literary Name: Gorbunov-Posadov) 111, 113, 138, 140, 268
Goremykin, Ivan Loginovich 161, 166,
Grigorovich, Dimitry Vasilievich 100
Grot, Konstantin Yakovlevich 288-90
Grot, Nikolai Yakovlevich 182-84, 194
Gusev, Nikolai Nikolaevich 251, 252, 255, 257

Heath, Charles 82
Hilkov, Dmitri Aleksandrovich 142-6, 148, 152-3, 163-4, 166-7, 197
Hiryakov, Aleksandr Modestovich 214, 262, 263,
Holevinskaya, Maria Mikhailovna 160-1

Ikonnikov, Anton Ivanovich 253
Ivan IV 251
Izyumchenko, Nikolai Trofimovich 162

Kalmykova, Alexandra Mikhailovna 90, 92, 98
Kaznachievsky, Afanasii 202
Kenworthy, John 159, 160, 169, 170, 176, 178, 179, 182, 186,
Kivshenko, Nadezhda Danilovna 134
Korolenko, Vladimir Galaktionovich 77
Kozhuhov, Yevgenii Alekseyevich 100
Kramskoy, Ivan Nikolaevich 79, 80
Kropotkin, Pyotr Alekseyevich, Prince 176, 177, 198, 200, 213, 220
Kuzminskaya, Tatiana Andreevna, nee Behrs 19, 58-9, 97, 150, 160, 167, 211, 242, 245

La Boetie, Etien 278
La Rochefoucauld, Francois 278
Lao-Tze 268
Leskov, Nikolai Semyonovich 77, 78
Lessing, Gotgold Efraim 100
Levashov, Nikolai Vasilievich 46

Makovitsky, Dushan Pyotrovich 198, 268, 280, 295
Malikov, Aleksandr Kapitonovich 22
Maltsev, Nikolai Sergeyevich 33
Maltsev, Sergei Ivanovich 25
Marakuyev, Vladimir Nikolaevich 58, 75

316

Marks, Adolf Fyodorovich 193-6, 216
Maude, Aylmer 182, 183, 184
Maupassant, Guy 152
Maximov, Vasily Maksimovich 136
Meklenburg-Shverinskaya, Princess Maria Pavlovna 46
Mohammed 286
Montaigne, Michel 278
Morozova, Anna Grigorievna 169, 170
Muravyov, Nikita Mikhailovich 28
Muravyov, Nikolai Konstantinovich 270, 271
Muravyov, Nikolai Valerianovich 161

Nechayev, Sergei Gennadievich 26
Nietzsche 241
Nikitin, Dmitri Vasilievich 284
Nikolaev, Sergei Dmitrievich 240, 268
Nikolai I 28
Nikolai II 37, 251
Northhampton, Lord 37
Novoselov, Mikhail Aleksandrovich 128

Obolensky, Leonid Yegorovich 59, 82,
Obolensky, Nikolai Leonidovich 172, 175, 206, 207, 214
Olhovik, Pyotr Vasilievich 234
Olsufyev, Dmitri Adamovich 251, 252
Orlov, Vladimir Fyodorovich 26
Orlov-Davydov, Andrei Vladimirovich 59
Ourusoff, Leonid Dmitrievich 24, 88
Ourusova, Maria Sergeyevna 25

Panina, Natalya Pavlovna 37
Panina, Sofia Vladimirovna 206
Pascal, Blez 230
Pashkov, Vasily Aleksandrovich 34, 108, 265
Paskevich, Irina Ivanovna 103
Pellico, Silvio 100
Peter I 73
Pisarev, Rafail Alekseyevich 36, 37, 39, 41, 44, 50, 51, 55
Plutarch 100
Pobedonostsev, Konstantin Petrovich 146, 161, 167
Polenz, Wilhelm 206
Popov, Yevgenii Ivanovich 158, 162

317

Potehin, Aleksey Antipovich 100
Prugavin, Aleksandr Stepanovich 75

Radstock, Lord Grenville 34, 66
Repin, Ilya Yefimovich 88, 93, 131, 250
Richter, Otton Borisovich 143, 145
Romanov, High Prince Mikhail Nikolaevich 46
Romanov, Nikolai Mikhailovich 46
Romanova, Olga Fyodorovna 46
Romanova, Maria Fyodorovna 46
Rossolimo, Grigorii Ivanovich 284
Rostovtsev, Nikolai Dmitrievich 134
Rousseau, Jean-Jaques 100
Rusanov, Gavril Andreyevich 51
Ruskin, John 89

Savihin, Vasily Ivanovich 82, 100
Schiller, Johan Fridrichs 100
Schmidt, Maria Aleksandrovna 123, 290
Semyonov, Sergei Terentievich 100
Sergeyenko, Pyotr Alekseyevich 275
Shakespeare, William 224, 234, 235, 241
Shaw, Bernard 244
Shkarvan, Albert Albertovich 169, 198
Shram, Vladimir Sergeyevich 39, 40, 45, 55
Shuvalov, Pyotr Andreyevich 28, 37, 103
Shuvalova, Elena Ivanovna 28, 46
Sidorkov, Ilya Vasilievich 268
Snegirev, Vladimir Fyodorovich 240
Socrates 90
Stasov, Vladimir Vasilievich 20
Stebut, Ivan Aleksandrovich 55
Stolypin, Pyotr Arkadievich 261
Strahov, Fyodor Alekseyevich 253, 270
Strahov, Nikolai Nikolayevich 18, 20, 21, 155, 216
Suhotin, Mikhail Sergeyevich 172, 263
Swift, Jonathan 100
Syaskova, Maria Vasilievna 174
Sytin, Ivan Dmitrievich 77, 78, 93, 94, 100, 107, 253, 262, 263, 268, 272, 285
Syutayev, Vasily Kirilovich 25, 26

318

Tchaikovsky, Nikolai Vasilievich 22
Tolstaya, Alexandra Andreyevna 18
Tolstaya, Alexandra Lvovna
172, 206, 210, 214, 239, 266, 268, 270, 280, 282, 283, 291, 293, 295, 296
Tolstaya, Maria Lvovna
17, 122-23, 125, 129, 170-74, 195, 206, 214, 239, 241-43, 247
Tolstaya, Maria Nikolaevna 295
Tolstaya, Olga Konstantinovna 206, 207, 211
Tolstaya, Sofia Andreyevna, nee Behrs
16-19, 22-5, 58-9, 88, 92-3, 124, 127, 150-1, 154-5, 160-1, 167, 172-75, 181, 183, 204, 209-11, 216, 217, 232, 239-42, 245-47, 250-51, 257-58, 266, 268-71, 276, 279-93, 295-96
Tolstaya, Tatiana Lvovna
16, 122, 160, 171-2, 174, 239, 247, 263, 265, 278, 283, 287, 290, 291
Tolstoy, Alexei Lvovich 16
Tolstoy, Andrei Lvovich 206, 258
Tolstoy, Ilya Lvovich 128, 247, 258
Tolstoy, Ivan Lvovich 129, 150, 155
Tolstoy, Lev Lvovich 148
Tolstoy, Mikhail Lvovich 258,
Tolstoy, Sergei Lvovich 16, 282, 290
Tolstoy, Sergei Nikolaevich 175
Tregubov, Ivan Mikhailovich 157, 161, 164-6, 214
Trepov, Dmitri Fyodorovich 43, 153
Tsetlin, Natan Sergeyevich 216
Turgenyev, Ivan Sergeyevich 41

Vasilchikov, Sergei Illarionovich 39
Verigin, Pyotr Vasilievich 162, 163,
Vladimir Aleksandrovich, High Prince 46
Volhovsky, Feliks Vadimovich 176
Voltaire, Francois 100
Vorontsev-Dashkov, Illarion Ivanovich, Count 103, 145

Weiner, Cecilia Vladimirovna 144, 145
Williams, Howard 136
Wright, Charles 267

Yaroshenko, Nikolai Aleksandrovich 95, 136

Zhuravov, Ivan Gerasimovich 100
Zlatovratzky, Nikolai Nikolaevich 75
Zola, Emil 15

1. L.N. Tolstoy and V.G. Chertkov at work. 1908

2. L.N. Tolstoy and his family. Summer 1884

3. E.I. Chertkova with her son.
Watercolor painting by August Delacroix 1860

4. V.G. Chertkov.
Portrait by I.N. Kramskoy 1879-1880

5. V.G. Chertkov.
Portrait by I.Y. Repin 1885

6. "Kursistka" ("A Student")
by P.A. Yaroshenko (Portrait of A.K. Dietrichs). 1883

7. A.K. Chertkova. 1886

8. The beginning of the letter
from Tolstoy to Chertkov on June 22, 1892

9. L.N. Tolstoy, V.G. Chertkov and P.I. Biryukov in Petersburg during the seeing-off (departure) of V.G. and A.K. Chertkov abroad in 1897

10. L.N. Tolstoy at the time of his illness in the Crimea in 1902

11. The Chertkov's home and
depository of Tolstoy's manuscripts in England

12. Yasnaya Polyana (Estate)

13. Yasnaya Polyana (Village)

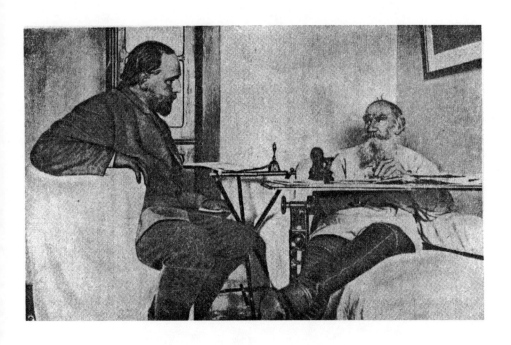

14. L.N. Tolstoy and V.G. Chertkov in 1908 during Tolstoy's illness

15. L.N. Tolstoy and A.K. Chertkova.
Winter 1908-1909

L.N. Tolstoy at V.G. Chertkov's
in the village of Suvorovo. 1909